This theoretical study is concerned largely with the works of two of the best short story writers in the English language – Mavis Gallant and Alice Munro. Although Gallant and Munro have received increasing attention in recent years, most critics have taken a general approach to their works, usually discussing the themes of memory and loss. In contrast, Karen Smythe focuses specifically on the importance of elegy in these fictions and on the role the reader plays in the work of mourning.

The title, *Figuring Grief*, refers to the narrative process whereby mourning is depicted and enacted by way of a performative "think-act," an interiorized speech-act. In her textual analysis Smythe explores various connections between representation and consolation. Drawing on genre and narratological theory, in the first chapter she outlines the development of the "fiction-elegy" as a sub-genre, and suggests that the modernist writings of Woolf and Joyce are paradigmatic examples of the form. In the chapters that follow she uses these paradigms as suggestive "reading models" for the interpretation of works by Gallant, Munro, and other contemporary fiction-elegists. *Figuring Grief* offers new readings of specific works and suggests that new ways of reading are both demanded and rewarded by a poetics of elegy.

KAREN E. SMYTHE is assistant professor in the Department of English, University of Regina.

Figuring Grief

Gallant, Munro, and the Poetics of Elegy

KAREN E. SMYTHE

McGill-Queen's University Press
Montreal & Kingston • London • Buffalo

For G.

© McGill-Queen's University Press 1992
ISBN 0-7735-0939-9

Legal deposit fourth quarter 1992
Bibliothèque nationale du Québec

Printed in Canada on acid-free paper

This book has been published with the help of a
grant from the Canadian Federation for the
Humanities, using funds provided by the Social
Sciences and Humanities Research Council of
Canada. Publication has also been supported by the
Canada Council through its block grant program, and
by the President's Publication Committee of the
University of Regina.

Earlier versions of material included in chapters 2, 3,
4, and 5 were published in *Studies in Canadian
Literature* 15, no. 2 (1990); *Canadian Literature* 129
(Summer 1991); *Wascana Review* 25, no. 1 (Spring
1990); and *University of Toronto Quarterly* 60, no. 4
(Summer 1991) respectively. The author gratefully
acknowledges the permission of the editors of these
journals to publish these articles in modified form.

Canadian Cataloguing in Publication Data

Smythe, Karen E. (Karen Elizabeth), 1962-
 Figuring grief : Gallant, Munro and the
 poetics of elegy
 Includes bibliographical references and index.
 ISBN 0-7735-0939-9
 1. Gallant, Mavis, 1922- —Criticism and
 interpretation. 2. Munro, Alice, 1931- —
 Criticism and interpretation. 3. Grief in
 literature. I. Title.
 PS8513.A563Z87 1992   C813'.5409'35   C92-090381-9
 PR9199.3.G35Z87 1992   75063

Contents

Preface and Acknowledgments

Mavis Gallant and Alice Munro are two of the most accomplished fiction writers in the English language. Though a number of book-length studies have been written on each in recent years,[1] the two authors have not been considered together extensively. Indeed, to the casual reader the work of these two authors may seem to have little in common except for their short-story form and frequent publication in the *New Yorker* (and of course the fact that both authors are Canadian). But Gallant and Munro share what I perceive as an elegiac attitude in their work. More specifically, they both present a poetics of elegy in their fictions, a variation on a poetics that was founded, I argue, by the modernist writers who preceded them. My readings are necessarily focused but are not meant to preclude alternate readings of these works, nor to suggest that everything produced by Gallant and Munro is elegiac and elegiac only. Some stories (and novels and novellas, in Gallant's case) are thematically elegiac, others structurally so; but in the majority of their works a concern with the effects of time on human life – that is, ultimately, with death – is translated to larger themes and figurations of psychological and linguistic modes of understanding: knowledge, memory, and writing itself. This generic study provides a theoretical framework for thematic, structural, and tropological readings of fiction by Gallant and Munro, and is meant to be suggestive rather than prescriptive.

The introductory chapter, which includes a brief discussion of the conventions and characteristics of elegy,[2] focuses mainly on the literary predecessors of Gallant and Munro by reviewing the work of Woolf and Joyce in the context of elegy. It establishes the elegiac fiction of these authors as paradigms – as models of fictionalized mourning – for the two later writers whose work forms the major focus of this study. By "model" I mean that the modernist texts are used as *reading* models against which the late modernist fiction might be read; I am not suggesting that Gallant and Munro directly model themselves after the earlier writers, and influence will not be an issue. In this chapter the more general term "elegiac fiction" is differentiated from my term "fiction-elegy," which identifies fiction written in a variant of the *form* of an elegy (and not merely fiction with an elegiac theme).

In the studies that follow, the theoretical emphasis shifts from generic and narratological to psychoanalytical and reader-response orientations. Chapter 2 explores the connection between empathy and the elegy, and develops a theory of a "transferential relation" between the reader – who is often positioned to empathize with the mourner – and the text. Silence as a response to loss is thematized in these works; it is also coded into the narratives in that a subtext of loss is used as a trope of elegy. The loss becomes displaced, embedded, and must be deciphered, or "plotted," by the reader.

In chapter 3 I theorize that the sequential structure of the Linnet Muir stories also contributes to Gallant's poetics of elegy and that a "temporality of discourse" is employed, providing a form of aesthetic consolation for the elegist-narrator. Gallant's use of the elegiac romance in *Its Image on the Mirror* and the Lena stories of *Overhead in a Balloon* is examined in relation to her concern with the events and issues surrounding the Second World War and with human responses to the crises and losses that it entailed. Models of mourning are explored in *From the Fifteenth District*, where Gallant seems to parody the use of prosopopoeia as a trope of consolation, a trope often employed in conventional and modern elegy. Gallant's texts usually resist tropological consolation, yet in this resistance there exists as well an affirmation of meaning. I also argue in this chapter that *The Pegnitz Junction* is about not only the effects of war but the ethical representation of those events and effects. The reader is positioned as cultural critic, responsible for reading history as accurately as possible and for condemning misinterpretations. I discuss Gallant's implicit critique of historiography (which she suggests is potentially distorting) and the ethical ramifications of remembering and writing of the past.

Munro's early stories, discussed in chapter 4, often use a death in the family as their point of departure. Influenced by James Agee's novel of this name, Munro explores a variety of responses to loss and renders the experience of recovery using narrative techniques within a realistic mode. *Lives of Girls and Women* also explores different models of mourning, though in a more self-conscious manner. The relationship between photography and elegy is detailed in the context of Munro's poetics, which involves an "ethics of seeing" (to borrow Susan Sontag's phrase).[3] Where Gallant focuses on world history, Munro, I suggest, details personal histories and the methods of writing those histories, and uses autobiography and the *Künstlerroman* as tropes in her stories. *Lives of Girls and Women*, often compared to Joyce's *A Portrait of the Artist as a Young Man*, does indeed employ the device of the epiphany, and here comparisons are made between Joyce's epiphanies, Woolf's "moments of being," and what Munro calls the "queer, bright moments" of her stories.

Many of Munro's stories portray a protagonist who mourns the loss of her mother. In chapter 5 the nature of that mourning and the ethics of translating a life into story are shown to be areas that Munro's work explores with increasing frequency as she develops a more complex narrative style to reflect the difficulties involved in such a translation. Not only the significance but the *signification* of death and loss is rendered in the metafictional stories of *The Moons of Jupiter*, which I argue are the epitome of Munrovian elegy.

The concluding chapter places the reading of fiction-elegy in the larger context of contemporary literature. Three other authors' works for which theories of fiction-elegy are useful are discussed in order to demonstrate the extensiveness of the sub-genre in late modern writing. By re-emphasizing the theoretical framework of fiction-elegy, I hope to show how the findings of the study may be extended beyond the boundaries that my use of particular authors may suggest.

J. Hillis Miller claims that "in the retrospective preface ... there is an obscure element of loss, regret, or even of mourning for the dead. This is the case even if the mourning in question is only regret for the death of that moment in the past when the original act of generative insight took place."[4] Perhaps this is true, but the pleasure I experienced during the process of writing this book surely must be a compensating element here as well, and thanks are due to many for contributing to its completion. First, my thanks to my parents, Margaret and Clifford Smythe, for their unquestioning support of my academic pursuits. The "original act of generative insight" from which this book began was a product of the input of several teachers. From David Shaw, whose graduate seminar on elegy at the University of

Toronto gave me the opportunity to explore my intuitions about elegy and fiction, I received intellectual inspiration; from Russell Brown I learned a great deal about Canadian literature and criticism, and received continuing encouragement; and most notably, from Linda Hutcheon, who supervised my doctoral dissertation at the University of Toronto, I was given friendship, moral support, and invaluable advice throughout my years of graduate work and beyond. The productive exchange of ideas with Deborah Esch and the carefully detailed suggestions of Patricia Merivale also contributed tremendously to the improvement of the manuscript, and for both I am very grateful. I am also greatly indebted to Professor Donald Hair of the University of Western Ontario, who, in teaching me about literature, verily "opened the world" for me.

Further, Gregory Betts has contributed significantly to the writing of this book, and my appreciation for his personal and intellectual involvement in the project is "figured," I hope, on every page.

Figuring Grief

1 Towards a Theory of Fiction-Elegy

In a brief study of melancholia and depression (recently expanded into a book, *Black Sun*) Julia Kristeva posits a general theory of the usefulness of literature, and states that literary representation is a "staging of affects" which "possesses a real and imaginary efficacy that, cathartic more than of the order of elaboration, is a therapeutic method utilized in all societies through the ages."[1] Though this statement as a generalization about all literature might make the reader sceptical, it may be accurately applied to the specific genre of elegy: elegy *is* a verbal presentation or staging of emotion, wherein the detached speaker engages the audience with the intent of achieving some form of cathartic consolation. According to Northrop Frye, "catharsis implies the detachment of the spectator, both from the work of art itself and from the author,"[2] and it is in this distance between the reader and the elegy that the literary work of mourning is enacted. For tragedy, Aristotle insists, it is the structure of the text that makes catharsis possible; for the elegy, too – which, though not dramatic, is a staged performance of grief-work – structure is partially functional. But how does the "work of mourning" *work*? The question that remains to be answered is *how* elegiac catharsis or consolation is achieved – through what type of literary representation(s)? In this study these questions are raised by the title: how do writers "figure grief"?

The importance of elegy as a genre in English (British–North American) literature has increased in the twentieth century, though the traditional elegy has undergone a great deal of change in terms of form. Elegy is a literary genre that has become increasingly marked by blurred boundaries, containing as it does an intricate mixture of other genres, sub-genres, and modes. Francis Cairns writes that "all the genres originate in important, recurrent, real-life situations" and that "important recurrent situations ... come to call for [culturally defined] regular responses, both in words and in actions."[3] The human need for "regular response" to its own mortal condition does not mean that those responses need be "regular" or conventional, however, and it is elegy's capacity to transform literary conventions that make it a viable genre of great potential for writers and of continuing interest to readers.

In choosing a generic critical approach to this study, I have had to confront the hermeneutical dilemma of which Günther Müller speaks, asking: "How can I define tragedy (or any other genre) before I know on which works to base the definition, yet how can I know on which works to base the definition before I have defined tragedy?"[4] The inseparability of the form and content of any genre is at the root of this problem. By first defining Woolf and Joyce as elegists, then, my intent is to circumscribe a particular *type* of fiction, such that the paradigms produced might be useful in reading Gallant and Munro within an identified tradition. Thus my ensuing attempt to define here certain characteristics of elegy serves to delineate some of the originating conventions of the genre that have come to operate in modern and contemporary fiction.

SOME VERSIONS OF ELEGY

To begin, my claim is that modern and late modern[5] narrative experimentation with elegiac tropes and forms results in features of elegy specifically identifiable in the fiction produced. The seeds of these features became evident in the nineteenth-century novel. In *Kinds of Literature* Alastair Fowler notes that the "expressive lyricism" of the nineteenth-century novel often produced an "elegiac strain" or "modulation" in fiction; focusing on Meredith's *Egoist*, he discusses the "prolonged meditations of feeling" and the "shaping of style, even of syntax, as a vehicle of passion."[6] But writers in the twentieth century so expanded such "prolonged meditations" on death and loss that a new form was required to structure the work.

Ian Watt writes that "what is often felt as the formlessness of the novel, as compared, say, with tragedy or the ode, probably follows from this: the poverty of the novel's formal conventions would seem to be the price it must pay for its realism."[7] What Watt perceives as a problem – the "formlessness" of the novel, its "poverty" of conventions – is precisely the source of freedom that provided writers like Woolf and Joyce the opportunity to experiment with and borrow from other genres and to create generic variations of the elegy. Edward Engelberg employs the term "elegiac fiction" to describe those nineteenth- and twentieth-century texts that manifest a "modern sense of personal loss and dispossession, and of a special kind of sadness that validates the belief that one's life has been a series of missed opportunities."[8] But this thematic definition disregards the formal and linguistic characteristics of fiction written within an elegiac framework.[9] The modernists' use of the novel as a form of and for elegy was indeed a "novel" idea.

This experimentation culminated in the production of the fictional sub-genre that I call "fiction-elegy," a term that differentiates fiction written in an elegiac *form* from the broader *thematic* category of "elegiac fiction." A sub-genre of the romance novel, such as the elegiac romance, would therefore be an elegiac fiction but not a fiction-elegy.[10] Alternative terms for the sub-genre might include "fictive elegy" and "fictional elegy," but because the word "elegy" is modified by an adjective in each case, both terms would seem to describe a non-occasional *poetic* text. Neither of these descriptive terms accounts for the structural and linguistic aspects of modern and late modern fiction written in the form of an elegy, while the compound noun "fiction-elegy" places equal emphasis both on aspects of form (fiction and elegy) and on content (mourning).

There are some obvious parallels between the sub-genre of elegiac romance and my description of fiction-elegy. For example, the elegiac romance is written in the guise of fictional autobiography, a form that the fiction-elegist also employs to varying degrees. Kenneth A. Bruffee states that "elegiac romance is also interesting epistemologically because it implies that emotional adjustment to the past plays a role in knowing."[11] "Knowing" also plays a role in fiction-elegy, as my readings of Woolf, Joyce, Gallant, and Munro will suggest. The fiction-elegy, like the elegiac romance, involves a quest for knowledge and self-identity (undertaken after a loss is experienced), which is accomplished by remembering the past and then *telling* it in a narrativized work of mourning. In modern fiction this subtextual quest becomes a quest for form, which, according to Eric Smith, is related to consolation since "the finding of the form coincides with the defeat of grief and the finished work is in some sense a triumph over Time."[12] This formal closure is one feature of modernist fiction-elegy that is modified by late modern writers, who both use and alter or disrupt the conventions of the sub-genre.

This sub-genre is fundamentally trans-generic in that it brackets other genres in their modal form while retaining the elegy as the generic "dominant."[13] The modal version of another genre within the elegiac form is, then, a portion of the elegiac text that has a synecdochic relationship to another, originating genre. Alastair Fowler differentiates between genre and mode: "Modal terms never imply complete external form. Modes have always an incomplete repertoire, a selection only of the corresponding kind's [genre's] features."[14] An example of an independent and earlier genre that has been transformed into a mode-as-trope in elegy is the pastoral. Clearly the pastoral elegy is a pivotal poetic sub-genre in terms of the development of the separate genre of elegy. Elegy and pastoral became mixed as early as Theocritus' Idylls, which employ what has been identified as the "melancholy mood" that is pervasive in pastoral.[15] Idyll i, wherein Thyrsis mourns for Daphnis (his predecessor as the best rustic poet), is usually considered the archetype of the pastoral elegy.[16] This apparent inseparability of the two genres at their inception is not surprising, considering that the ancient patron god of both pastoral and elegy is Pan. (Pan, of course, consoled himself for the loss of Syrinx by changing her altered form – she had become a reed – into a musical pipe.)[17]

When one genre is incorporated into another as a mode or trope in this way, the result is a certain self-reflexivity, since the presence of the distinctive "mode" draws attention to the form of the text. This is true of the earliest pastoral elegies: for instance, Moschus' "Lament for Bion" makes use of pastoral imagery in order to mourn a poet (and not a fictive shepherd, as does Bion's "Lament for Adonis"), such that the pastoral machinery is used in an allegory of mourning. The trope of the shepherd-as-poet comes to function as a symbol of "man" – "neither as *homo sapiens*, nor as *homo faber*, but only as *homo artifex*," as Renato Poggioli writes.[18] In the twentieth century this characteristic self-consciousness in elegy is emphasized to an even greater extent, since modern literature's heightened self-reflexivity focuses the reader's attention directly on the form of the work. Virginia Woolf's *Jacob's Room* is one early example of this kind of fiction-elegy; Joyce's *A Portrait of the Artist as a Young Man* is another.

The elegist, too (and not just the mourned poet-figure), is a member of the class of artificers identified by Poggioli, and therefore an emphasis on the art of mourning as well as on the mour*ner* – the artist and survivor – has always been a significant component of elegy (think of *Lycidas*, for example, where we care more about Milton's speaker/persona than we do about Edward King). Poetic continuity is achieved in the very writing of the elegy; in this sense, self-consciousness functions as a trope of consolation.[19] But the importance of the elegist's act of writing is often subsumed by the digressions about him or herself upon which the writer embarks. Thus the autobiographical comes into play in elegy as well. This genre-turned-trope would seem to constitute a "countergenre,"[20] but in fact forms of life-writing serve a fundamental purpose in elegy: as a trope of consolation, this use of autobiography distances the speaker from the scene of death and reminds the reader that life does indeed go on. In first-person fictions such as Gallant's Linnet Muir stories, or Munro's *The Moons of Jupiter*, the authors use this trope of autobiography such that it both distracts the narrator-elegist from the occasion of the narrative and at the same time depicts the genealogical relation of the speaker to the lost person – in these examples, to her dead father.[21]

As a self-reflexive trope of elegy, the inclusion of the autobiographical is directly related to the psychopoetics of the genre.[22] The speaker must focus on him/herself as the survivor in order to divert attention from the loss, and thereby create an inherent "self-privileging of the survivors ... as a way of keeping them in motion, ensuring a sense of progress and egress," as Peter Sacks writes.[23] Thus the autobiographical effort both subtextualizes the elegiac and accomplishes the purpose of the work of mourning.

This connection between autobiography and elegy requires closer attention, and the work of several rhetorical theorists who write of genre, language, and loss is in need of mention. Morton Bloomfield points to the dictum in Aristotle's *Poetics* (section 6) to the effect that all poetry arises in praise, blame, or hymns, and he therefore locates the origin of elegy in the speech-act genre of praise.[24] More generally, Tzvetan Todorov states that all literary genres "have their origins in human discourse," in speech-acts;[25] the human discourse at the basis of elegy would be the ancient discourse of human grief. "Mourning is a well-structured psychological process that people experience in a repeated pattern of ordered stages of behaviour," writes Ronald Schleifer in his recent *Rhetoric and Death*; the work of mourning – what Schleifer calls "the rhetoric of mourning" – aims at the "recovery of voice in the face of [death]."[26] Schleifer's description of the rhetoric of mourning is closely aligned with Paul de Man's definition of prosopopoeia, the "trope of autobiography" that gives a voice and/or a face to that which is absent.[27] But J. Hillis Miller identifies prosopopoeia as the "trope of mourning" in that it "is a cover-up of death or of absence, a compensation."[28] These two seemingly opposite functions of the trope might be resolved with attention to the fact that the prosopopoetic "voice" is a *double* voice in elegy: the voice of the absent as well as the voice of the survivor is figured in the performed and performative text.

It is in the latter voicing that prosopopoeia, the trope of mourning, also might be seen in a second doubling or echoing effect as a trope of autobiography, one that functions *within* an elegy or work of mourning. The genre of elegy transforms other performative literary genres (such as autobiography, praise, and the classical genres of lament and consolation) into tropological forms. An autobiographical segment of an elegy, for example, functions as a trope in that it signifies something other than the speaker's "life" – namely, a stage of the elegist's *textual* "work" of mourning, wherein grief is figured and survival is "voiced." The tropological function of a genre within an elegy also might be considered in terms of the liturgical definition of trope as an "amplification of liturgical texts."[29] Though elegy becomes separate from religious ritual in its modern and late modern versions, it is like prayer in that ritualistic components of the text (repetition and invocation, for example) are inherent in its structure. Thus the speech-act characteristic of these earlier genres is also absorbed by the elegy, which translates all such acts to an act of writing.

QUESTS FOR FORM

"Death is the mother of invention," writes Wallace Stevens ("Sunday Morning"), and for elegists, death is the muse. Generally speaking, in fiction written up to the nineteenth century, death – like marriage – was a theme used strategically to structure, and usually to close, the work. The nineteenth-century elegiac fiction of which Fowler speaks contains elegiac passages, or what he calls "strains," but the structure of these texts is not based on that of the elegy. Death is not a principle of closure in elegy (fictional or poetic) but provides the basis for writing itself, as well as for structural openness, for resistance to the universally thematic "end" – to death itself. The principle that does structure the end of an elegiac text, then, is consolation: whether explicitly or implicitly present or explicitly denied, consolation is the driving force and the shaping concept of elegy.

In the nineteenth century, what has been identified as the pastoral novel[30] proliferated, and in those novels that contain elegiac passages, pastoral was used as a balancing, consoling trope; the work of Thomas Hardy is an example of this type of fiction. But in the twentieth century pastoral is seen as an inadequate form of consolation;

the persuasive force of the imaginative representation has lost its power, as such pastoral fables as "the golden age, Eden, Arcadia, and various futuristic paradises"[31] have been abandoned by modern writers living in an industrialized, urban world. The issue of how to write loss or "figure grief" and how to console with words or a linguistic construct was suddenly called into question by the modernists to a greater extent than ever before in the history of the genre.[32]

In *Mourning, Gender and Creativity in the Art of Herman Melville*, a biographical study, Neal Tolchin writes that the author "came to implicate the form of the novel itself ... in the social control of feeling."[33] Melville's view of the novel as a structural constraint in the writing of elegiac fiction typifies the need for the subsequent modernist project whereby the transformed novel was made viable for elegy. Virginia Woolf comments on the "Victorian game of manners," which was "founded on restraint, sympathy, and unselfishness," and states that it was "helpful in making something seemly and human out of raw odds and ends"; but in terms of aesthetic activity, the "manners game" deprived the writer of elegy of an adequate form of expression (a deprivation that Woolf refers to as a "disadvantage in writing").[34] In seeking a more appropriate form, Woolf asks: "But can prose ... chant the elegy, or hymn the love, or shriek in terror, praise the rose, the nightingale, or the beauty of the night? Can it leap at one spring at the heart of its subject as the poet does? I think not. That is the penalty it pays for having dispensed with the incantation and the mystery, with rhyme and metre."[35] But Woolf does not divorce poetic conventions from those of prose. Rather, she uses the novel form in the exploration and alteration of elegiac conventions (such as incantation) that originated in poetic techniques. Her fiction-elegy novels evolved from her short stories and sketches, sketches that she thought were a "natural way of marking the past."[36]

The shorter form of fiction, by virtue of narrative concentration, seems to serve the needs of elegy quite well. In fiction-elegy a shorter form eliminates the novelist's need to elaborately emphasize plot and chronology, such that the intensification of a character's experience climaxes in revelation that is figured for the reader, if not the character/narrator. Meaning, more than plot, is foregrounded or dramatized to a greater extent than is possible in traditional novelistic narratives. In Joyce's short stories, for instance, the epiphanic moments are discrete and are located towards or at the end of a story (although they become more dispersed and generalized in *Portrait of the Artist* and *Ulysses*).

Experimentation with poetic and narrative forms led to the development of the elegy written in the fictional form. Extending those "elegiac strains" found in the fiction of the preceding era, writers began to break from the constraints of the traditional structure of poetic elegy while using that elegiac structure at the same time. Usually written on the occasion of the death of a real individual, the conventional elegy began to be replaced by a fictional exploration of the grieving process. Julia Kristeva writes that, like every affect, melancholy and depression are "irreducible to [their] verbal or semiological expressions" and that "no conceptual framework of the constituted sciences (linguistics, in particular) shows itself adequate for the comprehension of this seemingly very rudimentary representation (pre-sign and pre-language)."[37] Nevertheless, modern elegy demonstrates an attempt to find a framework of verbal expression for grief by using methods of psychonarration.[38] Modern elegy textually dramatizes the work of mourning on an extended and, in psychological terms, more realistic scale.

This work of mourning performs a quest for form, one that is inscribed in fiction-elegy by a story-within-the-story or *mise en abyme* narrative structure. The reader is implicated in the *mise en abyme* of stories, and the elegist uses the resulting temporal disruption as a counterpointing strategy against closure, against confronting the metaphoric "end." This structure constitutes what has been called a "mournful hermeneutics,"[39] since the reader's experience of the fiction-elegy is contingent upon the (mournful) experience of the narrator, who writes in the present or recent past from the more distant past of memory.

The presence of a story-teller within the fiction self-consciously points to the elegiac convention of communal commiseration, wherein "narration is an effort in effect to create a community of readers who share vicariously" the work of mourning.[40] Alan W. Friedman describes this relationship between mourning and aesthetics, and states that grief is both "experienced and recreated in the social form of telling."[41] Therefore grief-work itself *is* its own poetics of elegy: the process of the work of mourning involves narration, and what that narration produces is a *work* – a text – of mourning. Whether that work *works* in terms of achieved consolation depends on how "consolation" is defined; for late modern writers, for instance, formal consolation often is resisted, and the elegiac frameworks in the fiction of Gallant and Munro textually enact an obstacle to consolation. For them, "consolation," if it can be called that, is acquired in the reader's recognition of form, and in the apprehension of the meaning of loss in its relationship to presence – in the understanding of the role that memory plays in constructing necessary fictions of our lives.

The partially autobiographical narrative act of the late modern narrator-elegist also allows him/her to use memory to gain a kind of self-knowledge in that it usually progresses towards another elegiac trope: *anagnorisis*, which is variously translated as recognition, revelation, discovery, or disclosure.[42] For modern elegists the moment of discovery is a moment of clarification. In Woolf's work these textual moments are defined by the author as "moments of being"; for Joyce they are "epiphanies." Woolf's "moments" are "sudden shocks" that, although painful, are valuable because they are inseparable from the desire to "explain," as she explains in "A Sketch of the Past": "It is only by putting it into words that I make it whole; this wholeness means that it has lost its power to hurt me; it gives me, perhaps because by doing so I take away the pain, a great delight to put the severed parts together. Perhaps this is the strongest pleasure known to me."[43]

In Munro's fiction-elegies memory is thematized and performed, and "queer, bright moments" are produced that, though significant, remain unexplained to the reader.[44] However, the position and context of the moments indicate that they hold a significance beyond that which the text explicates for the reader; it is the very unresolvability of these moments that marks their meaning. Gallant's narrator- and character-elegists, who most often use memory to escape from the past rather than to understand it, rarely experience what is referred to in "The Moslem Wife" as "the light of imagination," the epiphanic understanding of themselves that the reader of the stories acquires from them. Thus a judgment of character and of self is implicitly demanded of the reader of Gallant's work. Neil Besner uses the phrase "the light of imagination" to title his study of Gallant's fiction; he writes that "significance plays over her stories in flashes and sparks."[45] But these various related terms used to describe the experience of the elegists inscribed in fiction do not name a new trope; rather, they provide new names and a new status for a traditional component of the genre.

Another modernist writer who used a term of his own for such anagnoristic moments is Marcel Proust. The "moment bienheureux" in *A la recherche du temps perdu* is a moment of revelation that interrupts the narrative of voluntary memory with what Jerry Aline Flieger calls "image-events"; these moments "figure" that which has been forgotten, that which is absent not only literally but in memory as well. Clearly Proust's narrative is an exemplary "elegiac fiction," and many of Proust's strategies participate in his "work of figuration" of the past.[46] But while his work is in some ways elegiac, it is largely concerned with *in*voluntary memory and is not structured as an elegy; rather, he translates "fragments of 'pure time,' apprehended in the difference between past and present moments, into a narrative technique that stimulates the reader to generate characters from discontinuous stills," writes Elizabeth Abel. In other words, Proust's text provides disconnected scenes that the reader "connects," whereas writers like Woolf "juxtapos[e] scenes to produce not synchronic understandings of character but fictions that join a moment in the present to its antecedent."[47] A fiction-elegy is more precisely a work of mourning wherein the memory-writing is not necessarily – and not often – pleasurable for the elegist. While both Gallant and Munro have stated that Proust was influential on their own artistic development, the direction taken in the works of the late modernists differs substantially from that of Proust, whose experimentalism exceeds elegiac form.

What is at stake in the modernistic fiction-elegies exemplified by the work of Woolf and Joyce is the ability of the aesthetic to console structurally or tropologically. The modernistic forms of consolation are altered in the work of Gallant and Munro, wherein a mourning experience is also induced in the reader; for these late modernists, however, the grief-work heightens the reader's awareness of loss but does not attempt to resolve or compensate for loss in aesthetic terms. Thus the disturbing empathy so induced often is not resolved for the reader, but insight is consequently produced *because of* the disturbance. D.W. Harding distinguishes between vicarious experience and empathic insight: "It seems nearer the truth ... to say that fictions contribute to defining the reader's or spectator's values, and perhaps stimulating his desires, rather than to suppose that they gratify desire by some mechanism of vicarious experience."[47] The desired "stimulation" of the reader of elegy produces a *simulation* – a version of the experiences of grief and consolation – and the evaluation of the appropriateness of emotional responses to loss. The ability of elegy to induce an empathic reaction in a reader who, prior to reading the text, has no relation to or knowledge of the characters is suggestive of its paradigmatic nature at the structural level. The reader, after all, has not personally "lost" Mrs Ramsay in *To the Lighthouse,* and the fiction-elegy enacts this distance in the narrative using a detached speaker, who has also not lost Mrs Ramsay. The aesthetic distance of the representation from the reader – a mimesis that both represents and performs a narrator's or a character's work of mourning – allows the reader to transfer meaning from the text to his/her own realm of experience.

Hermeneutically, this *epiphora* or transfer of meaning is analogous to a psychoanalytic "transference" between the analyzing text and the reader as analysand, and occurs when the reader recognizes the elegiac structure of the text and the psychology of its semantics. Metaphor is often discussed by theorists in terms of its etymological meaning of "transfer" or "transformation." In a discussion of the "semantic function" of the "psychological features" of metaphor, Paul Ricoeur concludes that metaphors "induce the reader ... to possess magically the absent thing, body, or person."[48] In the context of elegy this theory ascribes to metaphor the inherent ability to provide tropological consolation. While other tropes – such as prosopopoeia, which is metonymic – have been more common and powerful forms of consolation within elegiac aesthetic constructs than has metaphor per se, the ability of language to console at all on intellectual and epistemological levels is questioned by late modern writers such as Gallant and Munro, writers who most often disclaim the value of inventing a pacifying resolution of conflicts between memory and truth, past and present, life and death, life and writing.[49]

Schleifer suggests that metonymy is both "part of" language and meaning, and random or arbitrary, the "other" of language which provokes inarticulable feelings; he also aligns metonymy with death: death is both "part of" life (a stage of life) and the "negation of life."[50] Schleifer also insists that metonymy is not synecdoche. Metonymy is, I suggest, a metaphoric synecdoche, a paradigmatic synecdoche (for example, the crown for the king), whereas pure synecdoche is dependent upon the referential, syntagmatic function of language alone (for example, the hand for the arm). In my elaboration of the poetics of elegy, modernist writers who use metonymy as a trope of consolation (such as prosopopoeia, the voice for the life) emphasize the metaphoric characteristic of the trope in an attempt to mimic presence in the mental representation of the absent, whereas the late modernist writers emphasize the synecdochic characteristic of metonymy and of memory (which itself is a metonymy of the past).

The relationship between meaning and language is a common concern in elegy. Gallant and Munro explore what Karen Mills-Courts refers to as the human "need for language to be incarnative and our understanding that it behaves, instead, as representation."[51] The texts of these authors simultaneously employ, demonstrate, and question methods of mourning. In other words, they explore the human need to employ the metonymic *structure* of language – which seems to allow the retrieval of and connection to the past – in contrast to the metaphoric *characteristic* of language, metaphoric because the signifier only represents the signified in an arbitrary relation and because it transforms differences into similarities in the sign itself.

Fiction-elegy is a metaphorical or allegorical genre, then, because the representation refers to two levels of meaning – to the story and to the grief-work as a system of meaning, of figuring grief – as would an allegory, or extended metaphor. The difference between a modernist and a late modernist fiction-elegy is partially a difference between meaning-as-product and meaning-as-process. It is the performance of the work of mourning that, I will argue, Gallant and Munro emphasize in their fiction-elegies, rather than the consolation of closure and form of the modernist paradigms.

But first, close attention to the works of Woolf and Joyce as literary inventors is called for so that their models of mourning may be seen *as* models, as paradigms of fiction-elegy that the late modernists revise. Since fiction-elegy also provides a model for the reader, there are ethical implications of the genre as well. In "The Novel as Ethical Paradigm" Patricia Spacks provides a definition of ethical fiction that is useful for our purposes: "An ethical paradigm comprises an image of social behaviour. Although the word *paradigm* suggests a pattern for imitation, the idea of ethical paradigms need not imply a view of fiction as rule book. On the contrary, the paradigmatic force of narrative derives from its orderings of action, those fundamental dramatic structures that underlie plot."[52] In a sense, then, the fiction-elegies of Gallant and Munro may be seen as paradigms of a paradigm, models of "social behaviour" or "patterns for imitation" by the *reader*, derived from the modernist model of mourning.

MODERNIST PARADIGMS: WOOLF AND JOYCE

In her diary entry for 26 January 1920 Woolf writes of her "idea of a new form for a novel": "Suppose one thing should open out of another – as in An Unwritten Novel – only not for 10 pages but 200 or so – doesn't that give the looseness and lightness I want: doesn't that get closer and yet keep form & speed, & enclose everything, everything?"[53] Woolf used the structural techniques of the fragment, story, and sketch to compose *Jacob's Room*, which is an almost pure fiction-elegy,[54] and the elegiac novels that follow it. Indeed, at the time of writing *Jacob's Room* Woolf suggests "elegy" as the new name for her books, a name to supplant "novel."[55] Gillian Beer describes her style as "writing of the past as pastiche and celebration,"[56] and this dramatization of the past is typically achieved through the writing of fictional memories, which are themselves fragments of the past, made present.

If *Jacob's Room* is a fiction-elegy for Jacob as well as "an elegy for past youth and past summers,"[57] then the novel functions as an extended prosopopoeia, a verbal resurrection that both recalls Jacob to life and acts as a "cenograph": it marks his absence like a cenotaph, the body being elsewhere. The text opens with attention to Jacob's absence from a family scene. His brother's apostrophic call "Ja – cob! Ja – cob!"[58] becomes emblematic of the entire fiction-elegy, which is both an attempt to name and invoke the dead as well as a demonstration of the impossibility of its success. Bonamy's repetition of the incantation at the end of the text provides structural circularity (and formal closure) but not consolation for Bonamy himself. Jacob is supposedly the poetic inheritor, waiting to become initiated into an intellectual understanding of life and death; but he dies without completing the quest, leaving the reader as the next poetic successor in the reconstruction of the fragments of the elegy.

Woolf's novels typically consist of fragments that require the reader "to fabricate the links among scenes."[59] However, Carolyn Williams figuratively identifies *Jacob's Room* and *Mrs Dalloway* as "framed narratives" in which "issues of enclosure" are raised to "the level of self-conscious thematics and total narrative form."[60] In fiction-elegy a formal framing device is often instituted through multiple levels of story-telling. These frames produce the necessary distance for the narrator-elegist or narrated character-elegist. For example, the frame-construction of *Mrs Dalloway* situates the reader at the outermost frame, followed by Peter Walsh, who "reads" Clarissa, situated at the next framing level. At the centre of the frames is Septimus Smith, the "giant mourner"[61] whose death provides Clarissa (and consequently the reader) with an empathic understanding of the experience of death. The reader's "perusal of our doom in the death of a surrogate," as Garrett Stewart calls the reader's experience,[62] occurs via these narrative frames. Death is deferred in the narrative, which accomplishes "the displacement of fatality by effigy."[63]

Clarissa, a reader-figure in the text, witnesses death through its representation. She is the poetic successor, the inheritor of Septimus' vision, and a survivor: "She had escaped. But that young man had killed himself."[64] As a reader of the situation, she thinks: "here's death" (279). Peter Walsh, however, is "overcome with his own grief" (62) and, as a writer-figure, he fictionalizes his life "as one makes up the better part of life, he thought – making oneself up, making her up" (81). He writes the past, and he figures Clarissa herself: "It is Clarissa. For there she was" (296). Peter's invocational speech-act creates the figure of Clarissa in his (and the reader's) mind; the deictic "there" gives the reader a sense of his pointing to an objectified woman in the next inner frame – Clarissa as painting, as effigy.

The framing device also provides a paradigmatic structure for the reader, whereby a mournful hermeneutics is achieved in the figuration of the work of mourning as narrative. Fragments of fiction, then, quite literally make the fiction-elegy "framework" for the reader who reconstructs the work of mourning. For Woolf, descriptions of moments of being are induced by conceiving of that which is absent, an activity re-enacted by the reader of the fiction. Prosopopoetic "visions" (such as Peter's visions of Clarissa, which "ceaselessly float up, pace beside, put their *faces* in front of, the actual thing," 86; emphasis mine) replace the image of the real face with another image; this substitution, simulation, or image, which provides a mediating consolation, is inscribed in the text by the character-elegist (Peter, in this case), who is a model mourner for the reader.

Lily's attempts to invoke Mrs Ramsay in *To the Lighthouse* differ from Peter's memory-induced visualizations in that her silent cries of "Mrs Ramsay!" (throughout "The Lighthouse" section of *To the Lighthouse*)[65] are verbal apostrophes that fail as an invocation. Only a representation, a substitute language in the form of her painting (verb, not noun), allows her to perform an *ekphrastic* act: "Yes, she thought, laying down her brush in extreme fatigue, I have had my vision" (310). Elizabeth Abel argues that Lily's painting "functions as an alternative not to language but to Woolf's account of language acquisition, which she depicts through James and Cam as both compelling and dismaying."[66] The vision – the product of a performative act – consoles Lily, and in this sense the painting is a paradigmatic elegy, the line drawn an iterable mark, a sign that produces consoling thought. There are, then, two kinds of writing and two kinds of memory at stake for the narrator-elegist (and reader-mourner): while the painting is a repeatable *sign* for the writer of elegy, it becomes a *symbol* for the reader of elegy.

As designed textual constructs, fiction-elegies function in a paradigmatic manner, and the reader constructs a second paradigm – a model of mourning – from the text itself.[67] The act of reading requires that we "plac[e] our thoughts and feelings at the disposal of an unreality, bestowing on it a semblance of reality in proportion to a reducing of our own reality," as Wolfgang Iser writes. "Staging oneself" in this way is the "means whereby representation is transferred from text to reader."[68]

In fiction-elegy this means that the represented work of mourning leads the reader toward the experience of anagnorisis, that moment of recognition that Woolf describes with her phrase "moments of being." For Woolf such moments entail a heightened pleasure in and comprehension of reality.[69] This moment occurs when the non-sense of loss and grief begins to be replaced by some intuitive or intellectual acceptance of death, some "reason." The "moment of being" is often belated in elegy – it comes at the end of the work, not at the climax of loss and emotion. Thus the moment is partially a formal as well as a thematic property of elegy, and structurally it coincides with the moment of consolation.

Joyce's secular definition of the theological word "epiphany" suggests that it might be used similarly as a trope of consolation: "I mean that I am trying in my poems [and fiction] to give people some kind of intellectual pleasure or spiritual enjoyment by converting the bread of everyday life into something that has a permanent artistic life of its own ... for their mental, moral, and spiritual uplift."[70] This transubstantial transformation of life into art offers intellectual consolation for the ephemerality of that life, a consolation that for Joyce is related to the permanence of art. Such modernistic "art-as-epitaph" both encloses and discloses significance.

The reader of modern fiction-elegy experiences the epiphanic revelations that the character experiences, but at a remove. The epiphany is not primarily therapeutic, then (only an individual's non-literary work of mourning could be so described), but pragmatic and paradigmatic, in that it provides a model for the reader's "mental, moral, and spiritual uplift." This significant uplift is signified in the written epiphany, which is evoked for the character by the interaction of image and imagination. According to Stephen's famous description in *Portrait of the Artist as a Young Man*, first an object or image is apprehended (*integritas*); that apprehension is then analysed by the imagination (*consonantia*) and eventually comprehended in terms of its truth and meaning (*claritas*). The visibility of the image is essential for the epiphanic moment to occur; this "ineluctable modality of the visible," as Stephen Dedalus describes it, can be achieved concretely through the apprehension of an object, person or gesture; or it can exist only in the mind's eye, in a figurative seeing, as it is constituted in the aural experience of perceiving sound; memory also resurrects an image of the past in the present of the mind (this resurrection is figured by the trope of analepsis). Geoffrey Hartman refers to the importance of the "ineluctable ear" in

Joyce's fiction[71] and states that reading may be considered "an active kind of hearing,"[72] a parallel that is particularly useful in analysing the reader's experience of epiphany.

In the epistemology of the epiphany, the role of the subject that perceives and thinks is emphasized rather than that of the object, which discloses insight in the form of itself. Generally, epiphanic consolation occurs in and through this thinking, this grief-work. Recorded in words, the written epiphanic experience could be described in terms of a "think-act."[73] I define a "think-act" as an interiorized performative, an imaginative version of "doing things with words." Think-acts are performative parts of a narrative that are *thought* by a narrator or character and produce an effect (usually revelatory and/or consoling) on the thinker *and* on the reader. (Peter Walsh's invocation would be better defined as a version of this kind of think-act, for example, since it is an interior thought rather than a spoken phrase.) A think-act is a form of *anamnesis*, a recollection that, in a liturgical context, has a "sense of 'recalling' or 're-presenting' before God an event in the past so that it becomes here and now operative by its effects," writes Gregory Dix.[74] Using Austin's terminology, an elegiac think-act would be a "behabitive," which is "a kind of performative concerned roughly with reactions to behaviour and with behaviour towards others and designed to exhibit attitudes and feelings."[75] Elegiac think-acts originate with phrases that include "I mourn" and "I remember," and are therefore performed by an introspective as well as a retrospective consciousness.

Linguistic think-acts invoke memory, and seem to resurrect analeptically that which is absent. Though a speech-act "pledges only to what is mortal," as Derrida writes,[77] by implication an elegiac think-act often pledges to that which is no longer mortal. The reader performs the think-acts inscribed in fiction-elegy, too, since the think-act is an illocutionary performative: it is theatrical and staged, and thereby creates a contract with the reader; it can produce an effect of consolation, and therefore a think-act is potentially perlocutionary as well. Perlocutionary acts, says Austin, "produce certain consequential effects upon the feelings, thoughts, or actions of the audience, or of the speaker, or of other persons: and it may be done with the design, intention, or purpose of producing them."[78] By design, the think-act does have effects on the speaker (or character) as well as on the audience or reader, in terms of feelings, thoughts, and/or actions.

As textual acts, think-acts actively involve the "perceiver" of the fiction. But in the late modern fiction of Gallant and Munro, the connection between language and consolation is not as clear as it is in the modernist fiction-elegy, but is extensively explored by both authors, who suggest that memory's ability to "give voice" to the absent is fundamentally distortive. Munro's narrator- and character-elegists often undergo the same "queer, bright moment" that the reader does and are in this sense more in keeping with Woolf's moments of being, which reveal something of the "reality behind appearances," as Woolf writes in "A Sketch of the Past."[79] But in some cases the first-person narrator-elegist (or the character-elegist in a third-person narrative) does not complete the epiphanic experience, though the reader is positioned (via the third-person narrator, or through strategies of irony) such that he/she *does* acquire an understanding of the elegiac text. Munro's "moments" are less self-evident and more ambiguous than Woolf's; they do not offer closed, conclusive, or absolute answers to the issues explored by the elegist.

This situation is true for some of Joyce's Dubliners as well. R.M. Adams writes that the major theme of *Dubliners* is "that Ireland is a land of walking ghosts and barely vitalized corpses" (100). But in the *Dubliners* stories, Joyce uses the moment of insight, the epiphany, to revitalize both character and reader. Of the fifteen stories, five – "The Sisters," "Eveline," "A Little Cloud," "A Painful Case," and "The Dead" – fall into the category of fiction-elegy with their focus on death and/or loss. The collection ends with the aptly titled "The Dead," a framed narrative wherein the ceremonial speech or dramatic monologue that Gabriel Conroy performs publicly creates a contract with the textual listeners or audience; this relation, in turn, establishes a participative model for the reader. The elegiac subtext is indicated by the subject of Gabriel's speech, which is about the "memory of those dead and gone great ones" and "thoughts of the past, of youth, of changes, of absent faces that we miss here tonight" (203–4).

Gabriel learns that his earlier epiphanic "tide of joy" (212), induced by memories of "their secret life together" (213), was evoked by a falsity, by the fiction he had elaborated in his mind, when Gretta Conroy reveals her emotions for an "absent face" – a long-dead lover from her youth. A false epiphany, when revealed as such, breaks the contract between the think-act and the mourner; in J.L. Austin's terms, it is "infelicitous" or "unhappy" (14), a "Misinvocational Misfire" (17). Similarly, the contract between the elegist and the reader, who believes in the validity of the representation and bases a model upon it, is also breached at this point. But the contract is re-established in this story when the knowledge that Gabriel gains about his wife and himself leads to another think-act that produces insight, though hardly consolation – which is an important structural and textual difference. Gabriel experiences a subdued epiphany, the only "uplift" being the recognition of the universality of loss and mortality in nature's equal treatment of the living and the dead: his "soul swooned slowly as he heard the snow falling faintly through the universe, and faintly falling, like the descent of their last end, upon all the living and the dead" (223). After this revelation, we are told that Gabriel's "identity was fading out" (203), which indicates that he has been changed by the irony of his infelicitous epiphany. Indeed, consideration of his own mortality has been the basis of his speech early in the story, and even of the narrative itself; in elegiac fashion Joyce's narrative presents a portrait of Gabriel as elegist.

Adrienne Munich concludes that Gabriel's dinner speech is also a "self-epitaph, foreshadowing, if not his figurative demise, then at least sexual defeat."[80] Since elegy does tend to focus on the survivor, the genre could be considered "self-epitaphic" in this sense. It is the experience of the elegist, not of the dead or absent, that is of interest in this form of literature, and this experience is made most immediate for the reader by way of the think-act. While the think-act is what Joseph Frank would call a "time-act"[81] (whether figured using epiphany, moments of being, or queer, bright moments), the epiphany as think-act in elegy is clearly an atemporal experience wherein elements of the past, present, and future merge. This spatial fusion of temporal components creates a temporary eternity, a "timeless unity that, while it may accentuate surface differences, eliminates any feelings of sequence by the very act of juxtaposition."[82]

Another technique used to this effect in modern fiction-elegy is the manipulation of sequential time in the narrative. This is an effort to eliminate the sense of time passing, as the resultant "co-existence" of all time transcends the mortal present in a textual *otium*,[83] one that instals a "temporality of discourse." Jonathan Culler explains: "The clearest example of this [temporal] structure is of course the elegy which replaces an irrevocable disfunction, the move from life to death, with a dialectical alternation between attitudes of mourning and consolation, evocations of absence and presence."[84] This alternation, Culler states, "displaces the temporal pattern of actual loss" (67). In other words, elegiac literature that invokes the past (absence) and the present (presence) institutes a trope of temporal consolation.

Joyce's play with narrative chronology in *Portrait of the Artist as a Young Man* institutes this kind of temporal trope. Epiphanies interrupt the narrative that is a (third-person) elegy for an unhappy

childhood, and for Stephen's past selves. These epiphanies are provoked by images, and Pound's definition of the image is significant
in the context of epiphany: an image is "that which presents an intellectual and emotional complex in an instant of time" and provides
"that sense of sudden liberation; that sense of freedom from time
limits and space limits; that sense of sudden growth."[85] This definition[86] suggests that the image, like an epiphany, is able to produce a
form of the textual otium; its use may have a cathartic effect on the
reader, making it an appropriate tool of the elegist. The image is
thus a trope of consolation. The theme of language as resurrection
is Joyce's counter-argument to Father Arnall's warning that "there is
nothing in this wretched world that can make up for such a loss" as
the loss of man's "immortal soul" (110). Stephen attempts to recover
his "dead or lost" childhood and "soul" (96) – to reverse time – by
re-versing or re-writing it, by *imaging* it. It is language, then, that is
life to Joyce and to Stephen, and it is language that constitutes elegiac affirmation.

The trope of self-reflexivity proves to be the preferred form of consolation for modernist fiction-elegists such as Joyce and Woolf.
Munro, too, depends on story-telling as a source of wisdom and understanding, though her focus is on the *process* of story-telling and
less on a fixed product. But Gallant's "moments" cannot be aligned
with a consoling effect; they might be described as "disfigured
epiphanies" because her fiction-elegies are rooted in historical facts
outside of the text that prevent a Joycean uplifting revelation. Instead, history pierces the reader's consciousness and prevents epiphanic pleasure; in its place the reader gains the understanding that
the past cannot be rectified, is rarely pleasurable, and should not be
transformed into an atemporal deluding fiction.

Thus in the late modern fiction of Gallant and Munro, the trust in
language and art is questioned, and the exploration of grief and loss
is conducted not only on the formal level of representation but also
on conceptual and tropological levels in terms of figuring memory,
history, and the past. Ironically, the style of these later writers is
more realistic than both their predecessors' experimental prose and
their contemporaries' postmodern rewriting of history. However,
the late modern fiction-elegy reveals the traces and marks of its predecessor, as its literary-historical label suggests. The genre of elegy
has had to adapt itself to contemporary perspectives on psychology,
philosophy, and history as well as aesthetics. The studies of Gallant
and Munro that follow chart versions of this adaptation through
close analyses of the fiction-elegies themselves.

2 Gallant's Sad Stories

Though Mavis Gallant's fiction has received a great deal of critical attention in the last ten or twelve years, much of that criticism has been limited to noting Gallant's main themes: W.J. Keith states that "the concept of abandonment or betrayal" is central,[1] and Janice Kulyk Keefer and Neil K. Besner focus on the role that memory plays in her characters' and narrators' worlds. But few have attempted to relate the form of Gallant's fictions to their content. A special issue of *Essays on Canadian Writing* – the "Mavis Gallant Issue" – was published recently, and therein several articles explore structural and rhetorical facets of Gallant's work. Heather Murray insists that it is "the story rather than plot, the *way of telling* rather than what is told," that characterizes Gallant's narrative mode, a mode that demonstrates a "betrayal of generic expectations";[2] E.D. Blodgett, too, comments on the relation between Gallant's strategies and themes: "[Gallant] is an author who appears to know precisely, amid what often are no more than the fragments of a life, where to direct her reader, in such a way that even the *sense of loss* that *dépaysement* gathers in is *part of the plan*."[3]

Gallant's plan is, in very basic terms, to present the reader with segments of contemporary life as seen from her distinctly ironic perspective. In her oft-quoted brief essay "What Is Style?" Gallant writes: "Style is inseparable from structure, part of the conformation of whatever the author has to say. What he says – this is what fiction is about – is that something is taking place and that nothing lasts. Against the sustained tick of a watch, fiction takes the measure of a life, a season, a look exchanged, the turning point, desire as brief as a dream, the grief and terror that after childhood we cease to express. The lie, the look, the grief are without permanence. The watch continues to tick where the story stops."[4] Gallant does present us with measures of lives, with experiences of "grief and terror," and her fiction *represents* or *figures* this grief in a form that is self-conscious about its own language and structure.

Gallant's narrative strategies invite our empathic participation in the texts. J. Brooks Bouson, in *The Empathic Reader: A Study of Narcissistic Character and the Drama of the Self*, discusses the reader's empathic experience in theoretical terms: "At once affective and cognitive, the empathic event involves a dynamic interplay between objective and subjective, conscious and unconscious, the verbalizable and the unverbalizable ... Empathic reading also makes us aware of our affective and collusive involvements with literature, ... and of the ways in which we may act out our own self-dramas when we interpret literary works."[5] The reader is invited to experience in Gallant's fiction what might be called "mimpathy," a philosophic term that combines concepts of mimesis and empathy and refers to the acting-out of "our own self-dramas" when we interpret the suffering of a literary character.

The conditions of mimpathy require that this suffering "must already be given in some form before it is possible for anyone to become a fellow sufferer. Pity and sympathy as experienced are always subsequent to the already apprehended and understood experience of another person who is pitied."[6] Gallant portrays characters as they experience the apprehended "after-*affects*" of loss (rather than portraying the actual experience of loss), and so induces readers to understand that experience for themselves in the course of mimpathic involvement, in giving form to that experience outside of the story's frame of reference. This representation of grief necessitates by definition an elegiac form, and in this Gallant's work shares several features with modernist predecessors. Critics such as Robertson Davies and Donald Jewison have commented on Gallant's "modernist mode";[7] Ronald Hatch compares "The Other Paris" to *Dubliners*, for instance, and Elmer Borklund makes a similar comparison: "These anti-romantic glimpses of dislocation and despair are rendered in deliberately hard, dry prose, reminiscent, like their subject matter, of Joyce's *Dubliners*."[8] Lorna Irvine compares Gallant's fiction in general to that of Joseph Conrad.[9] But a thus-far unnoted similarity between Gallant and writers such as Woolf, Joyce, and even Conrad is that both Gallant and these modernists write using an elegiac perspective.

Gallant's world-view is quite close to that of Woolf, who wondered whether " 'sadness' ... is ... essential to the modern view."[10] In an interview with Janice Kulyk Keefer, Gallant discusses the relation between art and reality and states that "one is cheated in art"; "there's nothing pretty about [reality]. You know, there's pretty-sad and ugly-sad. Art is essentially a cheat ... being a displacement."[11] In this statement she denotes reality as "ugly-sad," while art *about* sadness produces a displacement of the ugliness and takes the form of "pretty-sad." In Gallant's view a mood of sadness might be said to dominate both contemporary reality and contemporary art – her own included.

Gallant's fiction, though contemporary, is not part of any postmodern agenda. Instead, with her social/moral realism, her focus on the past and on the *interpretation* of the past in the present, Gallant would be better described as a late modernist. Alan Wilde suggests that "late modernism interposes a space of transition, a necessary bridge between more spacious and self-conscious experimental movements";[12] he also states that "reading appearances correctly is, in fact, the project of late modernism." As a late modernist Gallant is concerned not only with issues of representation but indeed with the project of reading – with reading memory and the past, and with reading responsibly. Her work is usually less formally experimental than that of her modernist predecessors, and it questions the kind of perceptions and representations of the past that a modernist aesthetic tends to produce. The paradigmatic models of modernist fiction-elegies provided by Woolf and Joyce, I have argued, have been adapted by late-modern writers such as Gallant who aim to rewrite modernity – to "work through" modernism by confronting and challenging various of its tenets, usually in a more realistic narrative mode.[13]

Gallant's fiction-elegy employs strategies of "displacement" such as irony, allegory, and metonymy. Themes of loss, betrayal, death, and grief are presented in terms of these strategies, which, adopting Julia Kristeva's terminology, could be called "elegiac modalities of *signifiance*."[14] Kristeva uses the French term *signifiance* to refer to "the work performed in language ... that enables a text to signify what representative and communicative speech does not say."[15] Modalities of *signifiance* are necessary in literature since, as Kristeva writes, "representations proper to affects, and notably sadness," are "insufficiently stabilized to coagulate into signs, verbal or otherwise, actuated by the primary processes of displacement and condensation."[16] The work that Gallant's fiction performs in this way is the work of mourning, though this agenda is understated due to verbal displacements and condensations of affective response.

It is not only the understated that is of great significance in Gallant's work; what is not said, and what is unsayable, are crucial clues in reading her elegiac fiction as well. Wolfgang Iser's theory of literature as staging is particularly apt with reference to the unsayable in Gallant's elegiac fiction and fiction-elegies: "The recurrence of particular worlds in the literary text has always taken place on the prior understanding that it is a mode of enacting what is not there."[17] Gallant's prose makes use of the necessary conventions of elegy – what Iser would categorize as the "repertoire of the text," which create the appropriate conditions of the performance[18] – yet in terms of providing generic clues for the reader these elegiac conventions are very often obscured by the use of ironic allegories and alinear plot construction. As Heather Murray argues, it is the "way of telling" that dominates Gallant's stories, and it is the process of elegizing – the work (verb), not only the work (noun) of mourning – that structures the texts.

In other words, the reader's reconstruction of the textual, loss-dominated reality is made more difficult in Gallant's fiction than in fiction by Woolf, for instance. Though her fiction-elegies can be seen to derive from a modernist paradigm, the conventions of the genre are not often foregrounded as they are in the works of Woolf and early Joyce fiction-elegies, or even those of Munro. Hence the reader's paradigm, the model of mourning induced and produced upon reading Gallant's texts, is less explicitly directed by the author. We are, however, given contextual clues and markers of irony that assist us in the interpretative and reconstructive act, an act that Iser describes as a "staging" of oneself and that is "the means whereby representation is transferred from text to reader."[19] Just as Gallant selects from the modernist paradigm of fiction-elegy and then combines her selection syntagmatically into a new paradigm, the reader uses the new paradigm to select and construct a parallel paradigm of elegy. Iser argues that fictions are extensions of human beings and that "literature figures as a paradigmatic instance of this process [of world-making] because it is relieved of the pragmatic dimension so essential to real-life situations."[20] The reader's paraparadigm, so to speak, is a product of reading Gallant's (paradigmatic) text, of reading other elegies, and of personal experience of loss.

In his recent theory of fiction Michael Riffaterre refers to "mental frames of reference" to which the reader has access when reading. He states that these frames "are not just habits of thought; they constitute potential ministries, ready to unfold when needed and ready for reference when alluded to."[21] Such mental frames of reference contribute to the para-paradigm that, I am suggesting, the reader produces upon reading fiction-elegy. The active role that Riffaterre depicts for the reader of fiction in general is emphasized to a greater extent in the very structure and nature of fiction-elegy. In my modernist examples the reader is situated within the frames of the fiction; in Gallant's versions the reader is directed less explicitly to participate in the construction of a textual model of mourning, though Gallant, using detached ironic narration, does insist on this participation and also on identification with the situations and emotions of her characters – if only to disagree with or to reject them.

Constance Rooke claims that "the lure to character/reader identification is much less in Gallant's fiction than in Laurence's or Munro's, partly because the character/author bond is so much weaker";[22] however, I would suggest that a consequence of a "weak" character/author bond is that the reader/author bond is strengthened. Gallant's narratorial distance is used as a trope of elegy, one that often tends to replace the modernist method of frame construction that leads the reader to the central experience of the text (think of the reader/Peter/Clarissa/Septimus framework in Mrs Dalloway, for instance). The Gallantian narrators' textual distance from the story presents the reader with the independent perspective of the narrating survivor figure, which points to emotional and intellectual reactions, thereby authorizing the reader to appropriate or derive those reactions from or against the suggestive circumstances of the narrative. Thus the trope of distance is both displacing and deictic.

Despite Rooke's claim that there is "something chilling in Gallant," a fairly common evaluation, there is an emotional range in Gallant's fiction that has not received due attention. The narratorial detachment, which could be mistaken for a modernist's aesthetic of impersonality, tends to disguise this affective aspect of her work; she does not often render emotional realism at the immediate point of crisis, but rather depicts the after-*affects* of experience, a displaced form of affect. Paul Ricoeur writes of the "capacity of metaphor to provide untranslatable information ... [and] to yield some true insight about reality"[23] – and Gallant's texts are in this sense extended metaphors, allegories of remembering that provide what Ricoeur would call "models for reading reality in a new way."

The word "model" is of extreme importance in theorizing elegy. Jerome Bruner argues that a "mental model" of events patterned over time underlies all narrative,[24] but the genre of elegy – which has a particular function, a pragmatic function in its depiction of and insistence upon the reader's experience of grief – is a model in a particular way. For elegy to work, the reader must "place [his/her] own thoughts and feelings at the disposal of what representation seeks to make present in us," as Iser writes of the relationship between reader and text.[25] The emotions evoked for the reader who reconstructs a fiction-elegy are not the same feelings of grief and consolation as one has in actual life. The induced feelings are *modelled* on such authentic experiences of emotion, but as Ricoeur states, these literary feelings "are negative, suspensive experiences in relation to the literal emotions of everyday life. When we read, we do not literally feel fear or anger. Just as poetic language denies the first-order reference of descriptive discourse to ordinary objects of our concern, [modelled] feelings deny the first-order feelings which tie us to these first-order objects of reference."[28] This structure, which is divided or "split" between indirect representations of reality and models for reading reality (155), provides us with a point of entry into the elegiac text.

Gallant's narratorial distance creates this space or split between the structures of mourning. The text holds back emotion and resolutions, and provides a model of working through "real-life" confrontations with grief using an indirect form of guidance. Riffaterre provides a pragmatic explanation of the relationship between reading a text and applying it to "real life": "Narrative truth is thus a linguistic phenomenon; since it is experience through enactment by reading, it is a performative event in which participation on the reader's part can only serve to hammer the text's plausibility into his experience."[27] In this sense the narrative engenders a scene of transference, asking leading questions and giving no direct answers. Interestingly, Freud describes the psychoanalytic transference process as "a piece of real experience, but one which has been made possible by especially favourable conditions."[28] Gallant's stories construct analogous pieces of real experience. They are coded texts that create the possibility of a transferential model of reading, then: the reader, in the role of Freud's patient, is "led along the familiar paths to the awakening of the memories."[29] But the reader is also shown the *un*familiar, the strange. Ronald Hatch compares Gallant's strategy to a Brechtian *Verfremdung* (estrangement) device, and states that the reader of her fiction, like the audience of a Brecht play, "might return, changed" to daily life after engaging with her work.[30]

In the psychoanalytic model presented here, the text is not read as a patient; nor is Gallant. Instead, the text is the authoritative analyst and provides stories for the reader, the receptive analysand who must reconstruct and interpret the elegies by working through them. To extend the analogy, this model works Socratically, since the analyst (text), as Peter Brooks writes, "must help the analysand [reader] construct a narrative discourse whose syntax and rhetoric are more plausible, more convincing, more adequate to give an account of the story of the past than those that are originally presented, in symptomatic form, by the analysand."[31] Generally, the reader/analysand uses the text of story/self for the purpose of self-interpretation, which is the "event" of reading; in fiction-elegy, transference more specifically assists the reader to heighten awareness *of* and to grieve *for* communal and/or personal losses. This transference, which elicits interpretation, is invited by the text.[32] In Gallant's work the narratorial detachment invites the reader to enter into the transference relation; the invitation is reinforced by the use of irony, since it constructs double meanings that must be deciphered in context.

Ronald Schleifer suggests that irony is "the rhetorical trope that figures death: like the idea of death – like the very 'ideas' language gives rise to – irony is a material (linguistic) fact that creates 'immaterial' effects."[33] Irony has the potential to make the past present, then, as well as to create an *awareness* of loss and responsibility, as in the case of Gallant's fiction-elegy. Irony as trope is important in revisionist elegy such as Gallant's, in which the decorum of mourning is upheld but also is breached. Irony both constructs and disrupts meanings, and provides the distance required by the elegist and reader to construct the model of mourning, to locate oneself at a distance from the loss, *and* to critique the very model that the text represents on personal and cultural levels. Thus the reader's transferential reconstruction of the model of mourning in reading Gallant is most often *not* a duplication or re-presentation, but a re-vision.

Transference is both an activity involving reader and text, a rhetorical persuasion, and a *figuration*, a "mode of expression," as Cynthia Chase states, because it is in the process of transforming literary tropes during the act of reading that meaning and (variations on) consolation are produced. The former characteristic of transference is performative, and it obscures the latter characteristic – the figurative – with its "rhetorical designs upon the reader."[34] In modernist fiction-elegy, the tropological quality of transference is dominant; we seek consolation as a product, and the elegists within the fictions (Lily Briscoe, Stephen Dedalus) find such consolation in art, symbols, words in and of themselves. In late modernist fiction-elegy, however, it is the performative quality of transference that is emphasized by the authors; though the word "transference" is etymologically related to metaphor (*metaphorein*, to transfer), a particular *kind* of metaphor is used to figure the performative: metonymy. As Chase explains, "th[is] system of tropes [i.e., the "production of signs as action"] is fundamentally metonymic, a matter of *contiguity* between ideational representatives or signifiers."[35] Like the analytic aim to " 'destroy' ... persisting persuasion," Gallant's fiction-elegy aims to "destroy" a lack of consciousness about personal and public conditions of loss, and her realistic (metonymic) style serves to question metaphoric, tropological consolations – constructed fictions – that we too easily adopt for ourselves.

The reader's scene of transferential reconstruction is an activity that Peter Brooks calls "plotting"[36] – is a matter of "finding the right sequence of events, putting together the revelatory plot" (35). This readerly activity is heightened in reading Gallant's fiction-elegy, since Gallant's style of plot tends to be alinear and achronological – her narrators and characters are often exploring the past through memory. In fiction-elegy there is almost always a progression within the plot, a movement towards a revelation; for Woolf and Joyce that revelation provides consolation for character and reader alike. However, as Iser writes, "the greater the emphasis on compensation [in a literary text], the more dated the solution will appear to future generations of readers";[37] it is perhaps for this reason that the modernists' figuration of consolation in their fiction-elegies required revision in the first place, and that the late modern texts tend to raise more questions than they answer. Thus progression for the characters or narrators in Gallant's fiction-elegies is stunted; for the reader the progression is towards a consciousness of the character/narrator limitations as well as of a diminishment of personal and cultural values, both within the story and in society.

The transference produces consciousness, not consolation, and clarification, not obvious compensation, in Gallant's contemporary version of catharsis. For the reader (again, the analysand, not the analyst) the process of plotting (with the goal of anagnorisis) is an enactment of the work of mourning. The reader's plotting involves a sorting out of the temporal movements made by the texts. Keefer notes that "Gallant's fictive structures are dual: the backward spirals that give her characters access to memory are intersected by the forward hurtle of time."[38] It is to this forward hurtle or progression, to the "sustained tick of a watch,"[39] that the reader must become acclimatized, but Gallant places "hurdles" in the way of conventional consolation. The reading process involves metonymic transference (the work of mourning) as well as metaphoric transference (the transfer of meaning).

Gallant has described metaphorically the act of writing; she sees a story "build[ing] around its centre, rather like a snail."[40] This image is reminiscent of Woolf's description of "the house of fiction": "Dissatisfied the writer [Woolf] may have been; but her dissatisfaction was primarily with nature for giving an idea, without providing a house for it to live in ... the idea started as the oyster starts or the snail to secrete a house for itself."[41] But where Woolf's metaphoric fiction-elegy consists of (or houses) fragmented forms that represent multiple perspectives on reality (which, in capturing reality, have potential for consolation in aesthetic form), Gallant's metonymic fiction-elegy figures fragmented lives and societies and resists tropological consolation.[42] For Gallant, memory is accessible but it is only partial and selective, and it has dubious recuperative powers.

"I don't think the story should be a fragment. A short story is not just something snatched out of a larger fiction," Gallant states in an interview.[43] Even her segmented longer works consist not of fragments but of syntagmatically connected fictions (*Green Water, Green Sky* and *A Fairly Good Time* are examples). For Gallant, "content, meaning, intention and form must make up a whole, and must above all have a reason to be."[44] She revises the experimentalist, fragmentary, and symbolic narrative of modernist writing, then; for Gallant, the "whole" short story is not a fragment of a larger possibility but an independent narrative, precisely (though not chronologically) plotted. It is often this use of plot as trope in connection to the themes of loss and abandonment that connotes the elegiac in Gallant's work, such that the reader "plots" the work of mourning.

While W.J. Keith (surprisingly) states that Gallant's work "does not have any obvious thematic preoccupations," he also notes in a contradictory manner that "we come to realize that she continually concerns herself with human beings as they are affected by change and especially war."[45] One of her obvious preoccupations is with the occupation of Europe during the Second World War and with human responses to the multiple crises and losses that it entailed. With what could be called her social/moral realism Gallant confronts many of the issues surrounding these events, and is indeed as Keith states, an "excellent analyst" who depicts "mid-twentieth-century spiritual *malaise*" (158).

PLOTTING THE PAST: SAMPLING THE EARLY STORIES

The plots of Gallant's stories provide the reader with the repertoire of elegy: plot and story (*sjužet*) order the *fabula*, but Gallant's order is not one that satisfies the reader's idea of what reality *should* be like; instead of resolving tensions and consoling for losses, Gallant represents *dis*order, and the reader's habit of "reading for the plot" is disrupted, disturbed, forced to become a "plotting for the reading."

Peter Brooks believes that "plot is the internal logic of the discourse of mortality";[46] in a sense, this has been my argument for the proliferation of modern and late modern fiction-elegy, which is occasional only in that death is always an event: plot in fiction allows writers to explore psychological reactions to both death and loss, and it provides a structure for the narration of the work of mourning, which is, paradoxically, an act of narrativization itself. As Ricoeur suggests, plot has "a connecting function between an event or events and the story. A story is *made out of* events to the extent that plot *makes events into* a story. The plot, therefore, places us at the crossing point of temporality and narrativity."[47] In Gallant's stories "event" often is memory itself. This variation on the *fabula* does not eliminate plot, but it complicates its temporality.

Gallant's first collection, *The Other Paris* (1956), is admittedly less elegy-oriented than her later work. Two stories in *The Other Paris*, however, are early versions of the paradigmatic fiction-elegies in the first and third person that she later would write, "Wing's Chips" and "About Geneva." The former is a pseudo-autobiographical anecdote in which the adult narrator recalls a childhood summer. She recreates details based on "the picture in [her] memory" of the town that she lived in with her father.[48] The narrator, then, attempts to *read* her ekphrastic mental picture for its accuracy and truth. Though most details are recalled "with remarkable clarity" (142), she cannot remember the name of the town that she lived in with her father, and this paradoxical situation immediately provides us with a clue to the story's agenda: the forgetting of such a detail from childhood indicates an avoidance of what Freud would classify as "strong and often distressing affects" and suggests a loss or betrayal that the narrator must "work through" (or in terms of think-act theory, "think through") using narrative re-enactment. In analysis, "the process that should lead to the reproduction of the missing name has been so to speak *displaced*."[49] By analogy, as readers we begin to replace the process, to figure or construct a *fabula* from this plot, which is a "textual generator" in Riffaterre's terms.[50] Thus the reading of the fiction-elegy involves an initial *de*construction – what Jacques Derrida calls a form of "memory work" in itself[51] – before the model of mourning can be (re)constructed.

The elegiac repertoire of "Wing's Chips" includes the following: references to a harsh landscape (141); an "untended garden, in which only sunflowers and a few perennials survived" (142); the emotional detachment of the father, which implies parental neglect and a corresponding sense of abandonment in the child (145); unresolved affect, which becomes evident to the narrator only "years later" (147); emphasis on the artistic talents of the father, talents that are inherited by the narrating story-teller in displaced form as literary skills (150); and a semi-aesthetic object that stands as "proof" of her father's existence and identity (151).

It is the arrangement of these conventions or conditions of the performative text that is foregrounded, rather than the conventions themselves. The narrator explicitly draws attention to the fact that past events are not the same as remembered events. Her *father*'s narrative – which is an undeveloped plot embedded in the plot proper, and which serves as an inner frame of the fiction-elegy – is about "the England of his boyhood" (144) and is his conversational autobiography. Recalling pastoral-like details that he might have told her, his daughter thinks: "This was probably not at all what he said, but it was the image I retained – a landscape flickering and flooded with light, like the old silents at the cinema" (144). The tale is like a parable for the reader, advising us not to believe the story as told, for the events are likely different from the image retained and narrated as history. Her mental construction of a landscape "flooded with light" is quite fictive, then, though significantly the father's narrative has been translated by the child into a nearly ekphrastic, *wordless* visual image, one that represents a temporary closeness with her father and seemingly consoles the (now) narrating adult. But the consolation inherent in the symbolic version of the past is unsatisfactory, since it is not only fictional but knowingly false, and this is what the adult narrator comes to understand. Thus the narrator also questions the validity of such a trope of consolation. This is evident in the very fact that she consciously rewrites her past with the intent of a more accurate recovery, adjusting "the picture in [her] memory" in the process (141).

This conscious rewriting of the past is analogous to the reader's interpretive act, wherein the *fabula* is transcribed into another mental landscape. The words "Wing's Chips" both title the story and provide a clue to the meaning of the revelatory moment at the end of the narrative – they are the words on a sign painted by the girl's father, one that is a great source of pride for her. The sign is a metonymic sign of her father in that he produced it with his own hands, and it figuratively denotes her father; but it also displays the now forgotten name of the town where, we are told, the specific past summer in question was lived. Though the narrator looked at the sign every day of that summer and is able to recall minute details of other events – even of the colours of the sign, and the shape of the letters her father painted (150) – she cannot re-place the displaced name. The absent name on the consoling sign metaphorically denotes the void in the relationship with her father, and the metaphoric absence (via neglect and, later, death) of the man himself. It names him *in absentia*, and therefore names a lack as well. The sign, with the unnamed town in "P.Q.," is therefore contrasted with the landscape "flooded with light" as two different ways of figuring the past; the metaphoric sign is also a product of the narrator's memory, of the past reconstructed, but it contains the seeds of its own deconstruction – of memory work – within itself, and is therefore the more evocative way of figuring loss.

Derrida writes that "deconstruction is not an operation that supervenes *afterwards*, from the outside, one fine day; it is always already at work in the work; ... the disruptive force of deconstruction is always already contained within the architecture of the work."[52] In reading fiction-elegy, the structure of which contains a "deconstructive" code, the reader is directed to reconstruct his/her own version of events in a reconstructive process such as that Riffaterre describes as "mentally rebuilding or hypothesizing a pretransformation text."[53] The reader, I am suggesting, subsequently transcribes the pretransformation text (acquired in reading Gallant's paradigmatic story) to a post-transformation text, or perhaps a para-transformation text, as a useful model of mourning. Here consolation is found not in the form of symbolic signs but in the *formation* of signs; it is not the sign that reads "Wing's Chips" that leads the narrator to an affirmation of pride in her father, but the reconstruction of her past – a reconstruction that is admittedly never complete or completely accurate.

Thus the rejection of the symbol as a fictively "true" trope of consolation is another way that Gallant revises modernist tropes of elegy. Lily Briscoe's painting of Mrs Ramsay, for example, is a symbol, and consolation is found therein, not in the seemingly frustrating *process* of painting. Gallant seems to question the emotional validity of such a figure for the purposes of consolation, as she emphasizes the importance of signs – like the sign that says "Wing's Chips" – for memory work. But there are different kinds of signs, and different kinds of memory to consider in this context. The link between types of signs and types of memory is of interest to Paul de Man, whose interpretation of Hegel's concepts of sign and symbol leads him to suggest that since art is "of the past" and its paradigm is "thought rather than perception, the [temporal] sign rather than the [atemporal] symbol, writing rather than painting or music, it will also be memorization [*Gedachtnis*] rather than recollection [*Errinnerung*]."[54] In "Wing's Chips" the adult narrator does not recollect, nor use deluding symbolic recollection (as her father seems to have done), but she signifies her past, her father, and her loss in the metonymic act of telling.

"Wing's Chips" is a precursor story to Gallant's first-person fiction-elegies such as the Linnet Muir sequence in *Home Truths*.[55] "About Geneva" is a second story in *The Other Paris* that suggests an elegiac structure that recurs in Gallant's later third-person stories. The plot in this story consists of the attempt by the unnamed mother and "Granny" to extract the truth about the two children's visit with their father, who is living in Geneva with another woman. The broken-home scenario is presented *in medias res*, and the visit is over when the story begins. The events in the *fabula* consist of dialogue and mental reconstructions of the trip and of the past by the boy Colin, his sister Ursula, and their unhappy mother.

Neil Besner notes that "Geneva's appearance announces several realities,"[56] and indeed we are asked to consider the different versions of the reconstructed scene. The mother thinks, with reference to the children's accounts of the visit, "Which of them can one believe?" (198); the reader too must take this question into consideration. This issue of truth in story is, I have suggested, one of the central concerns in Gallant's fiction-elegy; the potential for a limited consolation depends directly on the capacity of a representation, constructed in memory, to embody a fictive truth. Colin's sudden statement early in the story, "I fed the swans,"[57] encapsulates the experience for him by evoking a fixed scene: "There, he had told about Geneva ... As he said it, the image became static: a gray sky, a gray lake, and a swan wonderfully turning upside down with the black rubber feet showing above the water. His father was not in the picture at all; neither was *she*. But Geneva was fixed for the rest of his life: gray, lake, swan" (196). Colin's declarative statement is a think-act that evokes this fixed scene in his mind, one that denotes his own emotional reality.[58] The static and false image functions as a symbol, one that leaves out the figure of the father and, though inadequate, is used by Colin to reconstruct his recent trip to Geneva.

Ursula's reconstruction is also produced by a verbal act, but one of a different order. She is writing a play based on autobiographical details of her father's lover, who is from Russia (and who suggested the name and the plot of the play; the woman is called "the original Tatiana" by Ursula's mother [197]), and in speaking the one line written thus far – "The Grand Duke enters and sees Tatiana all in gold" (194) – she produces a fable out of the *fabula* of the trip. Emotional reality, it seems, is too difficult to confront, and the distance of the fiction (in the form of an imaginary play) from reality is somewhat consoling for Ursula. The thought of a literal production of the play makes her cry, though (195), since the gap between the reality of the painful visit and the fiction she has constructed is thereby dramatized. Thus the mythological translation of reality is also shown to be an inadequate figuration of the past for the work of mourning.

With these different versions of the story Gallant condenses the (pre-transformation) plot of "About Geneva" into an allegory of plotting. In other words, the reader must consider the subtextual story of the visit and the portrayal of that visit by Colin and Ursula, and then assess the elements of the story proper, plotting them into a plausible subtextual paradigm. This transferential reading process is exemplified when Colin's mother interprets what she thinks is the authoritative version of events – Colin's version. Since "Colin seemed to carry the story of the visit with him" (197), his mother sees her son as an extension of the man who left her: "She thought of her husband, and how odd it was that only a few hours before Colin had been with him. She touched the back of his neck. 'Don't,' he said. Frowning, concentrating, he hung up his tooth brush. 'I told about Geneva.' " (197). The boy seems to understand his mother's need for a reminder of her husband, and offers his image to her again. Her version of the story becomes changed in the transference; the think-act "He had fed swans," which is appropriated from Colin's "I fed the swans," becomes actualized as a mental construction: "She saw sunshine, a blue lake, and the boats Granny had described, heaped with coloured cushions" (197). Thus Colin's symbol is transformed by his mother's reading into yet another symbol, one that represents not reality but her imagined version of the scene.

Because Colin's fiction is both possible and plausible, his mother temporarily believes the boy's representation (translated to her own vision) to be true, whereas Ursula's "one simple act of creating Tatiana and the Grand Duke" served to remove her "from the ranks of reliable witnesses" (197). But Colin's symbol is no more "true" than Ursula's drama, something that their mother cannot perceive. The ekphrastic image once actualized in her own mind, like the play, is seemingly unrelated to a reality external to the image-as-text, and is therefore not fictionally truthful or consoling. This revelation at the end of the story, though not a consolation, does indicate to the reader what a more useful model of mourning might entail: verbal versions of past events told in terms of signs, not symbols, would seem to provide a fictional truth.

Keefer paraphrases Frank Kermode and applies his ideas to Gallant, stating that "individual works of fiction cannot be too consoling, or they will not satisfy the reader's demand for 'complicity with reality.' "[59] The "effect of Gallant's vision," she suggests, "is not tragically cathartic but ironically disturbing" (46). I am arguing, however, that Gallant's fiction – elegiac, not tragic – directs the reader towards the construction of a parallel paradigm that simultaneously resists tropological consolation *and* encourages consciousness of tropological structures, and of the relation between memory and truth, language and fiction – even if, or rather *because* the characters in her stories do not arrive at this model themselves. Thus the reader is not only "disturbed" and abandoned, as Keefer suggests, but is stimulated *by* the disturbing events and characters to become actively involved in the rebuilding of the fiction-elegy. Character limitations, then, often can *move* the reader to move *beyond* disturbance.

Another early third-person story that demonstrates a failure of consolation for the *character* is "An Emergency Case" (1957), not collected until *In Transit* was published (1988). Again the significant events of the story have happened before the story begins: a little boy, Oliver, has been in a car accident with his parents, who did not survive. In hospital Oliver is talked *at* by several adults, though they fail to talk *with* him about his experience and loss. The doctor "had told Oliver that Oliver's parents were now in Heaven" (53), but this meaningless information is not retained by the traumatized child. The story portrays Oliver's emotional denial and the adult's emotional deficiencies. His lack of grief is a defence mechanism, or "the omission of affect" that often accompanies delayed mourning.[60] This omission is apparent in the story proper also; since the adults who surround the child have failed to grasp the boy's emotional condition, it is not rendered by the narrative voice either. Keefer's reference to the boy as "the unlikeable Oliver"[61] indicates, I think, a misreading of an intensely emotional story; if any of the characters are "unlikeable," the health-care workers might be.

The adults' inability to deal with the malaise of the mourner endows the narrative with a strategic coldness, one that has often been mistaken for authorial disinterest. Gallant's story demonstrates that the parent's death "hasn't been properly explained" to the child, as his adult roommate concludes (41). Details have been withheld from the boy, and narrative details have also been held back from the reader in a semi-Hemingwayesque style of narration. We must interpret the sparse story-line and construct a parallel fiction from our version of the *fabula*, just as Oliver must read the signs given him:

"The taking away of the toys, the unscheduled attempt to wash him suggested that something unusual was about to take place. It could only mean his mother" (41). In this literalization and reversal of the Freudian "fort/da" scene, Oliver expects the signs that represent his mother – toys – to be replaced with his actual mother. To him they do not signify loss, then, but presence and retrieval. Gallant contextualizes Oliver's misinterpretation of absence for the reader, who is led to conclude that the "absence-of-grief" syndrome has induced the boy to invent not a consoling construct but one that will re-enact only the experience of loss: his mother will not replace the toys but will be repeatedly lost to the child. The absence of toys does not symbolize the mother's presence, as Oliver believes, but is a figure of loss, as the reader perceives. Our plotting of the story, like Oliver's, is anticipatory ("something unusual was about to take place," he thinks), but we are directed to construct a model of psychological response and to become empathically involved with Oliver, in contrast to the adults in the story, who seem oblivious of the needs of the child.

The title story of *The End of the World and Other Stories* (1974) invites a similar anticipatory participation. In this first-person story (the narrator's name is William), the triggering event – William's father's death – has already occurred, but this monologue is an effort to narrate emotional response, to plot not only the after-affects of loss but the fore-affects as well. The first words that the speaker announces are "I never like to leave Canada, because I'm disappointed every time";[62] the subsequent statement "I had to leave Canada to be with my father when he died" (89) provides the reader with the implied information that being with his father is a disappointment, his death a double loss. Reader expectations of an emotionally charged scene are first constructed, then dismantled. The narrator, too, is disappointed: "I had expected to get here in time for his last words, which ought to have been 'I'm sorry' … But my father never confided in me" (90). In order to forgive his father, and to experience a memorable emotional bond with him before his death, William needs his father to apologize, to perform a consoling speech-act.

Instead, he is the one to perform a verbal service for his father: he "swear[s]" to him that he has tuberculosis, assuring him – promising him – that he will be cured (94). Since the man is dying, such a speech-act, though infelicitous under other circumstances, is not unsuccessful – the conditions of the promise are not expected to be fulfilled but are psychologically necessary none the less. Since the act is a lie, however, his father's statement "I knew you wouldn't lie to me" indicates to the speaker and the reader that the emotional bond

created in the speech-act, the recognition his father has given him, is
a fiction. The role of the narrator soon subsumes the importance of
the father's role in this story, which follows a pattern of elegiac romance; the narrator-elegist quests for knowledge about himself and
the world, though this knowledge is denied in the speech-acts exchanged between the two men.

The speech-act that his father does provide (he *thanks* his son for
the reassurance) is not the one William desires. This surprise, then –
not the death of the father – is what seems "like the end of the
world" (94) to William. The exchange of lies has shattered William's
imagined "world," his hoped-for consolation; what he had
"thought [he] wanted to hear" was a speech-act that would have
maintained his perspective on his father, the one he had constructed
in his mind over the years. The disappointment in not having the
long-imagined play performed becomes an experience of an unexpected, doubled loss. Again Gallant emphasizes the danger and fictive nature of conventional, romanticized expectations of consolation. She disrupts the reader's expectations of elegiac consolation in
her fiction-elegies; but the end of one world is also the beginning of
another, and her stories have the effect of heightening the reader's
awareness of the stories we tell ourselves, and of the importance of
their telling.

In *My Heart Is Broken* (1964) the majority of the stories are about
adults who are orphaned or abandoned – common Gallantian
themes. The characters aim to secure fictive consolations that will allow an acceptance of the ways of the world, to paraphrase one story
in the collection.[63] The title of the collection implies that loss and
grief are central concerns, and the fiction does portray characters
confronting these experiences. Bernice Schrank compares this collection to *Dubliners*, stating that "*My Heart is Broken* invites analysis
as a unified whole ... the stories collectively illustrate various per-
mutations of genteel angst and lower-class anomy."[64] The narratives possess the power to move the reader (as rhetoric is intended
to do) both emotionally and intellectually. They also focus attention
(often critically) on the ways in which characters figure their grief or
construct consoling fictions for themselves. Besner notes of this collection that the reader is invited "to discern characters as frames or
forms, as manners or idioms of perception,"[65] but while frames are
evident in narratological terms, the emotional import of the stories
certainly suggests that the characters are more powerfully present
than the terms "forms" and "idioms of perception" would suggest.
When confronted with loss in the outermost frame of the fiction-
elegies, we are moved to re-evaluate both the values portrayed in

the fiction and in our own lives, a re-evaluation that is not required of the reader by Woolf, and not often by Joyce either. Gallant's late modern fiction-elegy is less accepting of characters' fictive consolations and more meta-evaluative, then – it implicates the reader in what might be called an "ethics of grieving."

In "Bernadette" the ironically named Robbie Knight is a failed playwright, a frustrated artist-figure who is re-reading his literary influences[66] and mourning not only his lost youth but, eventually, lost love in his marriage as well. He is not moved to action by reading, however; the "only result of his [reading] project was a feeling of loss ... He felt only that he and Nora had missed something, and that he ought to tell her so" (25). Robbie's ineffectualness in life (and in reading literature, suggests Schrank),[67] and in dealing with loss, is contrasted to pregnant Bernadette's vitality; the contrast is also between Robbie's perception of a rural working-class lifestyle as idyllic and Bernadette's memories of what her life was really like. Her memories are think-acts that, once "set in motion, brought up the image" of her home life (27). While Robbie mourns the death of his dreams, Bernadette's (non)mourning for the predicted future death of her unborn child becomes the story-within-the-story. Bernadette's story displaces Robbie's self-elegy, and shows its relative insignificance, thereby calling the Knights' values into question.

Nora Knight resembles an unsuccessful Mrs Dalloway whose "party had gone wrong" (32); her failure became "a symbol of the end" of her world (37). Nora is also a failed reader, one who pieces together a plausible story from events and conversations but mistakenly accuses her husband of impregnating Bernadette. Readers are positioned outside of Bernadette's naïve frame of reference and must evaluate her ideas of life, death, and religious consolation as well as those of the Knights. The reader contrasts these opposing models and reconstructs an alternative view or frame outside of the narrative text. Though Bernadette does not read the books given her by the Knights (or any others), she does go to the movies, and it is in the cinema that she experiences a "comforting dark" protection (41) as a spectator of events: "She did not identify herself with the heroine, but with the people looking on" (41), we are told. For Bernadette, detachment allows her to accept and even to welcome the predicted death of her yet unborn child. Since we, too, are an audience, we are implicated in this protected spectatorship. Bernadette's adoption of conventional religious consolation for the imagined death of her baby is metaphorically aligned with her escapism at the movies: neither requires her to *think*, and Gallant indeed is making a moral judgment about Bernadette's "destructive placidity," as Schrank notes (67), forcing the reader to think.

In "The Moabitess" the protagonist, immediately identified in the first words of the story as "elderly Miss Horeham,"[68] is preparing for her own death. Her aversion to sexual activity, what she calls "that side of life" (43), provides a clue to the reader that her lifelong virginity is perhaps related to a misguided reading of the biblical line "A virtuous [hence virginal] woman is a crown to her husband" (50). This choice has placed her in the position of spectator, and our perspective as spectator-of-the-spectator aligns us with her narrow "vision of life" (47), where her eyes are the "centre of the house, of the world" (54). In reading the story we are presented with the memory of her father. The mention of his death makes her "stutter so ... that the others thought she would choke" (45). The fiction-elegy psychonarrates her alternating feelings of hatred and love for "Mr Percy Horeham, who had irresponsibly departed from life in 1946 and left his maiden daughter not a penny" (46). Here Gallant condenses the history of Miss Horeham and that of her father to a single paragraph, which is a think-act wherein Miss Horeham performs a wish that her father die a second death, "another annihilation after death" (46).

Like Mr Horeham's locked box under his bed, containing the money for which his daughter had to beg, Miss Horeham constructs her own locked box of fictive memories – an atemporal construct that David O'Rourke identifies as an "idyllic past" under lock and key in the present.[69] This crypt-like box consoles her for her deprivations, despite the fact that it contains only meaningless items that she has endowed with value. She even calls a stone thrown at her a "gift"; her misinterpretation of this abuse is analogous to her attitude towards her father's treatment of her, indicating that she is collecting her pain and translating her wounds into pleasure. In biblical law (in the Book of Matthew) stones are thrown as a form of punishment; the act also functions as an accusation of some kind of sexual sin, such as prostitution. To accuse is to label, to name. The protagonist's name, Miss Horeham, is appropriate then – despite the fact that she remains sexually inactive as an adult – because incestuous activity is suggested throughout the story.

Other items in her box that have symbolic significance are her father's butterfly collection, stored in a glass box (52), and the letters her father wrote to her when she was a schoolgirl (53), addressed in a subtly amorous tone. She reads the words written by a now-dead man and, putting on a scarf, enters a fantasy world that solaces her. She experiences an epiphany, wherein she actually sees her younger self in the mirror in the role of Ruth, remembering "how they had acted out the glorious [biblical] stories" of love and lust (53). The acting out "had all been harmless and a secret, and gave them the feeling that something rich was being lived" (53); the *think*-acting out of what she "acted out" with her father now provides Miss Horeham with a secretive pleasure, though clearly the reader evaluates the questionable morality of the originating act as well as the validity of the consolation attributed to its memory.

Her revealed hatred of her father causes the reader to contrast the consoling memory with the implied reality of Miss Horeham's past, and empathy is thereby stirred for the somewhat irritating old woman. Her fictions are, for her, necessary; but the story structure, which is also box-like, places the reader at the outer frame and allows us to evaluate her mental construction as one that reflects "love of established order" (49) and not true memory. Her epiphany occurs in her invented "small, clear field of light" (52), which is like a spotlight projected on the stage and emphasizes her role as actress, artificer, as well as the reader's role as artificer in reconstructing the story. The reader detects embedded works of mourning for Miss Horeham's past life with her father and for the life unlived *because* of that past. Gallant spotlights the fictionality of memory in this story, and by exposing a woman's secret self-vision she critiques the limited perspective produced by a veiled or boxed-in view of the past. The cost of the illusion of control over the past and life itself – the cost of the crypt – is life itself.

Peter Frazier is another character in *My Heart Is Broken* who creates illusory compensations at great cost to himself and others.[70] Described as one of the "peacock parents" (247), Peter enacts a work of mourning in "The Ice Wagon Going down the Street" by denying loss with distorted memory. The narrator asserts that "peacocks love no one. They wander about the parked cars looking elderly, bad-tempered, mournful and lost,"[71] which Peter certainly is. Peter is the dominant focalizer in the story, and the narrative begins and ends with Peter remembering a woman named Agnes Brusen. "Remembering the past" is a Sunday pastime for him and his wife Sheilah (246), and they speak names of people "as if they were magic," as if they could resurrect them. The Fraziers live in, rather than learn from, the past. Though he keeps the name Agnes a secret from his wife (272), Peter thinks of her when he remembers the past. The story opens and closes in the present tense, though throughout Peter's thoughts move back and forth in past time, narratologically indicating his (and Sheilah's) hollow repetition of the past. It is Peter's use of the past that is called into question by Gallant.

The story proper is about the Fraziers' loss of social stature and of the feeling of being in love; but perhaps more importantly it is about the recuperative power of memory, about significant moments of solitude and of union with another. The image of Agnes as a child watching the ice wagon is one of privacy and beauty; it provides epiphanies for both herself and for Peter, to whom she describes it (267). Peter *sees* the scene, and actually hallucinates a transferential epiphany: "He thinks of the ice wagon going down the street. He sees something he has never seen in his life – a Western town that belongs to Agnes. Here is Agnes ... Nothing moves except the shadows and the ice wagon and the changing amber of the child's eyes. The child is Peter ... He is there" (273).

Peter uses Agnes's name as a charm that triggers an epiphanic moment. Derrida writes that the proper name remains after death, that "in calling or naming someone while he is alive, we know that his name can survive him and *already survives him*; the name begins during his life to get along without him, speaking and bearing his death each time it is inscribed ... if at my friend's death I retain only the memory and the name, the memory in the name, ... this defect or default reveals the structure of the name and its immense power as well: it is in advance "in memory of.""[72] The name "Agnes Brusen" has this mnemonic power for Peter; the structure of the name-as-sign is symbolic, just as the name "Frazier," to Peter (and to Peter alone), is symbolic of power and prestige. In "The Ice Wagon Going down the Street" Gallant is depicting the process of epiphany, not just describing the epiphanic moment. She contrasts two different uses of memory in this allegory of grieving: distorting and disabling memory-as-symbol of the past – the Frazier's model of escape – versus memory as truthful fiction – Agnes's model of meaning.

Peter sees Agnes's epiphany and appropriates it, incapable as he is of having his own. His vision is an imaginative act that parallels the reader's, since Agnes's telling allows him to reconstruct her story and to interpret its significance. O'Rourke states that "ironically," Peter "does nothing with this epiphany" (106); but Peter does change because of this experience. The conversation that they have is of love and of death; the ice melts between them, so to speak, as they confide in one another about highly personal issues. The think-act Peter later performs brings him to a recognition of a potentially valuable vision of the past and of his emotions towards Agnes – but he does not act on this recognition. Though he returns to "a true Sunday morning" (273), he has identified the fictive truth of his constructed life with Sheilah and has seen, perhaps, the inadequacy of the Balenciaga dress as a talisman (248). He begins to think of Sheilah and his father as a couple in terms of their similar superficial values. He has also invoked Agnes with the think-act, since she speaks the last words of the story, reminding the reader of the peacock analogy: "Agnes says to herself somewhere, Peter is lost" (273).

Though "Peter [literally] lost Agnes" (273), he retains her unspoken name as his talisman and constructs a version of her from "the puzzle he pieces together" (272). The name functions as a prosopopoetic trope, but its ultimate effectiveness is dubious – not because the metaphoric vision of the moving ice wagon is invalid but because it is so easily appropriated and then rejected by Peter. Peter's reconstruction of Agnes, of the image of the ice wagon, and of the prairie paradise is paradigmatic of the reader's involvement in the fiction-elegy, and clearly a reconstruction of another person's story – or of an author's story – will not substitute for an individual's interpretation of his or her own experience. But the glimpse of meaning that Peter gets is a glimpse that the reader, too, gets in the act of reading fiction-elegy; it is a glimpse that Gallant urges us to hang on to.

A HAUNTED HOUSE: ITS IMAGE ON THE MIRROR

"Its Image on the Mirror" in *My Heart Is Broken* is subtitled "A Short Novel," and like Gallant's lengthier novels it can be read as an extended (and sequential) fiction-elegy wherein a female protagonist mourns for multiple losses.[73] Besner writes that one of its central themes is "the act and the art of remembering": "Showing that the processes through which memory asserts its truths are always significant," he states of the collection, "these stories invite readers to consider inventions, recollections, and recreations of the past by attending to the forms of the stories Gallant's narrators tell."[74] Jean Price, the narrator-elegist, mourns her dead brother and the "equally lost" sister[75] whom, she thinks, has abandoned her. She also mourns her lost "unlived self," as Donald Jewison notes.[76] The plot-trigger of the story is the sale of the house where Jean grew up with her brother Frank and sister Isobel. The dramatic-monologue form establishes the reader in the role of listener (and eavesdropper), as an audience that is given "misleading impressions" and edited or "corrected thought[s]."[77]

Though John Moss claims that Jean's "reason for speaking is never apparent,"[78] the telling is its own *raison d'être*. Jean's narrative is a prolonged, performative work of mourning, occasioned by the sale of the house and the incomplete mourning for her brother. Through it she confronts "the problem of [her] sister" (62) and seeks some understanding of her self, life, and death. The narrative has the basic structure of elegiac romance, wherein the narrator ostensibly narrates the biography of a dead or lost hero-figure, yet the biographical story is a thin disguise for the autobiography of the narrator who survives the hero and wishes to adopt the hero's identity for his/her own. Such autobiography is specifically confessional in nature. Besner notes that the novella is "both a report and a confession. Jean reports her memories as confessions: through changes in the way she calls up the past ... she comes to a fuller way of making sense of herself and of history."[78] The monologuic "Its Image on the Mirror" is an apostrophic confession to Isa, who is Jean's imagined confessor; but Isa will not speak to Jean "out of her own death," or even in Jean's dreams (97), and little is learned of this elusive sister by Jean or by the reader. Ironically, though, what Jean confesses is that by telling the tale she hopes to create a "dead-and-buried Isobel" (62) who could no longer threaten her sense of self within the family or with her husband Tom. Thus Jean's *use* of memory and story-telling is called into question by Gallant, since Jean is presented as a character with emotional limitations that she does not completely recognize; at least Jean does not *confess* to having the knowledge of herself that Gallant allows the reader to have.

Telling the story is a way of burying the past and of forcing "life to begin," something for which Jean "had waited years" (63). Confession, writes Dennis Foster, is a representation of "an attempt to understand the terms and the limits by which the people are defined, both as they listen to the confessions of others and as they recount their own transgressions"; "the importance of confession, and of the language of fault in general, lies in its power to interpret."[80] But in Jean's confession there is a sense that her story is not only a delayed reaction to her losses but a reaction that *perpetuates* delay and postpones a direct confrontation with herself. The flashbacks and achronology also work to subvert plot progression, to stop time and problematize the textual position of potentially epiphanic revelations. The successful burial of the past in Jean's aesthetic terms would create a kind of mental *crypt*, which, writes Derrida, is "not a natural place, but the striking history of an artifice, an *architecture*, an artifact: of a place *comprehended* within another but rigorously separate from it, isolated from general space by partitions, an enclosure, an enclave ... the crypt constructs another, more inward, forum like a closed rostrum or speaker's box, a *safe*: sealed, and thus internal to itself, a secret interior within the public square."[81] Jean's stated intent is to seal the past into its grave, to detach herself from it and to hide it within herself-as-house in an effort to make her life "safe" from the threat of Isa.

But Gallant's fiction-elegy "works" in spite of Jean's cryptographic goal because it is the "mode of narration that is responsible for the especial effect of this story and Gallant's other fiction," as Heather Murray argues.[82] Jean (s)crypts her past in front of the reader's eyes, and the reader uses what Derrida calls "the break-in technique that will allow us to penetrate into a crypt (it consists of locating the crack or the lock, choosing the angle of a partition, and forcing entry)."[83] The potential for the success of any method of mourning is limited by the capacity of the scribe or "scripter" to comprehend and to act on that comprehension – the latter being a dead-end for Jean, of course. But the efficacy of fiction-elegy depends upon the inducement of comprehension on the part of the reader, a goal which Gallant is able to achieve – despite her character's detached nature in this novella – by including characteristics of intelligence and signs of emotional suffering beneath her surface control of self and story.

Jean draws attention to her role as story-teller and elegist: "I am the only person who can tell the truth about anything now, because I am, in a sense, the survivor," she thinks (141). The story is about "vocabularies and grammars, and also about formal truths and fictional truths," notes Besner,[84] and Jean's (s)crypting is contrasted to Gallant's method of scripting the past. As the survivor the elegist stages a response to loss and grief and works through mourning in the act of staging, of writing. Jean's work is silent, though, and the entire fiction is in effect a think-act composition, since expression of emotion for Jean is nearly impossible. The Duncan family all suffered from "a fear of the open heart" (89), and even though the text is a work of mourning, Jean would never admit it as such – rather, she ironically claims at the end that the entire "story could wait" and that she "might never tell it" (153) to her husband, who knows few details about Isa's past or her relationship with Jean.

In claiming that "there is something in waiting for the final word," Jean is repeating her life-pattern of waiting, which turns her life into a kind of death. In this sense Jean is incapable of achieving the consolation that comes with acting on revelation. As Keefer writes, the telling of the story has no cathartic effect on Jean but leads only to a "passively ironic recognition" of her death-in-life condition.[85] Her reconstruction of memories is somewhat mechanical in that her think-acts produce not active emotion but tableaux, similar to her "last sight of the house at Allenton," which she compares to "those crowded religious paintings that tell a story" (57). Jean's memories do tell a story, but rather than producing a consoling fiction-elegy they often produce "discrete still-lifes," as Besner refers to them.[86]

Besner states that "Jean approaches her memories in a manner similar to the way in which readers approach fiction,"[87] as if they are not real, not her own. Though such detachment is a necessary part of the mourning process, Jean's approach to memories is undercut by Gallant, in that her methodology of memory and mourning is clearly so inadequate and stilted that we, as readers, can construct other versions that work. The reader becomes empathically involved while Jean remains emotionally reticent, paradoxically silent within her own retrospective discursiveness.

The Allenton house becomes a prosopopoetic figure that contains all deaths and losses for Jean: "Even before the house was sold ... it began to die ... Ghosts moved in the deserted rooms, opening drawers, tweaking curtains aside. We never saw the ghosts, but we knew they were there. We were unable to account for them: no one had lived here but our family, and none of us had died in Allenton" (59) – none except Jean's emotional self, that is. Since a ghost watched Jean watching herself in the glass on one occasion (60), at least one of those unaccountable spectres is Jean's lost version of herself, the one that had dreams of a possible love that might surpass what she finds in her real life. Gallant's characteristic contrast between romantic and realistic world-views is not a simple opposition, as this story makes clear; within the "real" the use of the imagination and memory is crucial to the construction of a fictional truth. Jean's rejection of the imaginative in life does not allow her to see the difference between life and illusion, as she believes; it identifies her instead as someone who sees life in terms of simple oppositions rather than a complex mixture of fact and fiction, and as someone who – because of this perspective – is doomed to a mournful, cryptic existence rather than a celebratory one.

A salvational crypt such as Jean's paradoxically "allow[s] death to take no place in life," as Derrida claims of such "sepulchre[s]."[88] Her insistence on "waking" and "return[ing] to life" (155) is, Gallant suggests, an insistence on permanent mourning, on endless wakeing. The elegiac markers are evident in this story from the start. The first mention of Jean's brother is made almost parenthetically, in relation to an anecdote about "poor Isobel" (61). It is Isa's near-death (threatened by a kidney ailment) that is narrated first, its significance established through a long digression that also describes her marriage to Alfredo. Isobel is perceived by Jean, who can't "figure" her (out), as a real ghost, returning from the dead as she "tricked [the family] by not dying" (62). She definitely haunts Jean, who tries to live Isa's life vicariously (she even marries Tom, who proposed to Isa first), and Jean only partially exorcises her past. Her expectation of "true justice," of achieving revenge for the past by building a family with Tom (77), backfires as Isobel remains unimpressed, and "thankful she had escaped" (77).

Frank escapes the narrow world of Allenton first through service in the war, then by dying. His death is mentioned only parenthetically in the second part of the novel, with variants on the phrase "dead brother" preceding his name, such as "our dead brother Frank" (71) and "my dead brother's daughter" (73). Frank's death is the explicit cause for grief in section five, though Jean here admits that she "scarcely mourned" him, and "ought to pay for [her] indifference" (129): "I withdrew from my brother's death into a living country of wrangles and arrangements and sharing taxis ... Although I speak now of his death, his death did not occur" (129). Speaking now of his death is her acknowledgment of that death as well as a version of delayed mourning. Her memory of the family scene reveals her mind performing this belated work: "The panes went black and reflected us: Isobel reading, our mother erect by the door, our father mourning and small. We were in a lighted cage. We could be seen from the street" (131). But Jean remains a spectator to her memories, which are sealed off, hidden in her safe.

The narration digresses to provide a trace of Frank; though "the ghost in the Allenton house cannot be Frank's," since "he left no trace" at all (131), Jean narrates a few days he spent with her and Isa to provide a sense of his presence, to invent a ghost and, with words, to replace the missing trace of her brother. But she also *displaces* that ghost, and focuses yet again on Isa's ghost and her capacity for love, which is so elusive to Jean that she can only be "warmed by the sudden presence of love" that she "could sense but not capture" (136).

What Jean perceives as a need for revenge on her sister is alternately a need for consolation, a need that is almost fulfilled: "I felt, that afternoon, the closest feeling I have to happiness. It is a sensation of contentment because everyone round me is doing the right thing. The pattern is whole" (75). However, this "pattern" seems to represent a negative, complacent, and mechanistic condition, and because Jean's use of memory and its translation to narrative are similarly attempts at making the pattern whole, but not necessarily true, the work of mourning is not completed. Her stifled, falsely ordered point of view produces instead an endless cycle of grief, as cyclical as Tom's unthought-out need to repeat his "parent's cycle – family into family: the interlocking circles" (79). Jean's recollection of the line Davy Sullivan quoted from *Anna Karenina* – "happy families are all the same" (79) – is, for the reader, ironic; the rest of Tolstoy's sentence, "each unhappy family is unhappy in its own way," is, of course, more apt. The most that the unhappy Duncan and Price families can say, as Jean does, is "we were still alive" (81).

Jean's comment about survival is juxtaposed with the start of the third section, which provides details about Frank's childhood and character. The information Jean gives contradicts her statement later in the text that she "had never known him" (145). Frank is a sign of absence for Jean, not only through his own death but even in his relationship to Isa when alive: she had written her name in his childhood books, thereby erasing his identity and ensuring the presence of her own. Jean's mother says "poor Frank" and "poor Isa" as if both offspring had been killed. Jean, reading these books to her children, notes that their inheritance from her will be "the assurance that there are no magic solutions" (84). Here Jean's displayed resistance to the imagination and her emotional limitations become evident; fairy tales, to her, are not imaginative stories but "stupid and a bore" (85). Her outspoken rejection of story suggests to the reader why Jean has had difficulty recovering from her past; but the telling of this story contradicts that absolute rejection, and its effect is potentially positive.

The reading of these books recalls memories for Jean of living "on the edge of [Isa's] life" (86), of putting herself in Isa's place, "adopting her credulousness, and even her memories, [which] I saw, could be made mine" (84). This adoption – typical of the narrator of an elegiac romance – had been part of her earlier effort to repair the wound of losing her sister's affection, a wound that affected her to the point where she referred to herself in the third person: "Isobel's sister, Jean Price, sits down, crosses her ankles, clasps her hands, smiles" (95). Jean cannot be consoled for the separation from her sister or from her entrance into the real world and her exit from the world of love and dreams.

Reading the childhood books provokes memory-digressions about Isobel, not of Frank, even though it is his absence that is the ostensible occasion for this narrative segment. Isobel's affair with Alec Campbell remains at the heart of Jean's grief: the real love she witnessed between the couple was a sight that awakened anguish in Jean (100), and still does. The story of her own marriage, described in part four, is eclipsed by Isobel, who, even there, "was center of things" (106). In this first-person story the autobiographical alternates with the biographical in a narrative of denial, delay, and waiting for mourning rather than a performance to that end. The act of waiting is implicitly compared to the act of dying: "The feeling [in Montreal] was of waiting, as the feeling in Allenton, years later, was of death" (108). Jean's life in Montreal is a stagnant one, and she is metaphorically dead in that she is waiting for her life to begin; but she is responsible for the state of emotional suspension she finds herself in, since it is Jean who is preventing herself from living by sealing herself off into a safe world.

In the last section of the story Gallant links the themes of life and death, biography and elegy by connecting Frank's death to Isa's first pregnancy (which was aborted). Isa confesses to Jean in Frank's empty bedroom, where Jean is to sleep (148); she has become Isa's confessor, taking Frank's place as she stands in for his ghost. The epiphanic moment for Jean occurs when Isa explains her ideas about love, which seem "astonishing and greatly intimate," and paradoxically cause her to understand "the inevitability of dying" (151). The union that Jean feels with Isa is the only possible consolation for her. Without it, she thinks, "we might as well die" (153). Jean's memory of this emotion remains in the present, and it is narrated in the present tense as she thinks of the scene: "There remains Isobel, then, cheek on hand, a little tired" (152). But Isa's rejection of Jean's hand signifies the return of death, of stagnation and the cold: "winter was still here and might never come to an end" (154).

In other words, Jean's life continues to be a survival, but little more:

I suspected, then, sitting in Frank's unhaunted room, that all of us, save my brother, were obliged to survive. We had slipped into our winter as trustingly as every night we fell asleep. We woke from dreams of love remembered, a house recovered and lost, a climate imagined, a journey never made; we woke dreaming our mothers had died in childbirth and heard ourselves saying, "then there is no one left but me!" We would waken thinking the earth must stop, now, so that we could be shed from it like snow. I knew, that night, we would not be shed, but would remain, because that was the way it was. We would survive, and waking – because there was no help for it – forget our dreams and return to life.   (155)

That there is "no help" for Jean is due to her refusal to risk, to question, to dream of real love, and to complete the narrative work of mourning by performing it as a reconstruction rather than as a record. She decides to believe of Isa's love affair with Alec that "a union of that sort was too fantastic to exist" (98); but while Besner suggests that Jean's conclusion demonstrates that "survivors must wake up to history" (87), Jean's awakening is merely a reinforcement of her mournful perspective on life. The rejection of the purely romantic for the purely realistic is not a revelation of the kind that allows a truthful awareness of self and world, and Jean's perceptions and interpretations have not been corrected in the course of her performance. Gallant's fiction-elegy suggests that a different *kind* of awakening than Jean's is required – that the reader must take the risk advised to the "fellow-wanderer" in the epigraph from Yeats's "The Shadowy Waters": to "mix ourselves into a dream / Not in its image on the mirror!" – for "beyond the world," there are possibilities for love and for life of which Jean cannot allow herself even to dream.

THE SILENT CRY: *GREEN WATER, GREEN SKY* AND *A FAIRLY GOOD TIME*

Though the short story is clearly Mavis Gallant's genre of choice, she has written two novels to date, and a third is in progress. Donald Jewison describes Gallant's techniques in *Green Water, Green Sky* (1959)[89] as "the methodology of … modernist realism," which, he says, creates a "tone of irony and elegy."[90] *Green Water, Green Sky* is particulary Woolfian in form and content; Jewison compares it to *Mrs Dalloway* with its themes of "ecstasy and madness" (95), but it is thematically and stylistically closer to *Jacob's Room* or even *The Waves* in that it consists of fragmented narrative, with a dislocated speaking subject and multiple points of view. Interestingly, the novella contains intertexts to Woolf's *The Voyage Out*, with references to Flor's metaphoric "journey out,"[91] the "journey away from shore" (82) that describes her movement into madness.

In *The Voyage Out* Terence claims that he wants to "write a novel about Silence."[92] In a sense Gallant's novel, composed of the four linked stories, is a literalization of Terence's desire in that it is about silence, about emotions withheld and withdrawn. It also renders silence through the narrative style of elision and through the transformation of point of view. The third-person speaker both describes and inscribes absence and loss in the text. The absence described is that of Flor's father, whose abandonment of Flor and Bonnie precipitates an incurable mourning in his daughter, such that she loses her sanity.

As Keefer writes regarding Flor, "Loss of one's native familial ground – of the past itself – is tantamount to loss of any convincing sense of self."[93] The inscription of Flor's subjective absence is accomplished by a parallel seeming-absence of the narrator; the reader is aware of its existence only by its absence, or rather its elusive presence. Each shift in point of view indicates that a speaker is at work, though the multiplicity of voices it projects obscures its own identity.[94] The unspoken in the text is an important part of its structure; Gallant employs a semiotic silence to represent both Flor's absence and her silent cry.

The speaker plays a game of *fort/da* with the reader, who must reconstruct the plot of the fiction-elegy from the fragments of achronological remembrances. John Moss states that "the reader seems to be inside the fiction, like a ghost inside other lives."[95] In *Green Water, Green Sky* the reader's role as spectral spectator is foregrounded. We see Flor alternately through the eyes of Bonnie, Wishart, Bob, and the two Georges (at the narrated ages of seven and seventeen), but the perspectives are not framed so as to enable the reader to situate him or herself easily in the text (unlike Woolf's fiction-elegies). Instead, the reader is abandoned to her own resources, an abandonment that parallels the fact that Flor has been abandoned by her parents at different times and in different ways.

Loss affects Flor to the point where, seemingly, there is no order left in life on any level, including that of language, society, or time: "Human cunning was keeping the ruin of Paris concealed. The ivy below Notre Dame had swelled through the city's painted crust: it was the tender covering of a ruin ... There was no present here."[96] Flor's mind is like a mirror on the world,[97] reflecting back "forms exploding with nothing to hold them together," like Bob's newly acquired painting, which she thinks is "absolute proof that the universe was disintegrating and that it was vain and foolish to cry for help" (43). Her cry is a silent one, internalized and unspoken, because, as she tells her husband, "Sometimes when I want to speak ... something comes between my thoughts and the words" (67).

Flor remembers fragments of poetry, reminders of the girlhood she spent reading (28). While Ronald Hatch, in discussing Gallant's modernistic methods, does recognize Flor's attempt to use fragments as a method of "shoring against ruin,"[98] he does not note that Flor's is a failed attempt, failed because it cannot resist a totalizing, negative vision of "a narrowing shore, an encroaching sea" (28). Literature (and/or language) is an inadequate means of expression and consolation for Flor's experience of melancholy. Julia Kristeva writes: "Melancholia then ends up in asymbolia, in loss of meaning: if I am no longer capable of translating or metaphorizing, I become silent and I die."[99] While Flor is capable of creating images that represent her state of mind, like the fox metaphor she uses to name her experiences of vertigo, she cannot read or identify the signified with the signifier; she cannot recognize reality, let alone translate it into words or signs that will communicate her experience to others. The fox metaphor is part of what Flor calls her own "private" language. She remembers a childhood fantasy, but "she could not convey this picture, an image of torment, nostalgia, and unbearable pain" (55). Flor is not a writer-figure in the fiction-elegy, but someone who is removed from the realm of language, incapable of using it to seek consolation in self-expression.

In rendering a mind driven mad by loss, Gallant does not use a modernistic stream-of-consciousness method, then, but one that simultaneously describes and enacts the impossibility of language's representing this state of mind. She suggests that, for Flor, consolation may not be accessible at all. In fact Flor's consolation is found in what Jewison calls her "psychic rootlessness" (95), in a pre-symbolic[100] condition of early childhood that protects Flor from the pain she experienced as an older child and adult. Her regression takes her to a point in life prior to the "mirror stage," when the division of self from mother occurs and the infant enters into the world of language, by recognizing the self as an image;[101] but Flor cannot recognize the image on the mirror as an image of herself, thinking instead that her reflection is some other person watching and witnessing her (77). Within her imagination she inhabits "a watery world of perceptions," of floating signifiers, and feels "a concrete sensation of happiness, as if happiness could be felt, lifted, carried around" (111).

The epigraph to *Green Water, Green Sky* is from *As You Like It* and encapsulates the theme of the fiction-elegy: "Ay, now am I in Arden; the more / fool I; when I was at home, I / was in a better place: but / travellers must be content." If to lose "home" is to experience psychic dislocation, then exiled "travellers" must find contentment – consolation – in imaginary realms. While Gallant is clearly not advocating madness as a solution to grief, she is showing that the former may result from the latter if the work of mourning is not performed. Flor's construction of a consoling scene wherein she "emerged in triumph ... and into her father's arms" (85), a result of a psychic introjection, is a pathological example of using memory and the imagination to achieve a symbolic and therefore tenuous continuity with the past. Flor's language, separated from reality, does not depict or represent the past – for her it constitutes the past itself.

In *Green Water, Green Sky* it is the other characters who enact versions of the work of mourning in and through memory and language. Flor's husband Bob is portrayed as an emotionally detached man: "Feeling came to him in blocks, compact. When he held on to one emotion there was no room for another" (36). He "tried to reconstruct their past, not sentimentally, but as a living structure of hair, skin, breath" (67), but now finds Flor's "hair ... a parody of Cannes" (65) – a parody of her old self and of the past. Bob's reconstruction is also a parody of elegy. The memories that he does have lead him to an epiphanic moment of re-experiencing their relationship in Cannes, to the point that "he thought he tasted salt" (68); but the memory sickens him: "he felt as if he might vomit ... He was appalled at the tenderness of the wound. He remembered what it was to be sick with love" (68). His work of mourning is incomplete. The reality of the past is not mediated in his memory by a fictive reconstruction or interpretation of its meaning; thus even pleasant memories are felt as cruel contrasts to the present, and are sickening.

George later believes that Bob's distant attitude "was probably a way of not hurting himself more than he could help" (146). For Bob memory is too difficult, but memory is crucial to the work of mourning and to the process of figuring grief, of elegizing. For Bob as for Bonnie (they have a "joint feeling" about Flor), "no present horror equaled the potential suffering of the past. Reliving the past, with full knowledge of what was to come, was a test too strong for their powers. It would have been too strong for anyone; they were not magical; they were only human beings" (69). Gallant does not make it clear if this last comment is an external judgment or the thoughts of the characters, but since the narrator is so detached we might assume the latter, and so evaluate both sympathetically and critically the values of Bonnie and Bob as mourners of Flor. Keefer states that the novel achieves an "accusatory order" (83), and I agree that, while the characters are indirectly criticized, their limitations are also contextualized such that we, as mimpathic readers, can understand their limitations, and in our own model of mourning – because the achronological text does force us to "relive" the characters' pasts – surpass them.

Bob prefers rooms that "contained no memories" (109) because he is a literal collector, not a recollector or an interpreter of the past. Even Flor had been, to him, "an object as cherished as anything he might buy" (37); for him possession and love are synonyms. Bonnie, however, is capable not only of recreating but of actually creating the past; while Bob, George, and Bonnie all "manufacture a past they can live with,"[102] it is the *process* of manufacturing that interests Gallant. Bonnie's self-centred construction of the past includes imagining an emotional bond between herself and Flor that may not have existed (especially from Flor's point of view): "Later, this was one of her most anguished memories. She forgot the time and the year and who was with them, remembering only that on a lost day, with her lost, loved, girl, there had existed a moment of unity while crossing a bridge" (52). This ekphrastic moment is subverted, since the narrator shows the truth-value of the image to be deficient. When Bonnie and Bob discuss Flor in the past tense, in a eulogistic manner, "as though Florence were dead" (151), George thinks that "they were creating an unmarred Florence, and through her a spotless Bonnie" (147). None of their memories is to be trusted, in other words – not even George's memories.

George knows, though, "that his isolated memories of Flor were right and Aunt Bonnie's fantasies wrong" (152). George is an empathic interpreter who reads his past as "a piling-up of hallucinations, things heard and seen that were untrue or of no use to him" (139). He is a survivor-figure,[103] and two of the four stories are told mainly through his point of view; the novel could be seen as *his* elegy for Flor, in this sense, as it demonstrates his developing understanding of loss, memory, and the fiction of consolation. George's "authentic hallucination" at the end of *Green Water, Green Sky* is representative of the entire novel's theme and structure, and of his entire sense of the past: details and images fuse, so that the past itself (not just images of Bonnie, Flor, and others) becomes "a changeable figure" (154) of suffering, given form. George's hallucination is a more truthful prosopopoetic figuration in that it is not fixed with Flor's idealized face as a symbol of an illusory, perfect past; instead, George's figuration is changeable, and it encompasses many perspectives on Flor, all of which contribute to a more truthful image of the past.

Those Gallant protagonists like George who literally or figuratively write of their dislocated pasts are, in effect, elegists of exile. In *A Fairly Good Time* (1970), which is composed of a mixture of "the 'sad' and the 'hilarious,'"[104] Shirley subtextually mourns her mother, her first (late) husband, Pete Higgins, and her second husband, Philippe Perrigny, who – having left his wife – is all but absent from the text, retrieved in Shirley's memory only. Shirley ponders her relationships with these three people; those with her mother and Philippe are shown to be particularly marked by loss in the form of emotional abandonment well before her mother's death and marital separation occur.[105] Since critics have commented on the novel, with its characteristic "hilarity,"[106] as a "comedy of manners,"[107] my designation of the novel as elegy may seem extreme; but Gallant uses the comic mode, I suggest, as a trope in the subtext of grief, one that counters the sadness and loss that is figured in the text.[108] Gallant herself has said: "I can't imagine writing anything that doesn't have humour. Every [tragic] situation has an element of farce ...

Look at the fits of laughter that you get at a funeral, at a wake. It's emotion and in a way it's relief that you're alive."[109]

The comic also undercuts the status of literature as a totalizing construction of consolation. Linda Leith says that the novel "mocks its own pretensions" (220) and that Gallant is suggesting "that literature is of no more help than any other semiotic system" (219). While it is true that "we not only read about the failings of literature as a guide, we experience them" (Leith 219), in Gallant's less political fiction writing does have the potential to console, since memories (once written and historicized, memorized as signs, in Hegel's terms) may then be forgotten and the unhistorical forgetting required of normal living resumed.[110] As E.D. Blodgett writes, Shirley's "power" in this text "derives from how she puts it [the text] to use."[111]

Thus Gallant uses the self-referential structure of the subtext as a trope of loss in A Fairly Good Time. There is a "common element" to the subtexts of all stories told by Shirley, as Blodgett suggests: the stories of Renata, James, and Peter "all address loss, as well as a sense of distinction" between selves.[112] Riffaterre writes that "the narrative is to the subtext as an object is to its sign";[113] the subtextual elegies in A Fairly Good Time function as "signs" that signify the larger meaning of the text proper as well as its status as a construct. Blodgett states that "the problem of the novel, then, is to find the right text, and, having found it, knowing the best way to put it to use."[114] While John Moss's overall evaluation of A Fairly Good Time is true – he says that it "is not a novel of psychological realism" – his suggestion that Gallant "never delves into the complexities of motivation or feeling" is dismissive.[115] These aspects of feeling are exactly what Gallant does delve into; she "operates directly inside the mind of her heroine."[116]

The epigraph Gallant uses for the novel ironically guides the reader away from the cynicism it advises: "There are lots of ways of being miserable, but there's only one way of being comfortable, and that is to stop running round after happiness. If you make up your mind not to be happy there's no reason why you shouldn't have a fairly good time." The epigraph reads like a parable, and establishes an allegorical significance of the novel at the outset. The novel depicts an allegory of the search for happiness, a search that entails the chaotic, though the novel is not "chaos for chaos' sake," as Keefer insists.[117] Shirley's search for happiness is an affirmative one, and her consolation for losses sustained in her life – her need "to be loved more"[118] – is found in the "chase for happiness" that Nietzsche suggests is what "keep[s] alive in any sense the will to live."[119]

"Meaning, discovery, and (self)-knowledge – Shirley's central projects – only appear possible as continual glossing upon other lives and the texts mutually produced," writes Blodgett.[120] And the reader glosses the losses in this novel in a re-enactment of Shirley's project.

It is Philippe's attitude that is captured in the epigraph, one that he assumed Shirley also held: "She could speak without weeping about her dead father, she never mentioned her dead young husband, she was not crying now, and so he believed that she cast sorrow off easily and that grief was a temporary arrangement of her feelings. He thought this to be an American fact [Shirley is Canadian] which made for a comfortable existence, without memory and without remorse" (49). For Philippe, who lacks any empathic ability, "you built a life around other people's leavings ... You built around a past of glass cases, shabby lighting, a foul-smelling guardian saying 'It is forbidden' " (154), whereas Shirley builds her life around love. Any chase for happiness eventually entails, according to Nietzsche, the "power of forgetting": "One who cannot leave himself behind on the threshold of the moment and forget the past, who cannot stand on a single point, like a goddess of victory, without fear or giddiness, will never know what happiness is, and, worse still, will never do anything to make others happy."[121] For Nietzsche and for Gallant, acting spontaneously does not mean acting immorally, and personally responsible action, not manipulative carelessness, is the intended ideal. Shirley does, indeed, respond "to situations as she-is-at-the-moment, not as some created *persona* who stands beside her," as Ronald Hatch writes (59). But finally, through her digressive narrational performance, she finds the balance between forgetting fact and remembering truth, and between caring for others and taking care of herself.

She has achieved the first kind of balance in her acceptance of Pete's death. Pete "did not exist, [but] stood in past time with heavy light around him" (154). In the imaginary letter to Philippe, Gallant devotes several pages of Shirley's thoughts to her first husband, his death, and her reaction to it.[122] "I am thinking years later now," she notes (231), when recounting what she put on his gravestone, and why. The narrative describing their honeymoon is a segment of the novel that shows what it is to have more than "a fairly good time": their activities "were all doing, using up your life; yes, it was a matter of living" (235), she thinks, which contrasts the rigid list-making life Philippe had planned and expected of marriage. "In Transit," the title story of Gallant's 1988 collection, had originally been part of the novel but was published separately (August 1965); there we hear that Philippe feels "as if love and travel were opposed to living, were a dream"[123] – a sentiment that recalls Jean Price's binary perspective in "Its Image on the Mirror."

Shirley's mourning for Pete seems to have been completed at the outset; she remembers realizing that "even if I were to visit the cemetery every day, he would never speak … The destination of a soul was of no interest. The death of a voice – now that was real" (241–2). Shirley does not try to revive Pete's voice, to speak for his silence or to attempt an artificial resurrection using apostrophe or prosopopoeia. She "forget[s] him for months" (245), and, feeling "responsible for something – for surviving, perhaps" (245) (typical guilt feelings of the survivor inscribed in elegy), she accepts the fact that part of herself died with Pete. She ends this part of her dream-epistle by thinking of herself in the third person: "She was someone belonging to me who had gone over to him. I knew I had lost two people, not one" (246). In reading about Shirley's life with Philippe, we become aware of this other, lost Shirley, and her fiction-elegy also mourns this loss of a past self and the life she led.

The last segment of Shirley's elegiac epistle is entitled "How I Happened To Write My Mother a Personal Letter," and it refers the reader to the novel's opening and the letter from her mother to Shirley. Linda Kauffman's general description of the epistolary genre relates it to the elegy: "The genre I shall question is epistolary; the mood is amorous and elegiac; the situation is the aftermath of abandonment. The heroine's discourse is meant as a performance to be spoken, a letter to be read."[124] In *A Fairly Good Time* meaning must be extracted from the fragments of narrative, and the meaning of Shirley's relationship to her mother surfaces as a significant subtext ("There's only one mother in anybody's life," Shirley is reminded by Cat Castle, her mother's friend [33]). Shirley's imagined letter of explanation to Philippe is a letter written but not sent, and it is simultaneously an apostrophe (explaining the failed marriage) to her now-deceased mother, whose death we are informed of at the end of the novel (300). Shirley's gesture is one of self-disclosure and hoped-for understanding and love, a gesture not communicated except in her imagination because the addressees would not have understood its meaning anyhow. Thus it is the writing of the letter that is a constructive act performed by Shirley, for her sake alone.[125]

The genealogical "female line" (40) between Shirley and her mother may exist, but a line of communication is never established. Blodgett writes that Shirley "becomes part of a matrilineal succession that Jonathan Culler describes as 'metonymical, maternal relationships based on contiguity,' "[126] but Shirley's efforts to make connections and to interpret surely oppose her mother's way of looking at the world; her interpretations are always, it seems, *unre*-lated to the signs she is given by her daughter. Of the actual letters sent between Shirley and Mrs Norris, Shirley thinks that they participated in "an uninterrupted dialogue of the deaf" (45) – just as her marriage was conducted in "a white silence" (125) – and that her letters to her mother were screams for attention (249). She sends a bluebell as a sign to her mother inside a letter, because, she says, "I thought that when she saw it she would know everything" (249). Shirley's bluebell letter, which is a request for consolation and for confirmation of her values, requires an empathic reader, though her mother is incapable of fulfilling this role.

One morning after being abandoned by Philippe, Shirley experiences a hallucinatory vision of her parents, who also abandoned her, first through emotional neglect, then by dying: "A milder lumination – of imagination this time – surrounded two middle-aged persons cycling steadily up an English hill ... The flower fragrance altered and resembled the scent of the aging lovers, of soap and of death ... Her parents, a lost pair, cycled off into the dark ... What she required this morning was not a reminder of the past but a harmless substitute for it" (9–10). Shirley voices this aesthetic of Gallantian elegy: symbolic reminders of the past are inadequate forms of consolation; the past may be replaced figuratively, however, in an empathic relationship with another person who would allow the mourner-elegist to narrativize the past and the emotional pain caused by loss – to tell a story.

Shirley had experienced an epiphanic moment while picking the bluebells, one of which she included in her letter to Mrs Norris: "Suddenly I saw a lake of blue. The blond girl clutched her golden heart and turned at the same moment. For a second only, the new, sweet fragrance that rose from the blue lake was a secret between us ... this color was true and the scent was real, and as I crouched down the better to see and touch I believed that you [Philippe] had led me outside the city after all" (249). Neither Philippe nor his friends attempt to understand Shirley's experience of pastoral-like bliss, which is "other" than their values, their "get all you can" philosophy (249). Ronald Hatch writes that "what appears to be merely an aesthetic experience for Shirley may well have moral and social ramifications" and that Shirley's story is that of "the individual struggle to claim victory over life."[127] Shirley certainly makes this kind of connection between her emotional/aesthetic experience and moral and social behaviour: the decay of the flowers coincides with the final disintegration of her marriage; she kept them "in water three days alive and four days dead, and then you [Philippe] left me," she remembers (250). The bluebells signify love to Shirley, then, and they are also metonymically connected to her father: "She remembered how her elderly father had called her Belle, first because he disliked the name Shirley, then because Belle corresponded to a generation and a measure of female beauty" (66). The flower is Shirley's real name, not a symbol of love but a metonymic marker of identity; it provides her with the anagnoristic sense of her real self, and allows her to reclaim part of the self that she had lost in her life with Philippe.

Mrs Norris's letter, written in response to Shirley's cry for help (though it disregards the cry entirely), is accidentally incorporated into the novel within the novel, fragments of the text written by Philippe's friend Genevieve (a novel appropriately entitled *A Life within A Life*). The *mise en abyme* shape produced by the embedded stories is a figuration of Shirley's own experience. As Blodgett notes, Shirley "finds herself in a labyrinth – literally *mise en abyme* – and her task is to come to terms with that subtle, shifting, heretical scene in which the self is to be created from the shambles it finds are the *donnés* of its existence."[128] Thus Gallant places the reader in the labyrinth as well, for the reader must reconstruct Shirley's 'self' by interpreting her relationships, her griefs, her stories of her*selves*.

Genevieve's novel is also a fictionalized cry, but it is a narcissistic parody of Shirley's; that her mother's letter of "good counsel" (25) becomes part of this novel demonstrates its lack of value for grief-stricken Shirley. Shirley recognizes that "Genevieve's language was a situation in itself ... Language is Situation ... The Silent Cry" (22–3). If language is indeed situation, is metonymically referential, then Shirley's sad situation is rendered in a rhetoric of mourning. Philippe's empty use of the phrase "the silent cry" in various of his articles is parodied by Gallant, and she endows it with significance when Shirley uses it; as Keith notes, the phrase "is suddenly seen to contain a potentially profound meaning."[129] The same phrase is shown to have two vastly different applications and interpretations, and it is the *use* of language that Gallant demonstrates to be either potentially dangerous *or* constructive.

Keefer writes: "Confusion, rampaging disorder, comic catastrophe reign supreme, and yet a kind of parity exists between the hapless Shirley, the author of all this entropy, and its helpless recipient, the reader" (83). Although the parity does exist, the reader certainly cannot be considered helpless; rather, he or she reconstructs the paradigm of mourning in a mimpathic encounter with Shirley, and with the text. Language is situation, and Shirley's situation is one of loss and isolation, of silence, and of internal narrativization. Hence this fiction-elegy is a silent one (the whole novel is Shirley's silent cry, notes Keith),[130] an unwritten think-act that the reader must reconstruct as Shirley reconstructs her past life with Pete – which stands as a "model of narrative clarity," writes Blodgett.[131]

It is narrative itself that is the primary model of mourning in Gallant's fiction-elegy. Shirley addresses her mother and Philippe in her think-acted elegiac epistle, wherein she attempts to "sum up the past and so make a future possible" (210) and with which she achieves "a measure of success," writes Neil Besner.[132] Her address to the absent is her silent cry, and as a result the past becomes "detached from her, and floated away like a balloon" (251). Her ability to remember, to write (or imagine writing), and then to forget and to continue seeking happiness is the model of mourning that the reader is able to decipher from the allegorical novel – a novel that consists of imagined dialogues with her mother;[133] with Philippe, either in memory, in "scribble[s]" (23), in epistles (211–50), or in absentia; and in "private dialogues" (179) with herself: "I congratulate you, Shirley said to herself" (265). Ultimately, the reader addresses Shirley with the same speech-act, affirming the affirmative.

In her novels, which are elegiac in theme, structure, and language, the emotional and empathic elements of Gallant's fiction involve the reader in the experiences of her characters. It is true that there is a judgmental quality to her fiction, in that the *uninvolved* reader is implicated in Gallant's critiques of non-comprehending, unempathic beings (such as Mrs Norris, Philippe, Bonnie, and Bob). Consequently, we are urged to take responsibility for our own readings of both the literary realities of the fiction and of the literal reality it serves to illuminate – to listen for the silent cry.

3 Gallant and the Ethics of Reading

In chapter 2 I argued that Gallant figures the elegiac in her fiction in a variety of ways, including the use of plot as trope, experimentation with contrasting points of view, and the subversion of sequential chronology. The work of mourning is demonstrated in Gallant's stories to be a form of "narrative thinking," which, according to John Robinson and Linda Hawpe, "consists of creating a fit between a situation and the story schema. Establishing a fit, that is, making a story out of experience, is a heuristic process," they continue, "one which requires skill, judgment, and experience."[1] The reader, too, enacts the process of narrative thinking in reconstructing the fiction-elegies using interpretive skill, responding to the narrative's insistence that the story-level work be judged, and integrating the story's meaning with experience.

Two other structural strategies are consistently evident in Gallant's fiction-elegies: the adoption and ironic adaptation of first-person elegiac romance ("The End of the World" and "Its Image on the Mirror," for example), wherein a narrator who is in the process of coming to terms with loss uses story-telling as a method of mourning and as a means with which to achieve self-preservation;[2] and the use of allegory, wherein the narrator's or character's process of representing the past constitutes another story level. Paul de Man writes that "allegorical narratives tell the story of the failure to read" and are therefore "allegories of the impossibility of reading";[3] this premise can be applied to Gallant's allegories, wherein narrators and/or characters very often are shown as failed readers of past and present.[4]

Allegory figures prominently in all fiction-elegy by its very definition, in that the reader enacts a work of mourning in the encounter with the text's story level.[5] Walter Benjamin's study of the German *Trauerspiel* provides many suggestive connections between mourning and allegory in his discussion of the genre of tragic drama – not unrelated to elegy – and the use of allegorical form: "Its dominant mood is that of mourning, which is at once the mother of the allegories and their content," he writes; "the only pleasure the melancholic permits himself, and it is a powerful one, is allegory."[6] The consoling pleasure found in the narrativization of grief – in the work of mourning – has its variations in Gallant's fiction-elegies, as I've suggested, and the sequences and allegories discussed in this chapter demonstrate an even wider range of the genre in Gallant's work.

Gallant has made use of the story sequence in a number of cases: the Linnet Muir stories, three groups of stories in *Overhead in a Balloon*, and the collected stories that make up *Green Water, Green Sky*. The sequence provides continuity within discontinuity in formal or structural terms. Elegies (l)inked in sequential fashion are connected metonymically, while the disruption that results from a fragmented whole emphasizes the reader's role in reconstructing the work of mourning, and the use of plot as a trope of fiction-elegy. Also, as Debra Martens notes, different character types found in Gallant's work produce a "tension between continuity and discontinuity": some characters are connected to the past through memory; others (who "cope better," Marten suggests) are forgetful and/or ignorant of the past.[7] Gallant's characters most often fall into the latter category, while the use of memory by the former is also questioned. Gallant's insistence upon the existence of a dialectical relation between fact and fiction, history and memory, is to be recognized by the reader who deciphers the code of memory in her fiction-elegies.

SECRETS OF THE SEQUENCE: THE LINNET MUIR STORIES

Mavis Gallant's Linnet Muir sequence in the collection *Home Truths* is an anomaly in many ways. On one level Gallant's use of Linnet as a first-person narrator constitutes a primary narratorial distancing technique (separating the implied author from the elegiac content of the story), but it also provides an inherent resistance to the efforts of some critics to read the Linnet stories as *Gallant's* autobiography.[8] In an interview with Geoff Hancock, Gallant insists that these stories are not "straight autobiography," which "would be boring. It would bore the reader. The stories are a kind of reality *necessarily* transformed. The people are completely other, and some characters two or three different persons all at the same time."[9]

Virginia Woolf says of her invention Mary Carmichael in *A Room of One's Own* that she is "tampering with the expected sequence. First she broke the sentence; now she has broken the sequence. Very well," writes Woolf, "she has every right to do both these things if she does them not for the sake of breaking, but for the sake of creating."[10] Gallant, I suggest, establishes her literary sequence only to break it by experimenting with the genre, for the self-reflexive sake of creating – and of re-creating. The linked Linnet stories are unique in that a single consciousness is presented in detail at various levels of time, thereby producing a multilayered single text in a form that Barbara Godard has recently labelled "modular fiction."[11] The result, as W.J. Keith notes, is "a splendid meditation on the very intricacies of thought and invention," akin, he states, to a "Proustian journey."[12] But as Jerry Aline Flieger writes of Proust, "it is forgetfulness, not memory, which performs the work of figuration" in Proust's text,[13] whereas in Gallant's work memory is a tool of figuring grief. Lois Marie Jaeck's assessment that Proust's involuntary memory "gave the past back to the narrator through the exact duplication in the present of a sensation that he had experienced in the past"[14] is in direct opposition to Linnet's own statement about memory: "When people say 'I know exactly how I felt' it can't be true."[15] Thus the writing of the past and of memory is more complicated for Linnet than a Proustian model would suggest, and Gallant's sequence formally experiments with these writings.

There are reasons for this innovative sequential experiment. Gallant has said that she wanted to restore "in some underground river of the mind a lost Montreal" with these stories;[16] but at the story level itself the Linnet sequence seems to be, among other recognizable forms, an exercise in elegy.[17] The focus on the almost silent father, often absent even while alive,[18] is one aspect of this elegy in its consideration of what Linnet calls the "principle of the absent, endangered male" (327). The absent father is a strong shaping principle in Canadian fiction[19] and is central to elegy in general, since (according to Peter Sacks) the patriarchal figure traditionally upholds social and familial structures.[20] Linnet herself is aware of this conventional structure, though clearly she undercuts and rejects it with ironic commentary: "It was the father's Father, never met, never heard, who made Heaven and earth and Eve and Adam" (269).

None the less, Linnet's father haunts both the text proper and the text-within-the-text, the one she writes in order to confront her loss and be consoled. Due to the covert nature of this intratextual elegy, Gallant's sequence might be read as a subversion, even as an anti-elegy or an "un-mourning." It is anti-elegiac for other reasons as well. For instance, the conventional pastoral contrast between the (ideal) rural and the (negative) urban settings is reversed. Similarly, the traditional longing for a Golden Age or paradisical childhood[21] is inverted: Linnet's childhood was marked by "a feeling of loss, of helpless sadness" (311), and by "a long spell of grief" (223), and she thinks of her youth as "the prison of childhood" (225). The ironic nature of this reversal emphasizes a "home truth" about Linnet's past: if a home truth consists of "the contradiction between what *is* and what *should be*,"[22] then it is true that her upbringing was not as it should have been. Consequently it is also true that after the loss of her father she is not consoled by what should comfort her; recollecting the past in search of factual truth is not a useful method of mourning, nor is writing about it in a documentary fashion. In order to find meaning Linnet must test the relations between fact and fiction, history and writing, using memory as a mediator.

The event of Linnet's father's death is described in abstract terms: "Peacetime casualties ... are lightning bolts out of a sunny sky that strike only one house. All around the ashy ruin lilacs blossom, leaves gleam. Speculation in public about the disaster would be indecent. Nothing remains but a silent, recurring puzzlement to the survivors: Why here and not there? Why this and not that?" (235) By telling separate stories about her past, Linnet appears to be instituting an orderly narrative sequence designed not only to answer these questions but perhaps also to console on the structural level of the aesthetic. But Gallant suggests that the sequence form may have the opposite effect; as Melissa Fran Zeiger writes, "the modern sequence reflects the tendency of modern elegy to create uncanniness by undoing narrativity, chronology, personality."[23] Clearly Gallant's sequence is less linear or chronological than that of a traditional or modern elegy, and though it offers a formally coherent narrative structure, it also paradoxically undoes chronology. Paradoxically, Gallant's undoing draws the reader's attention to the "doing," to the act of mourning with words.

This act of mourning is one method of interpreting the *uncanny*. The uncanny, that which "ought to have remained hidden but has come to light," as Freud describes it, is felt most "in relation to death and dead bodies, to the return of the dead, and to spirits and ghosts."[24] Linnet has kept some of her past hidden from herself, a past that – when confronted – has the sense of the uncanny; secrets are gradually uncovered in "relation" to her father's death. The story structure that seems smooth on the surface is, then, as Frank Kermode would argue, an "illusion of narrative sequence" that must be in conflict with narrative "secrets" that are kept from the reader.[25] For example, the mystery of Angus Muir (who had "nothing but" secrets himself [230]) surfaces only long enough to offer what Kermode would call "evidence of [an] insubordinate text" (83), the text that constitutes an elegy for Linnet's father.

Linnet's elegiac story sequence calls into question both the idea of narrative sequence and the potential of aesthetic consolation. As elegy it is fundamentally self-reflexive, drawing attention to its narrativity and artifice. What is at stake in Gallant's use of the elegiac genre is the convergence of the aesthetic and the epistemological as well as of the aesthetic and the historical, in terms of the possible recuperative power of such unions.[26] The breaking of the sequential form is accomplished with digressions on other familial relationships and parent/child politics,[27] and also by the movement back and forth in time and the intermittent focus on the self as an artist-figure.

This breaking has a double function: first, it literalizes a Kermodean-like theory of sequence and secrets, thereby drawing attention to the problem of accurately narrating the insubordinate texts of history; and second, the existence of a broken sequence is often one diagnostic test of the genre of elegy – it draws attention to the condition of the narrative as a drama of the mind, an internalization that works against narrative and what Jonathan Culler calls "its accompaniments: [chronological] sequentiality, causality, time, teleological meaning."[28] As previously noted, Culler goes on to suggest that this type of narrative posits a "temporality of discourse" and that the "clearest example of this structure is of course the elegy which replaces an irreversible temporal disjunction, the move from life to death, with a dialectical alternation between attitudes of mourning and consolation, evocations of absence and presence" (67).

This written repetition of her past makes Linnet a historiographer, if we characterize historicality as Paul Ricoeur does, "in terms of the emphasis placed on the weight of the past and, even more, in terms of the power of recovering the 'extension' between birth and death in the work of 'repetition.' "[29] The "concern for the past" is what generates history, Ricoeur writes (177); in Linnet's case it generates a particular history – her/story – and Gallant, through Linnet, explores different modes of memory and writing as well as their relationship to history and truth.

The broken-sequence form itself, then, enacts an aesthetic that re-covers life, that "extension between birth and death" of which Ri-coeur speaks. Linnet writes to attempt a recovery from the loss as well as to recover or regain the lost, only to re-cover it again by dis-tancing herself from her father. In the first story she recalls a time when she had yet to recover in any of these senses of the word. She is vulnerable, thinking "I had survived, but perhaps I had failed to grow some outer skin it was now too late to acquire" (232). On the actual return to her birthplace (Montreal) she carries her birth certif-icate and an object that synecdochically links her to her father: an Edwardian picnic hamper. She makes a metonymic connection be-tween the hamper, his death, and her life (which seems to be mourning-in-motion) by describing her luggage: "[It was] a prepos-terous piece of baggage my father had brought from England some 20 years before; it had been with me since childhood, when his death turned my life into a helpless migration" (219). Though she is "hampered" by memories of him, she chooses to remain attached to the inherited object that once belonged to him in his travels, despite her claim that she "did not believe in inherited property" (232).

Linnet not only inherits her father's identity as traveller but re-sembles her father physically as well: "I was so like him in some ways that a man once stopped me in front of the Bell Telephone building on Beaver Hall Hill and said, 'Could you possibly be Angus Muir's sister?' " (249) Linnet is bound so closely to the identity of her dead father, in fact, that three people in the story say on different occasions that they had heard *she* had died (224, 229, 249). Through the conventionally elegiac ritual of writing in response to loss she fills the basket with her own marks of life, her poems and journals. The stories in the hamper migrate with Linnet, and the fictional el-egy that they eventually compose moves in a migratory narrative pattern as well.

Gallant plays with the genre of elegy, then, and emphasizes the psycholinguistic components of the mourning *process* instead of a potential literary monument, which is the conventional product of elegy. Janice Kulyk Keefer suggests that Gallant's sequence achieves "continuousness" and "avoids programmatic closure,"[30] which are precisely the narrative strategies appropriate for elegiac fiction. In fact it is the paradoxical *dis*continuity of the broken sequence that prevents the programmatic closure often found in elegy. The quali-fied consolation in Gallant's fiction – brought about by an awareness of the significance and structure of the processes of memory – is found in the lack or disruption of closure, in the collision of history and fiction, and not in a structurally closed (and internally continuous) monumental piece of art.

Closure is also avoided by the inclusion of the autobiographical mode. While the first story in the sequence opens with the words "My father died" (218), and two of the three segments in the narrative begin with the phrases "my father's death" and "I know a woman whose father died," most of this story (like the five others in the sequence) consists of Linnet's overtly autobiographical anecdotes; taken in sum they emphasize her will to live and her roles as survivor and story-teller, both of which are crucial to the work of mourning. She believes that "having come down on the side of life [whereas her father chose death] ... writing now had to occupy an enormous space" (249).

Gallant uses Linnet's life-writing to fill the space of Linnet's mourning and to resist traditional elegiac consolation in closure. The autobiography often has a confessional tone, which also draws the reader into the immediacy and openness of the text; we are told things that Linnet never wanted "anyone to know" (226), things that she "never mentioned" to anyone (219). This mixture of genres and modes within the elegy emphasizes the fact that a crisis of representation parallels the crisis of loss experienced by the writer. The metafictional text thematizes an aspect of the elegist's mourning: the need to write. Since Gallant sequentializes Linnet's autobiography, she is fusing three types of fiction to create the fiction-elegy: the *Künstlerroman*, the autobiographical, and the elegiac. This combination of modes points to both of Linnet's crises, which themselves are linked: how to deal with her past as well as how to write, and thereby recover from, absence.

By exploring the relationship between the past and the ability of the mind not only to remember but to record or represent history, Gallant embeds an aesthetic of elegy in the stories. The use of repetition throughout the sequence is a significant component of this aesthetic. Different versions of events in Linnet's life are told in narrative variants (stories about her relationships with Uncle Raoul Chauchard, Olivia, Georgie, and fiancés, for example) and they become what Barbara Herrnstein Smith would call "modified retellings of a particular prior narrative text" (211). Subsequently, the reader is forced to face the unreliability of any one memory *and* of the act of writing down that memory. There is, after all, no single truth: only multiple (often painful) "home truths," as the repetition-with-a-difference of certain stories about her former home-life indicate.

Anecdotal wanderings or repetitions in and about the past are endemic to elegy. The subsequent temporal doubling-back in Linnet's writing is indicated by phrases such as "that *is* how it *was*," and "I *was now* eighteen" (219, emphasis mine), phrases that fragment the temporality of the story and suggest that a voice does exist in the present as well. Repetition both within each story and between stories in the sequence allows her to enact certain verbal rites that eventually complete the work of mourning. But the story sequence enables Gallant to literalize not only the psychological need of the grieving mind for repetition of memories; it also provides a form whereby she can literalize the primary characteristic of memory itself: fragmentation.

The digressions, narrative gaps, and non-linear story sequences within the stories work against chronology, as noted, and instal their own temporality of fragmented discourse. However, Gallant combines the referential and the discursive modes as the writing mimics the movement of Linnet's mourning mind and puts it on public display. The outer event – Linnet's story – and the inner event – Linnet's belated work of mourning[31] – become so closely aligned that the dramatic discourse is, in terms of the present mental drama, allegorical as well. Allegory institutes a dialectic of its own; Benjamin writes that it is both "convention and expression,"[32] and indeed the figurative and the performative characteristics of figurations of grief combine in an allegorical structure: the staged work of mourning.

Linnet's public story is clearly a staged one, whereby she speaks from a dramatic perspective.[33] Her techniques are the "staging devices" of an elegist,[34] and though her experience is private, her writings (on the surface at least) are not. Linnet mildly rebels against the "shamed silences" of people who refuse to display what they feel (227), a practice that she considers "murder in everyday life" (228). But she guards her own emotions despite this judgment and despite the writing of her elegy. Though she does address the reader directly at times, thus establishing a sense of intimacy, the content of the public address is often secretive, a mysterious piece of private information about her father and her past. For example, Linnet writes, "How I happen to know the revolver was loaded and how I learned never to point a gun even in play is *another story. I can tell you* that I never again looked in a drawer that didn't belong to me" (234, emphasis mine). Though the address is direct, the meaning is held back, the implication being that there is always "another story": either other versions of memory, or secret narratives embedded in the overt sequence, or both.

The public form of the elegy announces an attempt to assert a state of control over the emotions that underlie it, to make *"public* life tolerable" (228). Linnet comments early in the sequence that she admires people who, in a crisis situation, are able to retain control. Linnet's controlled writing style is at times blunt, factual, even clinical, and while this could relate to the fact that Linnet has been a journalist, more importantly it seems to suggest and endorse the emotional detachment of the elegist, which produces necessary control at certain stages of grief. Linnet becomes detached from herself as well. She simultaneously becomes both character and implied author of the text, and this doubling puts her at a remove from the life-story she writes, despite the fact that it is her own. She refers to herself in the past as "the smaller Linnet" (225), which also distances her self in the now of the text from her self then, within her own writing, and implies a splitting of the subject-past from the subject-present. The voice of the grieving self is, in this way, controlled and silent, as is the voice of the dead: Angus's.

Linnet suspects that "death and silence can be one" (228) and encodes this suspicion in her elegy for Angus who, it might be said, is implicitly represented in the white spaces on the page and between the stories in the sequence. We may be hearing him at one point, when Linnet breaks off a childhood anecdote about tulips, addressing the reader with the words "no, let another voice finish it; the only authentic voices I have belong to the dead" and then quoting one such dead person as if he (or she) could speak: "then she *ate* them" (283). The dead parent is seemingly her father, since the next line begins with "It was my father's custom" and since the story is at least nominally about his relationship with another woman. The title of the story is "Voices Lost in Snow," a title that would be suitable for the entire sequence.

That Angus is "lost" to Linnet, that his literal voice has been silenced, is obvious. It is how she finds him in memory and in writing that is at stake. Linnet's stories are not an attempt to capture her father in words. She collects three different versions (or "men's woolly stories") about her father's death and then has to assimilate them, to compose a story that lets her live with the death, the manner of the death, and the memory of the emblematic gun she found in a drawer. But she refuses to attempt to extract the true story from real events since she realizes that the impulse to narrativize events always gives rise to a form of fiction (in critical terms), to what Hayden White calls "an aspect of narrativity" (4). That is, Linnet has learned to distrust the ability of story to capture truth, and creates a vague story that encompasses most variants under the rubric of "homesickness": "I thought he had died of homesickness; sickness for England was the consumption, the gun, the everything," she decides

(235) – and her story is nearly as plausible as any other. Thus she is able to "settl[e] his fate in her mind," to "let go" (235).

Linnet's version of the truth, then, is as dubious as those of her father's friends. (Her unnamed acquaintance, who tells different invented versions of *her* father's death at dinner parties, is a parodic parallel to Linnet in this respect.) In "Truth with a Capital 'T' " Gallant explicitly plays with the idea of writing truth, and Linnet, from the vantage point of a "critical nostalgia"[35] through which she can "hear the past" (329), knows that the narrativized past is fiction. A voice, such as that of her godmother Georgie, is closer to truth than a written anecdote, since memory is unreliable: "Her voice, and her particular Montreal accent, were like the unexpected signatures that underwrite the past: If this much is true, you will tell yourself, then so is all the rest I have remembered" (325). Voice has an incarnative quality for Linnet, as it resurrects without translation into a prosopopoetic figuration by a mediating, writing voice. Voice acts as what Derrida refers to as an interiorized metonymy, one "where the part stands for the whole and for *more than* the whole that it exceeds. An allegorical metonymy, too, which says something other than what it was and manifests the other (*allos*) in the open but nocturnal space of the *agora* – in its *plus de lumière*: at once no more light, and greater light. It speaks the other and makes the other speak, but it does so in order to let the other speak."[36] But since memory is selective and inaccurate, not pure, and since to Linnet's mind "nothing but the present [can] live" (280), then even the pure recall of voice is an impossible source of consolation for Linnet. Hearing the past does, however, allow Linnet to interpret it from her present perspective, and to see her own past as well as her father's with greater understanding, greater light.

Despite the fact that Linnet thinks "one's impulse was always to write to the dead" (281), a traditional apostrophe to or invocation of her dead father is absent in this elegy. An elegy is usually addressed to an absent audience, but Linnet's address is a silent one. Her refusal to write directly to the dead, to resurrect the dead with words, is her refusal to mourn in the conventional sense. In other words, she recognizes the remembered past as a fiction, since in the present "she recognized nearly nothing and had to start from scratch" (235) – that is, to start remembering in the present, and to create new fictions based on the past. Linnet detaches herself from Angus, turning away from a type of "object-fixation" on the dead and lost to an intellectual acceptance of their unrecoverability. She has committed an "act of troping"[37] by putting distance between herself and the dead father and her past; she enacts a performative grieving in this focus on language, filling in the space left by the death of Angus by turning from object to sign, from father to story.

The resulting detachment takes the form of actively putting the past behind her, of "shedding past time" (222). "If I was to live my own life I had to let go," she writes, deciding that the "whole story [of her father's death] somehow became none of my business" (235). A verbal portrait of him would be the equivalent of "impersonations," like those "wash drawings of Canadian war graves" that her father's "painter-chum" sold to "heartbroken women" who "had them framed – the only picture in the house" (231). As Linnet implies in "The Doctor," it is not symbolic reminders that console but metonymic "true fragments" (301) – like the books of poetry the doctor-friend had written himself, secretly, or paintings her father had done, paintings that are now as lost as his voice.

Linnet's declaration that "mostly when people say 'I know exactly how I felt' it can't be true" (260) indicates a distrust of memory similar to Gallant's, and while what de Man calls the historical mode of language is, ideally, true referentiality, the best a writer such as Linnet (or Gallant) can do is to produce a field of interplay in which aesthetic and historical realms collide, in order to arrive at a version of history: written memory. The tension between textual opposites (history and story) is rendered through a near-historical mode of language such as that employed by Linnet in her clinical, unconventional elegy, a mode that provides a tenuous bridge or passage from the historical to the aesthetic.

This defiance of or resistance to codification in the work of mourning is a sign of what de Man calls "true mourning": "True mourning is less deluded than temporal harmony as voice and as song. The most *it* can do is to allow for non-comprehension and enumerate non-anthropomorphic, non-elegiac, non-celebratory, non-lyrical, non-poetic, that is to say, prosaic, or better, *historical* modes of language power."[38] And Derrida explains that true mourning "seems to dictate ... the tendency to accept incomprehension, to leave a place for it, and to enumerate coldly, almost like death itself, those modes of language which, in short, deny the whole rhetoricity of the true ... In doing so, they also deny, paradoxically, the *truth* of mourning, which consists of a certain rhetoric – the allegorical memory which constitutes any trace as always being the trace of the other."[39] The aesthetic (that is, narrative art) is considered to be false consolation in this poetics for the very reasons that Gallant distrusts memory and cannot claim truth for written versions of any single memory; a work of mourning is, after all, a work, a fictionalization.

In what might be called an "untrue mourning" Linnet attempts to construct this kind of bridge between history and aesthetics as her monument to place, producing a *"faithful record* [of a historical Montreal]" written by "a true survivor" (223, emphasis mine).[40] It is rebuilt from memory, like those "cities we build over the past to cover seams and cracks we cannot account for" (313), and it consists of "a superior civilization" where "the vision of a house upon that street was so painful that [Linnet] was obliged to banish it from the memorial." The city is memorialized, written down and forgotten as a "dream past" (228), but her father is not subjected to this somewhat ironic "faithful record"; in Linnet's textual performance he is mourned allegorically: indirectly, non-anthropomorphically and non-celebratorily – silently, in fact, since "true mourning" cannot be written.

Gallant seems to be advocating a Hegelian-like aesthetic wherein to write is to forget: in the act of writing down thoughts and memories we allow ourselves to forget them.[41] But Linnet's writing process (the embedded elegy) appeals to what Derrida calls the "living, knowing memory," or *mneme*. She avoids the construction of inventories and chronicles, which constitute "not memory itself ... only monuments" that are *hypomnematic*.[42] Though Linnet does memorialize *place* through the work of memory, her memories of her father reproduce not a localizable monument but an unwritten presence. Paradoxically, by *not* writing about his life directly in her elegy, Linnet does not forget him.[43] Whereas traditional consolation occurs in the conflation of art and history, in the creation of a lasting, closed verbal monument for the dead, Linnet's consolation occurs when writing and history are dialectically bridged but divided by memory and thinking – by what Derrida calls the "thinking memory" of *Gedachtnis* that goes "beyond mournful memory [*Erinnerung*]" and "def[ies] all reappropriation, even in a coded rhetoric or *conventional* [my emphasis] system of tropes, in the *exercises* of prosopopoeia, allegory, or elegiac and grieving metonymy."[44]

The relationship of memory to writing and of writing to history is problematic for Linnet because of her vocation as a writer. She thinks of her father's artistic failure on several occasions (253, 257), wondering if she "had inherited a poisoned gene from him, a vocation without a gift" (249). This issue of poetic inheritance is an elegiac convention, and Gallant treats it ironically by making Angus a failed artist. Though he was not a writer, and despite the fact that it is her mother who "rewrites" people's lives, "providing them with suitable and harmonious endings" (287), Gallant suggests that Linnet's artistic inclination and perceptiveness came from her father.[45]

Her evasion of closure is a rejection of her mother's aesthetic and an acknowledgment of the falsity of such truth claims.

This acknowledgment leaves Linnet on shaky ground, "between zero and one," to quote the title of another story in the sequence. The interrogatives that end this story leave the reader with the same uneasy feeling, asking with Linnet, "What will happen?" Linnet replaces the uncertainty by turning the unknowable into fiction (261), a fiction that remains in a state of artistic uncertainty and openness. She ends each story by beginning again with another – hence the sequence of stories, however broken. Mnemonic repetition – vacillation between zero (amnesia) and one (the knowledge of "whole truth") – becomes the only writable consolation for Linnet.

Paul Ricoeur asks, "is not repetition itself a kind of resurrection of the dead?"[46] Gallant's stories speak silently of Linnet's dead father in a sequence that seems to be without beginning or end, a sequence that ends but does not seem to conclude. The sequence that can be aesthetically "comforting" can also be unsettling, as Frank Kermode notes,[47] "unreadable," as is the text of mourning according to Derrida; but the failure to interiorize the past succeeds as well, because a recognition of the impossibility of figuring the dead is attained.[48] Linnet overcomes this discomfort and achieves a form of consolation by first understanding the relationship between memory, language, and history, and then responding to the past by being free to invent it over and over again. The need to start over, to repeat in language, is not only an elegiac method of achieving continuity, control and ceremony;[49] it also suggests that there is an inherent failure in the ability of memory and language to provide aesthetic consolation in the form of a single written historical truth, a failure that engenders a compulsion to repeat, to rewrite. Gallant's series of stories paradoxically emphasizes beginnings[50] and reinforces Linnet's resistance to closure, as is suggested in her affirmative yet oxymoronic and ambiguous motto: "Unless you died you were always *bound to* escape."[51]

ROMANCING THE STORY: *OVERHEAD IN A BALLOON*

There are three sets of connected stories in *Overhead in a Balloon* (1985), each of which focuses on the interconnections between personal lives and relationships, and political ideologies and actions. Many of these stories are comic, too, and Gallant's satirical edge is at work to bring the reader to a position of passing judgment on contemporary Western culture – especially in those stories that feature Sandor Speck, the art dealer, and Walter, his assistant. The last sequence consists of four first-person stories narrated by Edouard, and details memories of his two marriages within the context of such political and personal ideologies. He saved Magdalena – who is Jewish – from deportation and a likely death during the Second World War by marrying her; and he felt responsible for Juliette, who nursed injuries he sustained from a motorcycle accident in London (while being "trained" by the Free French after his return from Algeria). Neither marriage seems to have been "thought out," as Edouard notes of a conversation he and Juliette (almost) had about the number of children they would have. He is loved by both women but is in love with neither, and Gallant's fiction-elegy displays both Edouard's unacknowledged emotional emptiness and a confession of his refuted responsibilities.

Like the Linnet series, the memoir-like Lena stories are not presented in chronological order; they alternate between Edouard's distant and recent pasts within each story as well. But within the biographical and autobiographical frameworks of his fiction-elegy is a confession of emotional detachment. Gallant's use of parenthetical comments to represent Edouard's thoughts as he is writing direct the reader to evaluate his perspective and personality. After describing Magdalena, he thinks: "(Notice how soon after thinking 'cosmopolitan' I thought 'of her sort')."[52] He also corrects his thoughts: "(Wait, my memory tells me ...)" (152). We are positioned as critics, then, and asked to deconstruct Edouard's commentary, to question the validity of his values and morality. Keefer writes that the reader of the story undergoes "an emotional anaesthetizing"; but while it may be true that "we cannot admire, sympathize with, or even mildly like the narrator," as Keefer insists,[53] I would argue that issues of admiration and liking are irrelevant unless contextualized within a study of Gallant's strategies. The reader of these stories, then – rather than becoming numbed – reconstructs events from Juliette's intelligent and emotional point of view, and, recognizing *Edouard*'s anaesthetized responses, we reject them as inadequate and morally questionable.

The sequence, a prolonged four-part think-act, begins and ends with stories about Magdalena ("A Recollection" and "Lena," respectively), who is the "survivor" of the Second World War, of two near-deaths, and of Juliette. Lena metaphorically represents the past and the continuing effect it has on the present, as the return to a focus on her personality at the end of the sequence indicates. This repetition suggests a "return to a 'locked situation,' " as Besner writes of Gallant's "structural figurations," created by "evocations of returns";[54] though Edouard does not seem to recognize this pattern (hence its 'locked' quality), the sequence is patterned such that it "does more than just establish humanity ... 'in' time; it also brings us [readers] back from within-time-ness to historicality, from 'reckoning with' time to 'recollecting' it," as Ricoeur writes of the narrative structures of history. Ricoeur states that this "temporal dialectic, then, is implied in the basic operation of eliciting a configuration from a succession,"[55] and indeed Gallant's use of the sequence in the "Lena" stories forces the reader to historicize Edouard's recollections and to "figure" the stories' meaning using an alternate pattern of perception.

Edouard is seemingly unaware of the configuration that his invented recollection enacts. Nor is the effect of Edouard's past on Juliette explicitly considered by the narrator, although in the second story, "Rue de Lille," which begins with a statement of Juliette's death (161), he exposes his thoughtlessness and Juliette's vulnerability. ("The Colonel's Child" portrays a similar dynamic.) Having admitted that he begged Magdalena "to believe that [he] never invented anything" (152), Edouard calls attention to his stories as invention, as constructions that he thinks will explain his past and present; however what is revealed instead is Edouard's lack of imagination, of insight and empathy for others.

When Juliette learns of her husband's continued contact with Magdalena, she experiences one of the "unexpected visions" that she would prefer to have been "spared." Edouard relates that it was "as if three walls of the court outside had been bombed flat" and that he realized Juliette (a professional translator, and as such a reader-figure) was now reading him and his first wife "like characters in fiction" (165). Edouard, who ignores Juliette's reaction until he has seen some of a televised panel discussion "on the theme 'What Literature, for What Readers, at Whose Price?' " in which he participated, is, ironically, not capable of understanding that Juliette needed "to be covered," consoled for and protected from his betrayal and emotional negligence, as did "those [others] who outlasted jeopardy" (165). Edouard's inability to enter into the imaginative invention required of love is also evident in his refusal to look at Lena's "blue, enduring look of pure love" (187). Juliette's ability to imagine hope and love may make her a "hapless" character, as Keefer believes;[56] but it also makes her more of a fully human character, someone who does care for human beings other than herself (she turns to knitting a blanket for the needy after having had her "unexpected vision"), whereas Edouard seems mechanical and unfeeling. He admits to himself that, as a failed novelist, he cannot make life "sound true" (174), and he is incapable not only of finding a form of consolation in an understanding of the past, but also of seeking it, of imagining it possible.

If Gallant is asking the reader to criticize Edouard's written memories, his lack of empathy, and his inability to come to terms with history on personal and public scales, then in the "Speck" series she is using allegory to satirize contemporary misinterpretations, or misinventions, of the past. The type of allegory Gallant institutes might be described in terms of Paul Smith's categorization of modern allegory, one form of which "persuades the reader to construct a typology for the text from vulgar, shared assumptions (the old *paroemiae*) about, for example, 'human nature,' or 'common-sense.' "[57] In the Speck stories ("Speck's Idea" and "Overhead in a Balloon") the relationship between aesthetics and politics, art and ideology is questioned in a parody of what may generally be described as a modernist elevation of art to a religious status, at the cost of political and social morality. Though Speck, recently abandoned by his wife Henriette, imagines a "French film" setting around him, "in reality" he cannot "even hope for a subplot" (5); the reader of the sequence, however, is able to discern a sub*text* wherein modernist aesthetic conventions (including the elegiac) are ironically subverted and their consequences exposed.[58]

Sandor Speck's "floating sadness" (3) is part of his daily ritual of locking up the art gallery that he runs. The elegiac opening of the story parodically connects seasonal mourning (year-round, in Speck's case) and art: "Leaves from the church square blew as far as his door – melancholy reminders of autumn, a season bad for art. (Winter was bad, too, while the first chestnut leaves unfolding heralded the worst season of all. In summer the gallery closed)" (2). Though the narrator claims that "neither loss nor grief nor guilt nor fear had ever moved him to appeal to the unknown – any unknown, for there were several" (2), Speck eventually not only humanizes "the Grand Architect" (14); he invents him as a commodifiable artist-figure: "The Grand Architect, if he was any sort of omnipresence worth considering, knew exactly what Speck needed now: he needed the tiny, enduring wheel set deep in the clanking, churning machinery of the art trade – the artist himself" (14). Gallant's critique of contemporary culture-turned-machinery is both funny and disturbing.

Speck's silent apostrophe to an "omnipresence" is a parody of a religious invocation; his aim is the acquisition of cultural products that would be useful for his own material interests. The narrator refers to a recent newspaper article entitled "Redemption through Art – Last Hope for the West?" (8), a rhetorical question that Speck would answer with a "local but universal" artist who could "send rays, beacons, into the thickening night of the West, just as Speck's gallery shone bravely into the dark street" (8). But the politically suspect artist whom Speck chooses to revive suggests that this pseudo-apotheotic illumination is a dark one indeed.

Gallant's critique of contemporary values is implicitly a rejection of an unhistorical aestheticism that denies any political import or responsibility. This attitude is clearly to be questioned, as is its amoral gesture towards consolation for the decline of "Western European culture" in "the tattered [twentieth] century" (8). Speck's "faith" is really an idea, and he is ignorant of its inherent ideology. It is art alone that provides "inspiration" (9) for his ideas about the production of the Cruche show and for the artist's fictive biography – the rewritten and falsified history of his chosen saviour, who, we are told, "is coming back!" (16). Ironically, in the end Speck writes the catalogue narrative for the Cruche exhibit on the back of a fascist pamphlet, which he cannot interpret, and in looking for a clue to its meaning, he "forgot what he was seeking" (47). Though Besner suggests that "the epithet 'Fascist' has acquired a broader, more diffuse cultural and personal significance" in the contemporary Paris of Gallant's setting and that Speck is "indeed a 'Fascist' in the art world, dictating and regulating taste to advance his own abstract 'idea,' "[59] and despite Speck's distasteful values, Gallant is satirically suggesting, I think, that the label "Fascist" has been appropriated and commodified to the point of meaninglessness in contemporary society and that this commodification has contributed to the decline of historical consciousness on a large scale.

Speck's exploited assistant Walter offers a contrasting point of view. "Overhead in a Balloon," the story linked to "Speck's Idea," is told from his perspective, and the space created between the viewpoints of the different stories invites the reader to participate and evaluate alternatives to Speck's values. Walter thinks: "This gallery will be an oasis of peace and culture ... in the international desert" (11–12). Much is revealed about Speck in this story; he is satirically undercut for his ignorance of Walter's quest: he "understood now why Walter found [Bible reading] consoling, for much in it consisted of the assurance of downing one's enemies, dashing them against stones, seeing their children reduced to beggary and their wives to despair" (33). Clearly Speck *would* find consolation in acts of cruelty and revenge.

Walter also had looked to art for truth and consolation, yet he learns that he has misinterpreted an aesthetic experience for a spiritual one: "What he had mistaken for God's beckoning had been a dabbling in colors, sentiment cut loose and set afloat by the sight of a stained-glass window ... God is in art, Walter had decided; then, God *is* art. Today, he understood: art is God's enemy. God hates art, the trifling rival creation" ("Overhead in a Balloon" 60). Walter compares Speck's perspective with that of his friend Robert, whose patriarchal domestic attitudes lead to the exploitation of the women in his life and whose weekend hobby of ballooning provides him with a kind of escapism and silence (66). But Walter (who at first naïvely concludes that Robert's weekend escapes are retreats in a monastery) is very literal-minded and confuses the real activity of ascending in a balloon with engraved representations he has seen; since "virtually anything portrayed as art turned his stomach" (66), he is incapable of experiencing or understanding the perspective of Robert's philosophy, though the reader is able to connect the overhead position metaphorically with that of Speck's aesthetic stance, and judge it accordingly.

The title of the title story, "Overhead in a Balloon," can be read in several ways: as a satiric comment on Speck's contemporary perspective (a distortion of a modernistic position), which elevates art and separates aesthetic experience from other experiences in the real world;[60] as a metaphor for various attempts by characters (Walter, Robert) to achieve a consoling ascendence; or possibly as an allusion to Daumier's satiric lithograph depicting Nadar in a balloon over Paris, "Nadar Raising Photography to the Height of Art," wherein Gallant could be satirizing the satirist. The perspective Nadar acquired in photographing Paris from a balloon (in 1862) is not escapist but generative, where the familiar becomes both de-familiarized and contextualized, comprehended, and subsequently represented. The position "overhead" creates a space for a potentially more ethical creativity, then.

The position overhead does allow the reader, like Robert, to "reach a decision" (66); Gallant does not disallow choice but encourages it in the reader, and thus the alignment with Robert overhead is not really an alignment at all – irony creates more than one position overhead. The schema of Gallant's fiction-elegies opens up what Iser calls a "basic play space," which "is not dissimilar to imitation." Therefore the reader's participation in the enabling elegy is, as I have been suggesting, an imitation, a construction of events that, like the textual schema, "allow[s] us to adapt ourselves" to objects and to mark "our relation to the world."[61] Gallant's use of irony, allegory, and linked configurations – successions as structural metonymy – create the distance between self and world, past and present that is necessary for her readers to acquire the perspective from the balloon. "Overhead in a Balloon" is thus a figure for an advantageous vantage point and for the authorial stance taken by Gallant; it contrasts with the literal overhead perspective of Robert and the figurative overview of Speck, both of which take *ad*vantage of the detachment of the position without employing the vantage. Memory – the material and activity of the work of mourning, be it personal or cultural – is seen as a form of narrative itself, and is elevated by Gallant as a potentially powerful medium with which one can test the relations between fiction and truth, art and history. This is the position she is writing from in her late modern fiction: with her broad intellectual perspective, she does not con*descend* but rather situates the reader overhead, so that we may witness and evaluate, if not all, then all that we can see.

GHOST STORIES IN *FROM THE FIFTEENTH DISTRICT*

In an earlier collection, *From the Fifteenth District* (1979), Gallant explores the moral climate in post-war Western civilization using sometimes parodic, sometimes conventional modes.[62] Whether in Canadian or European cities, Gallant's characters – survivors of the war in one way or another – are often exiled not only from their homes but from their memories, identities, and from their values as well. Generally, the former form of exile leads to a sense of loss and dislocation, while the latter – which usually goes unnoticed by the characters themselves – produces certain ethical deficiencies that are detected by the narrating consciousness. In the act of telling, this narratorial voice simultaneously portrays and laments the resultant exile from morality.

Gallant explores different models of mourning or reactions to loss and grief in this collection, and uses the ironic distance between narrator and character to place the reader in a position of judgment. We judge the character in terms of the appropriateness of response, and compare responses between characters, as well as compare our own values to those represented in the fiction. Elegy combines both of the issues of morality and mourning: for Gallant, different versions of wartime (and post-war) suffering provide the kind of social critique that is often a subtext in elegy (think of *Lycidas*, for example). Conventionally, tropes of remembrance allow a figurative resurrection of the past; but in this collection such forms of literary consolation (including prosopopoeia) are subverted by the use of the ghost as trope, as phantom figure.[63]

Benjamin writes: "Ghosts, like the profoundly significant allegories, are manifestations from the realm of mourning; they have an
affinity for mourners, for those who ponder over signs and over the
future."[64] Ghosts in tragic drama and in fiction-elegy, then, are figurations or signs, representations of grief and – allegorically – signs
of the process of mourning that imaginatively link the realms of the
living and the dead. Freud's statement that the uncanny is experienced most "in relation to death and dead bodies, to the return of
the dead, and to spirits and ghosts"[65] is suggestive in reading Gallant's ghost stories, since she uses a familiar literary device in *unfamiliar* ways and thereby forces the reader to rethink conventional
representations of death and the past – to make the presence of the
past disruptive of our comfortable forgettings.

The most self-conscious use of the ghost trope in this collection
arises in the title story of the collection. The story is extremely brief
in comparison to most of Gallant's stories, though its significance is
highlighted by the fact that the story serves as an organizing principle for the collection. Gallant parodies the conventional tendency to
use prosopopoeia as a trope of consolation in this story, which is
deemed a "truly harrowing prose-poem" by Elmer Borklund, who
states that it "can hardly be called a story."[66] The figures are both
spectral and spectatorial in the title story, demanding that the end of
their lives be narrated from *their* perspectives; in these very demands they are writing the endings to their own biographies and
undermining the stories told by the living, proving them inadequate
interpretations of the past.

The three ghosts in the parodic "From the Fifteenth District" –
Major Emery Travella, Mrs Ibrahim, and Mrs Essling – are explicit
and fantastic reversals of the prosopopoetic trope; haunted by those
who survive them, they reject the versions of their deaths constructed by the living. Mrs Ibrahim, for instance, is haunted by two
people "without respite, presenting for her ratification and approval
conflicting and unpleasant versions of her own death;" similarly the
Major, a "man of feeling," "wishes the congregation to leave him in
peace."[67] Mrs Essling "complains of being haunted by her husband,
Professor Augustus Essling, the philosopher and historian," and
she is burdened with his gratitude, his insistence that she was an
angel; all angels are "stupid," she thinks. [68]

According to Walter Benjamin's philosophy, angels are inhuman
observers of the human world, capable of passing judgment though
powerless to effect change. Keefer uses Benjamin's "angel of history" as a phrase to title a chapter of *Reading Mavis Gallant*; for Gallant the figure of the angel, she suggests, is used to figure he or she

who measures the "pile of debris" produced by the "storm of progress" that is history, because – caught in the storm – the angel's face is forcibly "turned towards the past."[69] The angel of history sees "a single catastrophe" rather than "a chain of events," as the perspective of the angel is denied temporal contiguity; his back is to the future, which is visible only as it becomes the past, seen in the present. Clearly Mrs Essling is "no angel" in her husband's sense of the phrase, but she does seem to "see" the past as catastrophe now that she, like her future, is dead.

In "The Four Seasons" ghosts are used in a different vein. The passage of time is charted, as the title implies, with the passing months. While traditional elegies suggest that seasonal cycles are affirmative of ongoing life, in this story Gallant inverts the pattern, asserting that elegiac conventions are inadequate for the subject-matter at hand. "The Four Seasons" depicts the decline of morality in pre-war Italy, which is synecdochic of the movement towards war in Europe at large. The story is broken into five sections, each of these in segments, some of which begin with a statement of the month: June, September, October, and March. But in spring "the winds blew as they had in autumn,"[70] bringing disintegration rather than rebirth: the Marchesa's garden was "torn out by the roots," replaced by a bomb shelter the shape of a "large grave" (24) as war approached; the "flowers died off and the garden became a desert" when the rains ended (27). The ghastly, anti-pastoral landscape sets the stage for the entrance of the ghostly, of figures of suffering.

Gallant establishes Mrs Unwin's cruelty towards her great-uncle – whose ghost haunts the Unwin's house and the text – to contribute to the themes of both exploitation and grief: "Carmela felt the sad presence of the poor relation who had come ailing to a good climate and had been put in the meanest room; who had choked, panicked, grabbed for the bell, and fallen on it" (9). The prosopopoetic ghost, the resurrected dead man, is not a consoling figuration but a demonic hallucination that calls perception and comprehension into question.

There is no place for consolation in "The Four Seasons," a story that anticipates (in terms of its temporal setting) the atrocities of the Holocaust; the depiction of the deportation of Dr Chaffee, who is Jewish, provides the most haunting image in the story. However, there is an epiphanic moment at the end of story that does offer a sense of human hope: before being abandoned by Mr Unwin, Carmela's memory of the look of the ices brought to her at a restaurant induces a hallucinatory vision of "invisible glass" and "a fantastic tower of cream" (34). The resultant retrieval of memories, prioritized in terms of importance, not proximity to the present, lead Carmela not to the mere memory of Dr Chaffee but directly to his ghost, to the hallucinated, angel-like "Dr. Chaffee in his dark suit stumbling up the hill. He lifted his hand. What she retained, for the present, was one smile, one gesture, one man's calm blessing" (35).

This consoling figuration in Carmela's mind is not a prosopopoetic representation; rather, the memory – like anamnesis – brings past and present together, and the experience acquires meaning from its interpretation in the present. Though Carmela does not understand the intended message of the blessing, she interprets it and makes it a relevant and significant gesture for her; similarly, Dr Chaffee misinterprets Carmela's reaction to seeing him in the deportation line, but he too finds meaning in his interpretation of *her* gesture as one of shame for her country's treatment of the Jews. As Keefer writes (alluding to Walter Benjamin), this remembered moment where "fiction and history come together" stops "to awaken the dead and to make whole, however briefly, what has been smashed" in Carmela's world.[71] Dr Chaffee's unspoken speech-act – the gesture of the blessing – does indeed still exist in the present, and suggests that the contract between him and Carmela – like that between the text and the reader – can formalize an understanding of human experience and thus endow fiction with truth.

The dead are awakened in "The Moslem Wife" as well. In this story Netta, owner of a hotel in France and married to her first cousin Jack, lives through the Second World War in Italy, seemingly unscathed by political events. However, her historical consciousness is gradually awakened as she suffers the pain of abandonment: "The absence of [her husband] Jack was like a cancer which I am sure has taken root, and of which I am bound to die" (68). The narrator states that "love was memory, and [Jack] was no good at the memory game" (42); here we see Gallant weave the threads of the love story with that of the war by focusing on the role that memory plays in giving value to life on personal and cultural levels. The deteriorating relationship between Netta and Jack parallels the decline of European values at large, but Netta is a survivor and she adjusts to being abandoned by awakening herself to the presence of ghosts from the past.

In this fiction-elegy the ghost story is used as a trope. In sorting out her past and her relationship with Jack, Netta comes to understand that her imagination has played and will continue to play a large role in her perception of their marriage; "the ghosts, the candlelight, her tears on the scarred bar – *they* were real" (73), she concludes. That Netta values as real an imaginative figuration of her past demonstrates a marked shift in her attitude, as well as clarifies Gallant's conception of memory as a mode of narrative thinking. Earlier we are told that Netta "had no use for the past, was discovering a past she could regret. Out of a dark, gentle silence – silence imposed by the impossibility of telling anything real – she counted the cracks in the walls" (66). This silence has not prevented Netta from telling, and her idea of what, exactly, constitutes a real story has been modified. Thus the figure of the ghost also suggests the need to remember, to accommodate the past with an awareness of the difference between history and fiction, the recognition of which constitutes Netta's initiation within the story. She learns to differentiate between the "light of the imagination" and the "brightness on the looking glass," between the version of reality memory provides and reality as perception, and – though this act is seen negatively by some critics – she accepts Jack back into her life, as she again craves "something simple, such as true love" (73).

It is through the act of telling her story, of figuring her grief, that Netta is able to interpret her craving, her need for the "light of the imagination," and because of her interpretive act, her welcoming back the betrayer is not a simple nor a romantic decision. But before the telling can accomplish this acceptance, Netta confronts obstacles. One reason for the initial problem of telling of the past in general is, as Netta thinks, that people prefer to have short-term memories or no memory at all so that difficulties may be forgotten and responsibility evaded. For Netta evaded responsibility for her own past until she began to recognize its importance in her present. The telling of truth becomes problematic when the audience does not want the knowledge that his/story provides; perhaps this is one reason that Gallant's readership has been slow to evolve.

Jack's abandonment of Netta is, for her, his death, though she does not fulfil her promise to herself that "if Jack were to die she would search the crowd of mourners for a man she could live with. She would not return from the funeral alone" (59). Netta notes that during the Second World War "death made death casual" (66), and Netta's initial treatment of her loss, too, is casual. Upon losing Jack, she buries her feelings with him in a temporary grave, a crypt of memory, one that is vitalized only on his actual return. Previous to this loss she had thought that in her home environment, the hotel run by her father and then by herself, "the dead had never been allowed to corrupt the living; the dead had been dressed for an outing and removed as soon as their first muscular stiffness relaxed ... That is why there is no bad atmosphere here, she would say to herself. Death has been swept away, discarded. When the shutters are closed on a room, it is for sleep or for love" (38–9). The belief that death is discardable suggests an early naïve idealism on Netta's part, though the narrator's irony indicates to the reader that this idealism will not survive the story. Jack is not allowed to haunt Netta's memory – at least, not at first. But by the end of Gallant's story, Netta self-consciously compares her relationship with Jack to a ghost story, herself to a "burnt-out child" (73). Clearly the war imagery applied to the romantic lives of these characters emphasizes the inseparability of Netta's personal and cultural circumstances.

In Netta's version of the past Jack is never absent in the figural sense, though his presence (in spirit) is controlled: "Jack, as a memory, was in a restricted area" (61), the narrator notes, for Netta tries to contain the malignancy of memory, to control it, so that painful and ultimately inadequate resurrections are few. Hers is a stagnant mourning, then; she does not explicitly grieve, but she does not forget either. Though she "discovered the limit of what you can feel about people" (60), she learns that people also return "from beyond the limits, from the other side of the wall" (58) – as Jack's mother's imitation of death shows her – and the epiphanic moment is evidence of both her return from the position of detachment and of Jack's ghostly presence. Gallant demonstrates that some limitations in response to loss – both narrative and human limitations – need to be recognized in order that reality might be more truthfully represented despite loss and grief.

Netta eventually enacts this recognition and acts upon it. Since she "was not afraid of death or of the dead," she used to claim that "there are no ghosts" (39); yet Jack's presence is certainly of a ghostly nature. Only Jack, who has a very short-term memory (72), can be "closed to ghosts, deaf to their voices" (72), and he survives the better for it. In contrast, Netta (who has "an accurate, a deadly memory" [72]), makes close contact with ghosts from the past, which she claims are "real" (73). That memory is, though sometimes redemptive, also at times "deadly" is a risk that Gallant insists be taken. Gallant indicates not only that memory and morality are closely connected (Jack possesses little of either of these, which permits his infidelity, as Netta realizes), but that there are different types of memory, different *uses* of memory, and thus different degrees of moral behaviour. Jack's "short memory, his comfortable imagination" are critiqued by the narrator (72), and though Netta comes to realize that her own "automatic bits" of memory[72] are inadequate, she is also accepting of Jack's limitations.

Netta discovers that an accurate representation of death and loss is impossible. Similarly, writing the past is problematic because of the inability of language to render the past accurately. Her letter to Jack, an apostrophe written "in her head, on and off, for many years" (61), is both history and "fiction" (63). Her version of events, though the "true story" (64), seems "implausible" because, narrativized in epistolary form (though never sent), she realizes that it will fail to capture the interest of anyone (namely Jack) but herself, *because* of its fictive truth. "No one will ever realize how much I know of the truth, the truth, the truth, and she put her head on her hands, her elbows on the scarred bar, and let the first tears of her after-war run down her wrists" (68). Truth is later figured in the image of light on the looking-glass: "that unexpected play, at a remove, borne indoors, displayed to anyone who could stare without blinking, was a complete story" (73).

Gallant suggests that the telling is necessary none the less. Netta's unposted epistle succeeds as an invocation: the fantasy produces the phantom, and Jack returns, while Netta's prophetic, silent voice, saying "Not a hope," is given a new twist – for better or for worse. Though dangerous to her ordered psyche, Jack – despite his infidelity, the symbol of life-affirming sexuality, the return of "the same voyage, at the same rate of speed" (73) – is accepted by Netta because she has discovered the use of her imagination in the reconstruction of history; she walks with Jack but talks to "her ghosts" (74), asking them implicitly for their blessing as angels of memory. Thus she is able to tolerate their personal history by combining it with memory; for memory, she thinks earlier in the story, is love (42). Netta has learned to *read* memory and to see Jack realistically. Earlier she had been resistant to seeing any flaw in her version/ vision of Jack: "any alteration would have worried her, just as a change in an often-read story will trouble a small child," we are told (43). Netta's maturation allows her to read changes, to see that the "Jack" she had constructed was necessarily "dead" (72), and to reconstruct her life-story along more truthful lines. Interestingly, then, while Jack was always the one to read literature, "trying to make a world out of reading and sense out of life" (59), Netta is the one who learns to read history and memory.

Gallant also addresses the issue of emotional morality in the context of loss in "Remission." Alec Webb, the dying protagonist who haunts the story, is neither loved nor remembered. Besner writes that "'remission' becomes an apt metaphor for the lingering, ultimately fatal illness suffered by a whole generation of Englishmen after the war – a generation which saw its cast of mind, its notions of civility, its entire worldview fade out of sight."[73] But my focus will be on the immediate familial genealogy of the Webbs, who are exiled from home since Alec chooses to die in Italy, and on their adjustments to Alec's death.

The story is a narration of a prolonged dying, a postponed event that has already happened. Written in the past tense, with an obituary embedded in the second paragraph, the characters' anticipation of the death controls our reading. The reader is a spectator of the spectral, since Alec's death is inscribed at the start of the story. The actual death is narrativized succinctly: Alec was "breathing deeply and ever more deeply and then no longer" (109). But the textual markers of delay, such as "Alec drifted away from life altogether" (97), "it happened at last that Alec had to be taken to the Rivabella hospital" (98), and "the hospital stood near the graveyard" (98), not only foreshadow the eventual event; they cause the reader to imagine a reaction to this type of extended emotional ordeal. Our comparison of this model to the characters' seeming detachment from the experience reveals the inadequacy of the mourners' acts and the necessity in our act of reading allegorically to construct a moral model of mourning.

Diana, Alec's sister, is a true mourner in the story. She is a seamstress of sorts, and had made a baptismal gown out of the silk Alec had brought back from India. She connects the gown (celebrating life) with Alec (who is now dead), and being "beyond remedy" for her loss, sees "that absolutely no one in the cemetery looked like Alec – not even his sons" (111). If her grief is beyond remedy, then the prosopopoetic illusion of resemblance would not be a consoling one. Keefer says that Diana is "a kind of memento mori for her niece,"[74] who, despite Alec's unresponsiveness, seeks her father's love even after his death: "How will he hear me, Molly wondered. You could speak to someone in a normal grave, for earth is porous and seems to be life, of a kind. But how to speak across marble? Even if she were to place her hands flat on the marble slab, it would not absorb a fraction of human warmth" (114). This kind of apostrophe, a trope that is traditionally consoling in elegy, necessarily creates ghost-figures in this text. But just as Alec's death was delayed, so will be any trope of consolation. The invocation figures a haunting of the present by the past, haunted because the past has been left unread, its significance uninterpreted.

That all events are postponed in the text is implied in the anticipatory conditional tense used by the narrator: Alec insisted that "his children *would not remember* him unkempt or dishevelled" (77); "the children *would recall* later on that their cook had worn a straw hat in the kitchen" (84); Barbara "*would remember* what it had been like when the children were babies still, and hers alone" (84); Alec "*ought to have died* that night. It *would have made* a reasonable ending" (90, emphases mine). These characters seek reassurance in endings, and endings entail forgettings. Since Alec's illness is metaphorically the "social malaise which has afflicted all the men of his background and experience," as Besner writes,[75] the forgetting of Alec is also a cultural and historical forgetting, his unremembered life a mark of the futility of his loyalty to the monarchy and of the vanished order it represents. The delayed closure for the characters' pseudo-work-of-mourning finally occurs as a displacement, a form of forgetting: "It then happened that every person in the room, at the same moment, spoke and thought of something other than Alec ... [It] was enough to create the dark gap marking the end of Alec's span. He ceased to be, and it made absolutely no difference after that whether or not he was forgotten" (116). There is no mourning by the characters in the fiction-elegy (even Diana's emotions are said to be "not worth a mention" [111]); the closure that they select is, for Gallant, equated not only with death but with lack of memory and of emotion (as was suggested by Jack in "The Moslem Wife"). Total narrative closure is a "dark gap," a phantom mark of death, wherein interpretation and thinking – intelligent thought – stops too.

The lack of closure in "Baum, Gabriel, 1935–( )" is announced in the parentheses of the title itself, which signifies that Gabriel is a survivor as well as that the story is about his lifespan. Indeed, the title consists of the words that appear on the mentally constructed "Baum memorial" (143), and the parentheses signify his future mortality and "en-Baum-ing," so to speak. The atmosphere of the story is, as Gallant states, "of a fading world," and the story itself is "about loss and bewilderment."[76] Gabriel is identified by a pseudo-journalist in the story as "spokesman for the flotsam of Western Europe" (148); the personal story is coexistent with the historical in that the narrative is partially a gesture of genealogy, of tracing ghosts in the closet, but one placed within a political context. The impact of the Holocaust on the life of this individual character is typical of Gallant's elegiac agenda, wherein personal fictions assume public and cultural significances as well. As Gallant states in her introduction to *Home Truths*, while "the seed of our sense of culture" is etched upon the mind during the early years of one's life, "a deeper culture is contained in memory."[77]

Gabriel examines his culture and his memory in this fiction-elegy, the occasion of which is the death of Uncle August Baum (the name "August" has a seasonal significance in the context of mourning as well). His arrival in Gabriel's life in Paris in the 1960s is crucial to Gabriel's sense of self, since his uncle is his "only surviving relative"

(139). August is described as an "unyielding remainder of the European shipwreck" (140), a survivor, unlike Gabriel's parents. The textual structure of August's biographical data mirrors Gabriel's: "August Ernest Baum, b. Potsdam 1899–( )" (140); the blank date is later filled in, when he dies in 1977. Proper names are extremely valuable to the characters in the story; as permanent traces, they signify a person's selfhood and integrity, and they remain as metonymies, Derrida writes, after death in the memory of the living.[78] Indestructible, names of certain cities remain on bottles of liquor, though their names have been literally "swept off the map" (141). As August states, "I have lost everything and everyone but I still have a name" (141), and the mention of Gabriel's parents' names is the catalyst for the young Baum's retrospective tale. The names still exist, says August, in "the trace of a marriage certificate somewhere," though nowhere else; "even when the registry office was bombed. Even when the papers had to be left behind" (141), the name stands in memory.

That Gabriel's parents were captured in the Second World War and that consequently he was separated from them at age eight is the central loss in the story. The "small, invisible version of himself" – the eight-year-old Gabriel – actually haunts the adult version with his promise to "settle" the scores for his parents' sake (141), due to the unresolved mourning, the inconsolable trauma that he suffered. Uncle August's questions about acquiring compensation from the German government seem ridiculous to Gabriel, who could not "equate banknotes to a child's despair" (146).

The divided identity in Gabriel's consciousness (adult/child) is a literalization of the divided subjectivity experienced when one attempts to write about loss. The elegist inscribes him/herself in the fiction as one who has had a relationship with those now lost; yet this elegist is a different individual, one who is now distanced enough to write about that loss. Gabriel's child-version is still present within him, however, and he therefore is unable to elegize, to comprehend and accept the past. He still hears "his unruly tenant ... screaming for a child's version of justice, for an impossible world" (158). Gallant uses an inverted version of the childhood pastoral to contrast its idealism – within a single character – with the adult's view of reality. Gabriel has not yet exorcised his childhood and therefore cannot mourn it from the distance required of an elegist.

But when August dies, Gabriel "truly mourned him," and it is at this point that he invents the Baum memorial, marble surface and all, for his entire family. The mental construction, with his own name and open date inscribed within it, "created a new difficulty: it left the onlooker feeling that these dates and names were factors

awaiting a solution. He needed to add the dead to the living, or sub-
tract the living from the dead – to come to some conclusion" (143).
The memorial remains open-ended, memorized and stored "in his
head, where it could not be lost or stolen" (143) – or forgotten. Total
closure would signify complete absence in the form of Gabriel's
death; as in "Remission," it would also suggest that there are no
longer any surviving memories of the Baums.

Gabriel's memorial is a concise version of the story itself, containing the facts of Gabriel's family history; Gallant institutes a *mise en
abyme* structure that imitates the story- and memory-begetting nature of genealogy, of written personal history. From the memorial,
the narratives of his parents and uncle, and of Gabriel himself, can
be constructed. Though not closed, the constructed list and potential stories offer some consolation in that they provide an identity, a
proper name – concreteness as well as necessary distance from the
"terrible story" (142) of the family's past. For a time he is "immersed
in the present moment" (150) while the "child-Gabriel had grown
still" (152), the spirit put to rest. Memorial replaces haunting and para-
lysing memory, therefore, and signifiers replace ghosts as tropes of
grief; ghost stories become stories – writing that is mediated by
memory and responsibility.

The complexity of this story, like that of others in *From the Fifteenth
District*, forces the reader to assess human sadnesses and the potential to overcome sadness – to remember and to survive. The stories
involve an "ethics of reading" in J. Hillis Miller's sense of the phrase:
"By 'the ethics of reading,' … I mean that aspect of the act of reading
in which there is a response to the text that is both necessitated, in
the sense that it is a response to an irresistible demand, and free, in
the sense that I must take responsibility for my response and for the
further effects, 'interpersonal,' institutional, social, political, or historical, of my act of reading."[79] Gallant combines issues of morality
and mortality to explore human responses and responsibilities. Confrontations with ghosts – and with tropes of representing the past –
may lead us to re-evaluate *how* we structure the past for ourselves.
This is one aspect of Gallant's revision of modernist fiction-elegy; we
not only read of epiphanies, but we read about the validity of such
aesthetic moments and thus evaluate their truthfulness as well as
their usefulness outside of the text. Besner writes: "Gallant's fiction
demands that we recognize how significance plays over her stories
in flashes and sparks, and that we develop the imaginative agility to
respond to these moments of light."[80] By subverting elegiac conventions, and in using the ghost as trope, Gallant tests our responsive
agility – insisting that we question not only the past but also our

writing and reading of the past, and the ethical efficacy of our elegies.

THE USE AND ABUSE OF MEMORY: *THE PEGNITZ JUNCTION*

Paul de Man writes that "allegories are always ethical, the term ethical designating the structural interference of two distinct value systems ... The ethical category is imperative (i.e., a category rather than a value) to the extent that it is linguistic and not subjective ... The passage to an ethical tonality does not result from a transcendental imperative but is the referential (and therefore unreliable) version of a linguistic confusion. Ethics (or, one should say, ethicity) is a discursive mode among others."[81] The truths that narrator- or character-elegists quest for in Gallant's inherently ethical allegories of mourning – often focused on the events and effects of the Second World War – go beyond the personal confirmation of self or the public affirmation of life; what they approach is an anagnoristic understanding of the human potential for inhumane behaviour, and of the necessity of remembering ethically, so that the extremes of sentimentality and irresponsible forgetting – both of which allow the evasion of responsibility for the past – are condemned.

In "The Pegnitz Junction" Gallant requires the reader to decipher the "junction" of the history and fiction, the past and the present as posited by the text. The theme of the junction (the German word for which, *Knotenpunkt*, also means "knot"[82]) is structurally encoded in the novella, which is, at times, quite resistant to interpretation, and in the stories collected in *The Pegnitz Junction* as well. However, there is always a progression, a movement towards the kind of revelation that is fundamental to elegy, for the reader if not the characters. As Ronald Hatch writes, "in Gallant's narrative schema, the reader exists for moments in both the past and the present, and therefore perceives the past as it continues to exist unrecognized in the present – a perception for the most part unavailable to, or denied by the characters in the stories."[83] Thus anagnorisis is not denied the reader, though the revelation that usually consoles in elegy is most often that which *disturbs* in Gallant's fiction-elegy.

Gallant positions the reader at the crossroads of memory and history; we become cultural critics, responsible for reading history as accurately as possible and for condemning misinterpretations. The novella questions what might be called the 'plausibility principle' of constructed historical fictions, to show that such inventions – which might make sense of the world, and seemingly might be true – can be an abuse of history (to paraphrase Nietzsche) as well as an abuse of memory. Gallant accomplishes this analysis of ethics with a technique of *dis*junction – fragments, elliptical passages, gaps, embedded stories and irony both construct and disrupt meaning, forcing the reader to participate in its reconstruction. Neil Besner notes that the novella, like "the constellation of stories" also collected in *The Pegnitz Junction*, "experiments instructively with mixed modes, with polyphonic narration, with literary parody, caricature, and extended metaphor";[84] indeed, the experimental form of "The Pegnitz Junction" self-consciously emphasizes the "displacement" that is characteristic of art and the need for the reader to re-place it in the context of history. The invitation to reader participation is reinforced by the use of irony, since it constructs double meanings that must be deciphered in context.

Paradoxically, the play with form in "The Pegnitz Junction" draws attention less to the text as artifact than to its messages about the non-sense of the post-war world. But the two are connected; as Hayden White writes, narrativity "is intimately related to, if not a function of, the impulse to moralize reality, that is, to identify it with the social system that is the source of any morality that we can imagine."[85] Gallant is intensely concerned with the impact of the Second World War, with the concept of history (that is, narrated events), and with the moral politics of art and memory. In "The Pegnitz Junction" her move towards anti-narrative (in combination with allegory) implies that the morality of the Western social system itself is questionable. Hayden White suggests that the form of allegory allows a text "to achieve *both* narrativity and historicality."[86] Thus the allegory of mourning for the social and moral disintegration during the war functions on levels of fiction and of fact.

"Allegories are, in the realm of thoughts, what ruins are in the realm of things."[87] Benjamin's parallel between a literary structure and historical fragments might serve to explain Gallant's use of allegory in her fiction-elegies. Allegory as a signification system works for Gallant's work because it posits not only "the nature of human existence," as Benjamin writes of the "allegorical way of seeing," but "also of the 'historicity' of the individual." In allegory, he argues, "everything about history that, from the very beginning, has been untimely, sorrowful, unsuccessful, is expressed in a face – or rather in a death's head."[88] That "The Pegnitz Junction" gives a "face" to history is straightforward enough, but what *kind* of face is constructed with the figure or trope of allegory? The conventional prosopopoetic face is *dis*figured in this novella, which makes us *see* the significance of the past in the present anew.

The historical subtext critiqued by the allegorical narrative is created with allusions to history. For example, if the "cultural leader" of the opera fans represents the anonymous, unnamed authority figure that the civilized citizen endows with political power, as the word "leader" (*Führer*) implies, his comments about "the Adolf-time" being "a sad time for art"[89] – presumably an allusion to the fact that art was then censored and used propagandistically – are indicative of the post-war population's fairy-tale-like displacement of Hitler's atrocities through denial and forgetting. This distancing method also releases the "average citizen" from responsibility, imposing a cultural distance between the present and the events of the past by interpreting them as aberrations of a single Satan-figure.

Though this history is difficult to read, it is not (as cliché would have it) beyond comprehension. For Gallant, it seems, the Second World War cannot be interpreted until those who refuse to confront and take responsibility for the very human nature of the crimes stop using incomprehensibility as a blinding forgetfulness. She is not suggesting, however, that the answer is for everyone to take equal responsibility; as she makes clear in her essay on the Gabriel Russier case, "when everyone is responsible then nobody is, and that is comfortable, finally."[90] In her novella what Gallant reveals is the "banality of evil" (Hannah Arendt's term)[91] and that "the origin of the worm – the worm [fascism] that destroyed the structure" is in "every day living."[92] The trivialization of the events, epitomized by the reduction of the period to the term "Adolf-time," is the amoral human reaction that "The Pegnitz Junction" condemns. Such a reduction is made possible through forgetting on both a large scale and at the personal level, a forgetting that is symptomatic of a Nietzschean "malady of history": "we must know the right time to forget as well as the right time to remember; and instinctively see when it is necessary to feel historically, and when unhistorically. This is the point that the reader is asked to consider; that the unhistorical and the historical are equally necessary to the health of an individual, a community, and a system of culture."[93] In Nietzsche's terms the "capacity of feeling 'unhistorically' " is equated with "the power of forgetting," (8) and while this is necessary for an individual (or culture) to retain the ability to look forward – to set "limits to the memory of the past," for the purpose of "healing wounds, replacing what is lost, repairing broken moulds"[94] – forgetting can also be dangerous in that it may allow history to repeat itself. Thus Gallant suggests with her historical fiction that the intermediate step of *interpreting* the past, of learning from it, prevents one from becoming either rooted in the past or forgetting it.

In "The Pegnitz Junction" history does seem to be repeating itself: the description of the train ride recalls images of those trains that prisoners rode to death camps during the war: they "sounded sad, as though they were used to ferry poor and weary passengers – refugees perhaps" (15); the windows are sealed (35); Christine "imagined the holocaust they might become" (36); they pass through barbed-wire frontiers (54) and fire zones; the "bun-faced conductor" terrorizes the passengers, then asks Christine if she would testify for him if asked (81). Keefer, who has noted these passages as well, argues that the metaphoric train journey has "an immediate application to the mechanics of plot – getting travellers to the junction from which they board trains to their respective homes – and to the enormous historical questions about the Germans and Nazism with which Gallant is preoccupied." Keefer's statement that there is a "sense of doubleness" in the narration of the trip, what she calls an "inverted parody," leads her to the conclusion that "the journey from Paris to an uncertain destination in Germany is an ironic mimesis of the trip to 'Pichipoi,' "[95] but more specifically Gallant makes the metaphoric train ride an ironic *allegory* that depicts not forward movement but the "decline of the next generation" (42) and the lack of human progress that results from the personal and cultural refutation of the past.

The social disintegration with which Gallant is concerned is mimetically represented, then, and the inability of language and art to render historical truth unaltered also is indicated, allegorically. What I have called Gallant's anti-narrative stance in this text exemplifies a gesture towards what White would call "a refusal of narrative [which] indicates an absence or refusal of meaning itself."[96] Though clearly *Gallant* does not "refuse" narrative, the historical events that she is dealing with in "The Pegnitz Junction" have been "refused meaning" in the sense that they have been forgotten, denied an appropriate textual form by Western culture's interpretations of the past. With the novella Gallant is writing about the extreme difficulty of writing this particular history, and about the absolute necessity of *reading* that history.

Writing memory will lead us to a fictional truth; though necessary for us to "bring the past to the bar of judgment, interrogate it remorselessly, and finally condemn it,"[97] any written version of history is, of course, falsifying. Written history is an interpretation, a re-vision and thus a selective forgetting, and therefore identifies the site of an impossible mourning. Language often may be an inadequate instrument with which to represent reality and reactions to it, as Gallant noted to herself while working as a reporter during the

Second World War. After being asked to write captions for the first available photographs of concentration camp victims, she thought: "there must be no descriptive words in this, no adjectives. Nothing like 'horror,' 'horrifying' because what the pictures are saying is stronger and louder."[98]

Gallant is averse to the abuse of language, then, and her rejection of lyricized descriptions or falsely narrated events (for the newspaper as well as for her own historical fiction) is a gesture towards the kind of "true mourning" that de Man describes in a passage already cited: "True 'mourning' is less deluded than [the attempt to find consolation or] temporal harmony as voice and as song. The most *it* can do is allow for non-comprehension and enumerate non-anthropomorphic, non-elegiac, non-celebratory, non-lyrical, non-poetic, that is to say, prosaic, or better, *historical* modes of language power."[99] Though "The Pegnitz Junction" is not entirely written using such a prosaic, non-elegiac historical mode of language power (though more so than the Linnet Muir sequence, for example), we are not deluded by tropes of consolation for the crises of the past.

De Man uses quotation marks to imply that elegy or written mourning is a rhetorical figuration, an approximation of the human experience that distances writer and reader from the actual event. However, his suggestion of non-anthropomorphism would, it seems, eliminate the human element from the process altogether, and Gallant is certainly not doing this in her novella. Neither does Gallant allow the reader to be distanced from history; rather the reader is forced to participate in the interpretation of her disjointed text. For Gallant true or historically accurate mourning necessitates an ironic stance in that self-consciousness about one's situation as a survivor is necessary in order to acknowledge and accept the extremes of death, loss, destruction (and the often extreme situations surrounding them). The novella is an example of what could be called historiographic memory-fiction[100] because the text refers to the historical but also contests the graphic representation of history by challenging its origins in personal memory *and* by critiquing its abuse, either through wilful distortion or through forgetfulness.[101]

"The Pegnitz Junction" positions the reader as historiographer, one who must interpret both the text and real history, thereby rewriting both. The schism created when the moral, grieving "I" (which acknowledges the shambles of the present and the significance of the past) becomes exiled from the dominant functioning "I" (which denies the past, loss and/or responsibility) constitutes a negative distance that allows amoral forgetting – a forgetting that is, arguably, the malaise of contemporary Western civilization. True mourning, ethical grieving, is possible when this gap becomes ironic, when the "I" assimilates the grieving memory yet continues functioning, remembering *and* forgetting. Reading *is* writing in this sense; reading first necessitates remembering the past, then interpreting its significance, and then eventually an informed reading of the *present*.

Since the majority of characters in the novella do not remember, they are non-mourners, non-readers, non-interpreters, and are voluntarily blind. Herbert "would not have moved an inch to see the film" of his mother's life had it been recorded, for instance (14). The embedded story about Uncle Ludwig, Uncle Jurgen, and family (names "lifted out of old German comic strips," says Gallant)[102] seems to be a random depiction of members of contemporary German society; these caricature types travel to a castle (à la Kafka)[103] that is, they think, a museum, only to find that "there had not been all that much to see" (31). Because they are incapable of observing and interpreting an architectural "fragment" of the past, a restored "ruin," as a significant presence in the present, and because Christine imposes certain distasteful characteristics on them, this absurdist segment of the novella seems to suggest – in parable fashion – that a general detachment from the meaning of history is a symptom of contemporary society.

These caricaturized figures, whose actions Christine alone seems to be seeing before her eyes and whose future she projects (imagining what their fate will be), are actors in a surreal drama that seems to relate only tangentially to Christine's act of looking out the train window. They are "all too human" (Nietzsche) in their somewhat exaggerated deficiencies and moral vacuity; they have stories told *about* them, as does Bruno (the anthropomorphized sponge), who is also used by the adults to tell didactic tales of varying degrees to Little Bert. But Christine also reads (significantly, she is carrying Dietrich Bonhoeffer's *Essays* with her, essays that detail the difficulties of acting on ethical principles, written by a religious man who *did* act), and since she reads minds as well as situations, we become aware of an array of perspectives on the past, and we must evaluate the validity of each.

The "scarred stranger" who telepathically transmits his autobiography to Christine gazes at, measures, and memorizes (57) the "dead landscape" (60) of the town from which he believes he escaped with his family. His thoughts are narrated, but he contradicts his own memories and claims that in 1943 he "wasn't born yet" (62), and since public history in the form of the "newspaper account of [his] adventure" contradicts his own personal knowledge of the events (60). This man, with a face "of infinite sorrow" (60), remembers and interprets the past, but Christine, while questioning the accuracy of the account, cannot interpret it due to "interference" from other minds. That the effect of Christine's sensitivity to the thoughts of other people can vary from insightfulness to interference suggests that awareness must be co-ordinated with *interpretive* space, or else "information" – perceptions of past and present – becomes muddled.

George Woodcock writes of "The Pegnitz Junction" that there is "no attempt at that special Gallant realism where the web of memory provides the mental links that make for plausibility. Here [Gallant] is trying to create, in a structure that is as much dramatic as fictional, a kind of psychic membrane which replaces recollection by telepathy."[104] As Christine enters a telepathic relationship with other consciousnesses, we enter into a transferential relationship with the text and must make the mental and representational links ourselves. As receptor of the text the reader mirrors Christine's role as receptor of those autobiographical anecdotes embedded as narratives in the novella, and contextualizes the narratives in history. Gallant refers to the actual junction at Pegnitz as "the nerve centre of the railway system in that part of Germany" and confirms the suggestion that "nerve centre" might be a neurological metaphor as well.[105]

Walter Benjamin writes that "thinking involves not only the flow of thoughts, but their arrest as well. Where thinking suddenly stops in a configuration pregnant with tensions, it gives that configuration a shock, but which it crystalizes into a monad."[106] The *reader's* crystallization of the narrated thoughts in the novella is imaged in the "fine silver crystals forming a pattern" that Christine sees when she hears the information transmitted to her from the woman passenger's mental autobiography. The text itself might be seen as a monadic figuration of the reader's thinking engagement with the novella; the thinking, too, must stop long enough for the reader to judge, to evaluate, to interpret, and to conclude. But while Christine is a model for the reader, she is not a model reader in that she doesn't seem to empathize, judge, or condemn explicitly; at the end of the novella she closes Bonhoeffer's book. Everything remains uncertain to her (she apologizes for this to little Bert [87]), and she fails to finish any of the stories she begins to tell the child (37, 86), just as she fails to finalize the historical fiction accumulating in her own mind. It is as if Christine is unable to narrate events into story, just as she is unable to provide closure; closure would imply that Christine had the answers and that her interpretation had been completed, whereas in actuality Christine has only begun to think.

Hayden White states that "the demand for closure in the historical story is a demand ... for moral meaning, a demand that sequences of real events be assessed as to their significance as elements of a *moral drama.*"[107] But "The Pegnitz Junction" cannot provide such closure, since the characters, Gallant implies, do not desire such an assessment and because the moral of the story is that the "demand for moral meaning" must be an ongoing demand; the significance of the drama of the past must not be closed, forgotten. As readers we are placed in the ironic space between this human moral deficiency and the mimpathic potential for ethical reading, for "true mourning." Gallant's highly political fiction forces the reader to recognize the necessity of remembering, of reading memory, and of differentiating between constructed plots and history. "We must know the right time to forget as well as the right time to remember," says Nietzsche, and it is through appropriate and appropriated memory that the work of mourning is performed. And by reading "The Pegnitz Junction" we perform a version of this memory and "read ourselves home," as Besner suggests.[108]

Though White states that "the moral sense that is conveyed by the representation of past public events differs from that conveyed by the representation of personal memories,"[109] Gallant's short stories in *Pegnitz Junction* dispute the claim. The first-person stories in the collection ("An Autobiography," "O Lasting Peace," and "An Alien Flower") detail the effects of loss and dislocation resulting from the Second World War – from political events – on the personal lives of individual characters, two of whom Keefer accurately labels "survivors."[110] Their personal stories/histories are embedded in what Benjamin would call "natural history," a phrase that refers to the use of world events as a method of contextualizing the story events.[111] This narrative style is used in *From the Fifteenth District* as well, wherein Gallant depicts post-war social attitudes and individuals' responses and responsibilities.

As the title suggests, "An Autobiography" is a generic experiment; it is also a variation on the elegiac romance. Erika, the narrator, is confronted with her past, which intrudes on the present with the reappearance of her one-time lover. The digressive story structure is divided into two segments. The first opens in the present tense as a type of dramatic monologue: "I teach elementary botany to girls in a village half a day's journey by train from Montreux" (101). Initially a detached narration, Erika's tale-turned-meditation reveals her philosophy of dealing with a painful past. Referring to the attitude of her students' parents, she thinks: "Home is built on the top layer of Ur. It is no good excavating; the fragments would be without meaning ... It is easy to put an x over half your life (I am thinking about the parents now) when you have nothing out of the past before your eyes; ... There are no dregs, except perhaps a carefully sorted collection of snapshots. You have survived and the food you eat is new–even that ... not even an unpleasant taste in the mouth will remind you (103)." The assurance that Erika is defining the attitudes of others is not convincing. As readers we have been given enough information about Erika herself to know that her story will be an elegiac excavation, anecdotes of a survivor who has eliminated traces of the past – reminders – in order to forget, and to become released from "the grip of the past," as Kenneth Bruffee would say.[112]

Until she writes "An Autobiography," Erika harbours memories that maintain a "grip" *on* the past that has provided her with pathological protection from the present for years. In "The Pegnitz Junction," where political history is the allegorical story, remembering, interpreting, and reading are vital for the construction of a historical account that goes beyond mourning. And in the type of fiction where a personal past is the basis of the work of mourning, forgetting – which might involve *selective* writing – is often the antidote of choice to an interminable mourning. However, *interpretation* of the past must be performed by these characters, just as it is demanded of the politically maimed, such that the past is not merely repressed or forgotten but managed, accommodated within a truthful framework.

The autobiographical details surface, in part one of the story, in the form of an anecdote about her father: "I recall, in calm woods, searching for poison mushrooms. He knocked them out of the soft soil with his walking stick" (104); thoughts of her present students are mingled with thoughts relating to her parents: "My father was a non-believer, and my mother followed, without conviction. He led her into the desert. She died of tuberculosis, not daring to speak to God for fear of displeasing her husband" (105). The narrator's autobiographical excursions into the personal past are triggered by the present situation and by observed relationships between children and adults (the character of Veronique serves as the allegorical abandoned child in this respect).

Here think-act memories induce and constitute the fiction-elegy, while the metonymic mementos that one would expect to have strong effects are oddly inert: both her father's book, *Wild Flowers of Germany* (104), and her mother's photograph (106) are examples. The past is inescapably present, though: Erika's resemblance to her father (106) and the return of Peter are two such emblems of and connections to the past. Erika must re-evaluate her methods of mourning, and the subtextual meaning of her narrative eventually surfaces to prove that there have been "worms eating at her heart" (128) despite her denial that she regrets her decision of years before to leave Peter.

Peter's several (invented) autobiographies are embedded in the story via Erika's memory. Erika had been "greedy for more of the past" at one time in her life, when the maternal aunt who disowned her gave her the photograph of her mother (113). She becomes conscious of the importance of the past again with Peter's presence. She had left him in her youth because he made her feel insecure to the point of vertigo; she had been "on a sea without hope of landing anywhere" (121) because "he was a person who would keep moving from one place to another" (121). Her secure world is mechanical, though, and in this sense Erika is reminiscent of Jean Price: "I have learned to be provident. I do not waste a sheet of writing paper, or a postage stamp, or a tear," she thinks (129). But in the reader's reconstruction of the story it becomes clear that her love for Peter still exists: she looks fondly at the "pattern on the carpet where he walked, and the cup he drank from," displaying more emotion at these metonymic signs than she had towards Peter himself.

Erika's versions of past events are "briefly and accurately remembered," she claims (120), but her construction of events that might have happened, the narrativization of the future, is a consoling fiction: "or perhaps this time one of us would have stayed forever," she thinks (129). Erika's thoughts are a creative fantasy in Freud's sense of the term: "A strong experience in the present awakens in the creative writer a memory of an earlier experience (usually belonging to his childhood) from which there now proceeds a wish which finds its fulfillment in the creative work. The work itself exhibits elements of the recent provoking occasion as well as of the old memory."[113] In reading the story we too construct a creative work from the information provided in the plot. But Erika's constructed safety net, like the plot she has charted for her life and the narrative she "thinks," is, in a moment of revelation, recognized as a destructive fiction, for her fantasy is capable of "rot[ting] the fabric" of her constructed real life (129). The chronology of her autobiography is replaced with an atemporal think-act, an event that demonstrates her decision(s) to leave Peter were based on a fabrication or fiction that has protected her from abandonment but has also, paradoxically, caused "such a waste of everything" (129).

Peter also has misused personal history, albeit in a different way; he "never told the same story twice" (120); he "lived in a fantasy of false names, false fortunes, false parents" (122); he was even "inventing things to be remembered" during his stay in Switzerland (125). Subsequently, he "would never be certain if the memory he was feeling tender about was true" (126), notes Erika. It is his falsification of the past, his ability to forget and therefore his potential to abandon Erika, that explains her desertion of him years before: "I had not gone to him out of duty and had not left him out of self-preservation. It was not that simple," she confesses (127).

It is at this epiphanic moment that the reader must piece together the truth of Erika's loss and grief. Peter would have left her eventually (as she predicts in her later consoling fantasy [128]), so her abandonment was, in effect, self-preservation after all. Her original wounds (aside from those caused by her parents' deaths) are dual in this fiction-elegy: she was rejected by her sole surviving relative, and projects rejection by her lover. What these abandonments have in common is the "one idea" she clings to – that they resulted from her being lured out of Switzerland (124). Her method of protecting herself and of healing the wounds, however, proves inadequate: the attempt to forget does indeed prevent dust from accumulating on memories, as the first-class train carriages are protected (128); but the artificial existence that it produces with the "worms eating at her heart" is as "hideous" as the train's decorative iron roses, with the iron worms eating at their hearts.[114]

The image of "unrotted fabric" at the end of the story is a blank sheet of writing paper (129) on which no written narrative appears; it represents the unrepresentable, a deconstructed past. Erika's plan to "write about everything, all of the truth" (128) proves impossible except in terms of her memories, her constructed think-acts (both of which are fictional, by definition). Lorna Irvine writes that in both "An Autobiography" and "O Lasting Peace" Gallant "pits loss against narrative sequence, showing how the ego struggles to master plot."[115] Here the word "plot" also implies secrecy and mystery. With her narrative sequence, the narrativization of her personal history, Erika unconsciously plots and displaces the story of her life in an unconventional autobiography in an effort to master the real "plot" of her life-story. While she might not understand rationally the compensatory nature of her story-telling, the reader hears another story. As the reader reconstructs the plotting and de-plotting, she re-enacts Erika's quest for an honest, ethical interpretation of history and recognizes that perhaps certain stories we tell ourselves are, indeed, necessary fictions.

"O Lasting Peace" is another story that consists of "tightly controlled patterns of revelation," as Besner notes of all three first-person stories in *The Pegnitz Junction* (80). The melancholic narrator uses narrative ruses to deflect attention from her own repressed emotions and grievances. Gallant's ruse, the dramatic monologue form, implicates the reader in the reconstruction of the motives and emotives of the speaker, who asks: "Why is it that everyone is depressed by hearing the truth?" (162) Hilde, the speaker, is also depressed by the truth. She cannot answer this question, and uses the fictional form for her life-story to escape it.

Hilde narrates her mother's personal history, her family's "lies and their mysteries" (151), all of which has affected her and turned her into a bitter cynic awaiting the fictional "end of the world" – the end of her constructed vision of the world – just as Uncle Theo waited for an actual apocalypse in India on 5 February 1962 (154). Theo's need to lyricize the truth, to cover its depressing essence, is evident in his poems, two of which are set to music – though Hilde ridicules them, significantly, for having no (or only minimal) effect on the listener (155). The title of the story is also a title of one of these songs, and while neither the music nor the narrative is capable of producing a lasting peace, the story does produce an effect in the form of the reader's mimpathic response.

Poeticisms cannot console Hilde, for whom life is extremely sad; when told not to "think of sad things" (157), her answer is "What else is there?" (158) Gallant uses questions to urge the reader to take Hilde seriously, to consider possible answers. With similar effect Gallant contextualizes Hilde's personal grief in historical events: "I could have piled all our sad Christmases on the counter between us – the Christmas when I was thirteen and we were firebombed, and saved nothing except a knife and fork" (158). She then makes mention of her father's departure, the main loss mourned by her mother and, it seems, Hilde herself; she was both abandoned by him and left with responsibility for her siblings, mother, and uncle. The cultural and the private memories presented by the story are contiguous.

Uncle Theo mentions her mother's sadness at being abandoned, and this leads Hilde to note that "everyone has a reason for jumping out the window at Christmas and in the spring" (159); "With all this behind me, the Christmas memories of my life, what could I say except 'What else is there [but sadness]?' " she asks the reader (160), who is also told in the present tense to "*now* consider my [Hilde's] situation" towards the end of the story (163, my emphasis). The interrogatives serve to draw the reader to Hilde's viewpoint, to see the world as Hilde sees it, so that the reasons for and limitations of that viewpoint might be understood. In a plea for empathic understanding Hilde asks "What shall I do when I have to bury the family?" (164) It is her emotional situation, then, that constitutes the elegiac subtext, the secret of the story proper. Secrets – hidden facts and fictions – can serve as a form of forgetting a past that has become taboo; if "language is situation," as Shirley comes to understand in *A Fairly Good Time*, then silences – unspoken secrets – figure a situation of absence, of loss.

Hilde is desperate for knowledge of the truth of family history: "'Tell me everything you remember,'" she begs of them (163). But she receives no reply, because her family "can't keep their own histories straight" (163); they forget their pasts so that they cannot be hurt by them, but their lives consequently are empty of meaning, and of this Hilde is aware. Thus Hilde is think-acting in order to keep her own history straight, to give her own life meaning – or so it seems. Her narrative secrets are as puzzling as are her relatives' mysteries, since she reveals nothing of herself in trying to deny her emotional needs. The "one last thing" (165) that she narrates for the reader is one of the most significant pieces of information available to us as we try to plot Hilde's life: a potential husband, who answered an advertisement published by Theo without Hilde's knowledge, rejects her. It becomes obvious that Hilde's triple rejection – by her father, by her family, secretly trying to remove her from their home, and by this peasant-like stranger who never returns – is at the core of the story, which is Hilde's self-elegy masked by the monologue-as-complaint.

In "An Alien Flower" Gallant also uses a dramatic-monologue narrative style (and the form of the elegiac romance) to render multiple melancholic personal histories, and she uses tropes of autobiography and biography. Political history is foregrounded to a greater extent in this story than in the others, but again it is interwoven with the personal. Thus the elegiac romance also takes on allegorical characteristics. In this story the effects of cruelty enacted in personal relationships (the "sub-themes" of Helga's life, as she calls them) are made analogous to those committed in war by the seemingly naïve, ahistorically minded narrator. But Gallant would not make such a clichéd parallel between betrayal and literal atrocities.

"Bibi" is a nickname derived from her full name, "Beate Brüning," and in referring to it as a "diminutive" the narrator reveals her condescending attitude (174). Bibi is a Silesian refugee, though her background and wartime sufferings are not revealed to the narrator or to the reader. Her history does include the fact that she twice attempted suicide and was successful the second time. But ironically it is not her experiences during the war that drive her to this act twenty years or so later; it is a broken heart, and the loss of an illicit relationship with the husband of the narrator. Helga, the wife of Julius, tells Bibi's life- and death-stories – Bibi's eulogy – herself, and indirectly writes her own autobiography in the process. The detached voice of the narrator creates a personal history of Bibi – whom Helga considers an "alien flower," drawing an analogy to an inferior "other" plant species – that contrasts with both the truth of Bibi's secretive past and the divine-like Julius's invention of "convenient fables" (173, 192). The label of "other" is analogous to the "impure" plant life to which Helga compares Bibi (173), and reveals Helga's (allegorically representative) potential for fascistic attitudes and behaviour. Her protests that Bibi was never treated as a servant in her household (167) are hardly convincing.

The two women are closely identified in the text; both are "war orphans" (176), and "there was also a joint past that lay all round us in heaps of charred stone. The streets still smelled of terror and ashes, particularly after rain. Every stone held down a ghost, or a frozen life, or a dreadful secret" (168). Both women love Julius, and both are figuratively killed by his betrayals and rejection. But the real pasts of these two women were very different, and the point of view of the narrator emerges as a detached and amoral one, one that cannot read the ruins of the past with any historical consciousness at all.

Julius denies reality even more vehemently than does the narrator: he vindicates himself from an adulterous affair by claiming that "there was no evidence that I was involved. My name was not mentioned anywhere" in the diaries of his lover (191). His philosophy is to reject the past and all responsibility for his own actions as well; he advises Bibi to disassociate herself from other war refugees: "Julius did not want her to waste her mental energies talking about the tides of history. I can truthfully say that Julius has never discussed historical change," his wife reports to us (172). He also refuses to consider the distinct possibility that Bibi committed suicide due to Julius's abandonment of her, insisting that she had "an incurable disease" (173) – a fact that Helga (who is also unreliable) chooses to believe, though the reader remains sceptical.

Bibi's version of her own history remains mysterious. Helga chooses to think that her past was non-existent (169), that Bibi's experiences were forgotten and forgettable because she was "swept clean of friends and childhood myths and childhood itself" (174) in the war. Rather than try to ask questions of Bibi, or try to read the clues Bibi *did* provide, Helga merely labels Bibi as "other" (174). We are told that Bibi "hinted that once she had not lived like other people and had missed some of her schooling on that account. Why? Had she been ill or delinquent? Was she, as well as Silesian, slightly foreign? Sometimes male ancestors had been careless about the women they married. Perhaps Bibi had been unable to give a good account of herself" (173). Helga takes it upon herself to provide this naïve, vindictive, and untruthful account of Bibi's past, and her capacity for ignorance, or for absolute denial (we are not sure which), is made to seem both cruel and morally destructive.

Thus Gallant counterpoints various versions of the past, including Julius's deliberate rejection of history; Bibi's unspoken remembrance of history (which she cannot or will not narrativize); Helga's naïve plot construction of Bibi's life experiences; and the reader's reconstruction of the story, which involves deciphering Bibi's clues and contextualizing the narrative within historical events. Gallant insists that we locate our own ethical position upon reading the elegiac text that mourns both Bibi and the history that she endured. Helga's narratorial detachment from both of these provides a negative model against which the reader must measure him or herself.

Since Gallant often does not render emotional realism at the immediate point of crisis but rather as a displaced form of affect, her characters are in a position to interpret their experiences and to make moral *use* of their memories in constructing individual views of the world. Most do not make constructive use of the past, however, and Helga exemplifies the kind of character Gallant holds up for judgment. As a result of these narrative conditions the moral component of allegory – the face of history – is fully functional in Gallant's fiction-elegies, narratives that often present the reader with unflattering pictures of contemporary society. "In allegory, history appears as nature in decay or ruins," writes Susan Buck-Morss;[116] Gallant's vision of history certainly is one of ruins, and allegory serves to figure the "enormous upheaval – not just in history, but in one's life" that created "the world today," as she explains it.[117] The indirectness of her fictional representation of reality is a product of Gallant's focus on the work of mourning, a process that is inherently allegorical, as Benjamin insists, and that requires the reader's participation in order to work.

As noted earlier in this study, Ricoeur writes of the "capacity of metaphor to provide untranslatable information ... [and] to yield some true insight about reality." Gallant's texts are in this sense extended metaphors, allegories of remembering that provide "models for reading reality in a new way."[118] But it is not only a new reading of reality that Gallant encourages with *The Pegnitz Junction*; it is also a new model of reading, one that de-familiarizes and has the potential to effect change in the reader's thinking. If allegories are to thought what ruins are to things, then Gallant's allegorical representations of ruins serve to deconstruct our ordered versions of the present reality so that we might reconstruct meaning from the fragments of history.

4 Munro and Modern Elegy

In answer to Alan Twigg's question, "How much do you think your own writing is a compensation for loss of the past?" Munro states: "My writing has become a way of dealing with life, hanging onto it by re[-]creation. That's important. But it's also a way of getting on top of experience. We all have life rushing in on us. A writer pretends, by writing about it, to have control. Of course a writer has no more control than anybody else."[1] Munro's subject-matter, like the aesthetic her answer implies, is fundamentally elegiac in that an effort to control loss often is depicted in her work. Munro writes fiction-elegies within a late modern framework, though her earlier stories especially are marked by more modernist characteristics. George Woodcock argues that Munro partakes of a "European realism of the early part of the century that trembled on the edge of modernism, without herself going forward,"[2] but his criticism fails to recognize the innovative use to which Munro puts her so-called modernism. Ronald Schleifer writes of the "*quality* of modernism" in his *Rhetoric and Death: The Language of Modernism and Postmodernist Discourse Theory*, arguing that "a revelation of the other in the same is the secret melody of death that Spengler describes in the traversing counterpoint of modernism … [and] a revelation of *negative* materialism. It makes the accidents of existence, including the material 'accidental' formation of codes of signification, and including contingency and death, resonate in art."[3] That Schleifer's rhetoric should (accidentally) include two of Munro's story titles ("Accident" and "Material") perhaps is telling in itself. Munro's fiction does display "otherness" in the familiar, thereby de-familiarizing the reader and drawing attention to the codes we use to figure life and death.

Several critics argue that Munro's aesthetic of order provides "an antidote to confusion and drift, a balm, a saving grace," as Joseph Gold, for example, suggests;[4] others insist, as does Helen Hoy, that Munro allows us to be "protected from nothing"; Hoy notes that a "vision of desolation is increasingly prominent in Munro's later stories."[5] The later stories, less modernist than late modernist, have more in common with Mavis Gallant's work in this latter regard. But both Munro's style and subject-matter are different from Gallant's in a number of ways. First, Munro writes much more self-conscious fiction than does Gallant. J.R. (Tim) Struthers succinctly states: "The imagination serves as the principal *theatre* of Munro's work, as a favourite *subject* for reflection, and, increasingly, as a guiding *form*."[6] Her stories are very often explicitly about story-telling, whereas Gallant's thematization of the act of writing is more often allegorical. Both authors emphasize the necessity of fictional truth, but where Gallant opens our eyes wide to *see* the truth and emphasizes the necessity of judgment using characters who fail to judge, Munro creates revelatory moments most often by demonstrating the process of unravelling judgments made in error by relatively perceptive characters and narrators. Gallant directs our judgment precisely; Munro, too, insists that judgment is essential but does not answer the questions raised by ambiguities perceived by the characters. As Janice Kulyk Keefer says, "Munro is as fine a stylist, as accomplished a word-artist, as Gallant, but there is a saving, softening element of mystery to the world of horrible, yet necessary, peculiarities her fiction reveals."[7]

Another difference is the avowedly apolitical subject-matter that Munro addresses.[8] Where, in her moral/social realism, Gallant uses the personal to parallel the political, juxtaposing memory and morality in an ethics of grieving, Munro charts not world history but ancestral worlds and private histories. Her realism, then, involves the anti-entropic documentation of life as a stay against the natural process of decay – as a kind of shoring against its ruins. She says that "with me it has something to do with the fight against death, the feeling that we lose everything every day, and writing is a way of convincing yourself perhaps that you're doing something about this."[9] Although Munro's fiction is engaged in this fight against death, the goal of that fight is not a sentimental and escapist notion of conquering death with literature; she is not inscribing a Freudian theory wherein, writes Jacques Derrida, a view of "death as an internal necessity of life" produces a "domesticity of death" that is "nothing but a consoling fiction."[10] Rather, Munro stages the fight so that what she has called "the fact of death" might be accommodated within life, but figured in such a way as to represent life as a resistance to order and "all attempts to render it comprehensible."[11] This accommodation is not, then, what Derrida refers to as "the poetics of the proper as reconciliation, consolation, serenity";[12] Munro's poetics of elegy is a poetics of the *im*proper, the *un*familiar, the *un*resolvable.

What Eileen Dombrowski calls Munro's "vision of ephemerality"[13] leads to the production of fictions wherein death "emerges as a narrative device; it evokes conflicting responses in characters; and it challenges them to define its significance" (22). Munro's texts encourage such responses in the reader, too, challenging us to define both the significance and the signification of death. Her narrative style constitutes an elegiac rhetorical ceremony, which, as Frederick Hoffman says of such rhetoric, "prevent[s] the corporeality of fact from communicating with too intense directness."[14] In other words, Munro uses a rhetoric of realism as a trope of persuasion or, in Roland Barthes's terms, a *"referential illusion"* in the mode of modern *"vraisemblance."*[15] This narrative trope serves to present the "fact of death" in such a way that the reader engages not only with a familiar fiction but with the unknown as well. The effect created by the strategy, then, is to induce a process of *de*familiarization or "estrangement" in the reader. Helen Hoy uses this Brechtian term in her discussion of Munro, and it recalls my discussion of Gallant's use of ironic distancing to induce a form of estrangement in the reader as well.[16]

More specifically, though, Munro's rhetoric produces what many have called a type of photographic realism. Susan Sontag writes: "Photography is an elegiac art, a twilight art. Most subjects photographed are, just by virtue of being photographed, touched with pathos ... All photographs are *memento mori* ... Precisely by slicing out this moment and freezing it, all photographs testify to time's relentless melt."[17] The "luminous shadow" of photographs is what signifies a "true shadow," writes Barthes.[18] Munro's realism produces such oxymoronic moments – both bright or luminous, and odd or shadowy – in an affirmative magic reality[19] that enlightens the reader with characteristic "queer, bright moments."[20]

The component of photographic realism in Munro's work might better be considered photographic elegism,[21] one that provides the reader with "intense, but not connected, moments of experience," as Munro says in another interview.[22] As participating readers we must make the connections between moments for ourselves.

Munro's queer bright moments are used as tropes of partial consolation for the reader, to whom "some of the seeing is always left," as
James Carscallen notes.[23] The queerness of the experience is a modification of the conventional modernist revelatory moment. Munro's
epiphanies, like Woolf's moments of being, possess "shock" value
in that they surprise the character/reader and provide heightened
awareness; like Joyce's, they are bright in that they provide a revelation that invites a positive response in (mental) action, and therein
lies a form of consolation. The moment is necessarily bright (photographs, too, require a flash of light for their production). The queerness arises from the juxtaposition of unexpected, surprising phrases
or ideas, which results in a de-familiarization of the ordinary.

Munro implies that there is a strange aspect to the insights with
which the reader is required to come to terms. While epiphanic moments are used repeatedly – ritualistically – in the work of mourning, and eventually produce the effect of knowledge and certainty,
for Munro they leave tensions *unresolved*. Helen Hoy quotes an important sentence from *The Moons of Jupiter* in this context: the narrator recognizes that "something unresolved could become permanent,"[24] that the only thing permanent in life is irresolution.
Because of this lack of resolution, Munro produces fiction that "is
not a memory ... but reality in a past state: at once the past and the
real," as Barthes says of photographs.[25] The reader's initial experience of epiphany is one of surprise, an experience that is analogous
to Barthes's "photographic 'shock,' " which "consists less in trau-
matizing than in revealing what was so well hidden."[26] The revelation is produced by the co-presence of what Barthes calls the *studium*
and the *punctum*: the former means "*average* affect," the "cultur[al]
... participat[ion] in the figures, the faces, the gestures, the settings,
the actions"; the latter is "an element which rises from the scene,
shoots out of it like an arrow, and pierces."[27] In Munro's stories the
studium is that which produces the "reality effect," then, while the
punctum produces the surprise, the shock of revelation.

In a similar vein Walter Benjamin writes of the relation between
thought and photography, and his comments (previously cited with
reference to Gallant in another context) are particularly apt in considering Munro's photographic elegism: "Where thinking suddenly
stops in a configuration pregnant with tensions, it gives that configuration a shock," he writes.[28] Shocks, suggests Benjamin, are unconscious impulses that break through the protection of consciousness.[29] But he also compares the function of the camera to that of
psychoanalysis, since the former "introduces us to unconscious op-
tics."[30]

It is this connection between shock and knowledge, epiphany and disrupted consolation that is at stake in Munro's photographic elegism. Where Gallant writes of the ghostly, Munro writes of the ghastly, the grotesque that is more common than we readily recognize or admit. According to James Carscallen a "feeling of meaningfulness" is achieved in reading Munro's fiction that "seems to depend on a sense that two different things are the same or at least alike"[31] – in other words, it depends on tropes of metaphor or metonymy. But "meaningfulness" in Munro is produced more notably by observation not of similarities but of the differences between "things" – of paradox. Munro's use of paradox is paradigmatic of her vision: two (usually opposite) words or scenes have intertwined underlying meanings. The perception of paradox produces a queer, bright moment, then, and in that moment mysteries are illuminated, though not resolved.

As in Gallant's fiction, the underlying sadness in Munro's work is both a textual mood and a transference phenomenon that instigates an empathic encounter with the text. E.D. Blodgett claims that metaphor is the dominant poetic figure in Munro's work,[32] and since metaphor both is and requires a transfer of meaning, the reader of a metaphoric mimesis *re*places the meaning in a parallel version of the story. Munro has stated that "every final draft, every published story, is still only an attempt, an approach, to the story,"[33] and her fiction-elegies do invite a readerly response that contributes to the production of meaning in the reconstructive act – an act that is another "attempt" to write the still unfinished story, in Munro's terms. J. Brooks Bouson writes that "the model of reading as an empathic event furnishes yet another 'story' of reading,"[34] and it is by way of this empathic exchange that the reader reconstructs self and story in the experience of reading fiction-elegy such as Munro's.

It is in this exchange that Munro's works of mourning provide an angle of approach for the reader's ethical participation. W.J. Keith notes that "Munro's refusal, at least explicitly, to influence our moral responses to her characters forces us as readers to relate their actions to our own ethical principles."[35] Reading Munro is therefore an act of "reconstructionism" – it involves the reader's response in terms of reconstructing Munro's fictive world as well as our own responses in and to the real world. W.R. Martin writes of Munro's work that "in its final effect it is just, rising above all the snobberies of fashion, class, and the intellect;" but if, in her moments of illumination, Munro achieves an acceptance of the ironies of life and death, as Martin suggests,[36] it is because her narrators seem to accept the queerness – the strange, the mysterious – rather than subject it to sustained intellectual analysis. Further, notes Keefer (in an article on Gallant), these narrators seem to implicate themselves "in the judgments [they] make of the steady human aptitude for smallness, failure, betrayal, loss,"[37] thereby softening those judgments with acceptance.

Since Gallant, as we have seen, is also just in placing the reader in the role of "judge," Munro's method of mimesis must be analysed in order to discover her own morals in and of mourning. Munro's photographic elegies seek to render what Barthes's grief required: "both justice and accuracy – *justesse*: just an image, but a just image" as well.[38] The reader of Munro must be "flexible both in sympathy and in judgement," concludes Margaret Anne Fitzpatrick.[39] Where Gallant guides the reader towards judgment, often denying pity for her characters, Munro allows characters and the reader to ponder ambiguities without pronouncing final judgment. This is the trick of Munro's technique: photographic elegism not only implicates us in a mode of mourning but implicates us in what Susan Sontag refers to as an "ethics of seeing."[40] The sense of photographic reproduction in Munro's work leads to a condition that, as Sontag writes of the visual art form, "feels like knowledge,"[41] but this knowledge of reality is questioned both within the stories and by the reader.

Munro's narrators, who frequently have an ability to involve us in their vision or witnessing of reality, are observers of life, most often shamed by emotional display. They also reserve a "tentativeness of judgment," writes Hoy of Munro's strategy.[42] As elegists the narrators privatize their emotions because they are ashamed to discuss them directly, and in psychological terms this shame distances them from themselves. Hence Munro's indirection, and the need for readers to reconstruct the basis of the story-telling in order to reattach form to content for themselves.

Irony is the trope of indirection that allows for the detachment of the narrator and insists upon the involvement of the reader. Linda Lamont-Stewart writes that "the only protection from the absurdity and horror of life" in the fiction of Alice Munro "is irony. The character who acknowledges his essential isolation, the dreamer who recognizes the artificiality of his idea of reality, has at least a measure of security in an insecure world."[43] Some psychological detachment is necessary for the elegist to "get out of" a "messy" situation. Munro's comments about a character in "An Ounce of Cure" and about herself point to the necessity for irony in writing of "hopeless" situations: "When the girl's circumstances become hopelessly messy, when nothing is going to go right for her, she gets out of it by looking at the way things happen – by changing from a participant to an observer. This ... is what a writer does ... I made the glorious leap from being a victim of my own ineptness and self-conscious miseries to being a godlike arranger of patterns and destinies, even if they were all in my head."[44]

The role of the observer allows Munro (as model reader) to employ the "twentieth-century hybrid" of "sympathetic identification and aesthetic detachment" of which Lorraine York speaks.[45] This detachment of the mourner is a modification of a modernist aesthetic of impersonality. Life is turned not so much into pure "art" (specifically, grief is not turned *directly* into elegy), but life and grief become *story* – yet another *version* of life, but a mysterious, legendary, and mythical version rather than an historical one. The lines between art and life are questioned by Munro, then, and we, as participants in life, mourning, and their respective narratives, seek what truth or meaning may underlie the realities of life and of death.

SHAPES OF DEATH: THE MEANING OF LOSS IN MUNRO'S EARLY STORIES

Munro has said that she was significantly influenced early in her writing career by James Agee's *A Death in the Family*,[46] the realism of which both portrays and embodies a psychology of grieving. While the unconnected stories in her first books – *Dance of the Happy Shades* (1968) and *Something I've Been Meaning To Tell You* (1971) – are not all about specific familial deaths, the majority of them are concerned with the passage of time and human responses to it. Munro's characters consistently confront the significance of death: a parent is often mourned (as is the mother in "The Peace of Utrecht," "Images," and "Ottawa Valley," for example); lost loves are frequently lamented as well. But Munro does not merely thematize such losses. She "probe[s] inner dimensions" in her early stories, as Struthers notes,[47] wherein death (whether figurative or literal) is her point of departure; the experience of recovery is then rendered in an elegiac manner through psychonarrative techniques.

In "Walker Brothers Cowboy" Munro combines themes of lost love and potentially fatal danger using a narrator who retrospectively identifies the essence of her *father's* emotional existence. With the title "Walker Brothers Cowboy" Munro renames the protagonist's father (Ben Jordan, also of *Lives of Girls and Women*) with the nickname he invents for himself, the one he uses in an invented song about his current occupation as a salesman for the Walker Brothers company. The name ironically identifies another, romantic side of himself, a successor to the dead Ned Fields, of whom the narrator thinks: "Who is Ned Fields? The man he has replaced, surely, and if so he really is dead; yet my father's voice is mournful-jolly, making his death some kind of nonsense, a comic calamity."[48] The child recognizes the paradox that is built into Ben's autobiographical, parodic elegy for Ned, the "mournful-jolly" tone (reminiscent of Gallant's "pretty-sad" reality) that blends truth and fiction, and she suggests that while Ned's death may be an invention, Ben is the successor to an at least figuratively dead man.

The renaming of Ben seems to separate him from the mortality associated with his predecessor by fictionalizing his very identity, reinstating a side of himself that he lost or left behind when he assumed the conventional roles of husband and father. As John Orange writes, there is a sense of transience and loss in the story.[49] The narrator can hear sadness in her father's voice after they have left his one-time sweetheart's (Nora's) farm: "the words seem sad to me as never before," she thinks (17). Soon Ben stops singing altogether, and his silence indicates a gradual dissolution and disappearance of the cowboy self: "I feel my father's life flowing back from our car in the last of the afternoon, darkening and turning strange, like a landscape that has an enchantment on it, making it kindly, ordinary and familiar while you are looking at it, but changing it, once your back is turned, into something you will never know, with all kinds of weathers, and distances you cannot imagine" (18). The story documents a fragment of Ben's life, and it presents a queer, bright moment wherein the narrator recognizes that this fragment belongs to an alien landscape – "another country," to quote from "Dance of the Happy Shades" (224) – one that is also, paradoxically, enchanting.[50]

As part of the legendary past Ben's "dark" side is as dangerous as death. Munro's juxtaposition of the words "strange" and "enchantment," "ordinary and familiar," produces a tension in the narrative moment that is reproduced in the reading of the story. Though it is "story" (for the narrator and for us), not anecdotal fact, there is what the narrator of "The Shining Houses" calls "a pure reality" (19) existent in the moment that consoles through cognizance, through recognition. This kind of knowledge is acquired in the transformation of fact to fiction.

The tension between fact and fiction is explored by the first-person narrator of "Images." This fiction-elegy might be described as an achronological memoir (wherein the death of her mother is evaded by the focus on her father's trapping activities); the story moves back and forth through time as the narrator eventually allows herself to address her fear of death through a displaced telling. The mother is dying in the "now" of the text (30), cared for by a cousin who also nursed her grandfather when the narrator was "so young" she slept in a crib (30). This young narrator seems to remember, thinking about "all this life going on," a house where "dim wasted space," "emptiness," and "stained corners" signified death. In the mind of the narrator the nurse is "held responsible" for the mother's death and symbolizes death in her mind (31); but it is the narrator who has turned her mother into an inhuman effigy: "This *Mother*," she says, has become "an everlastingly wounded phantom" (33). The effigy haunts, then, and does not console; prosopopoeia erupts in the work of mourning to impede its progression.

Her quest initially is for "the fact of death-contained, that little lump of magic ice" (31), and also for a written account of it, one that would reveal death's secrets; if she could confront that phantom, humanize it, and "live happily ever after," as she knows children do in fairy stories (43), her work would be done. When Mary moves in to nurse her mother, the narrator "watch[es] the shadows instead of the people … trying to understand the danger, to read the signs of invasion" (35). This reading and interpretive quest involves questions, which the narrator asks herself and the reader: "What was her [Mary McQuade's] smell like?"; "How could my parents not know" about the taste that "was in all the food Mary McQuade prepared?" (32) And in the course of questioning, the goal of the quest is seen to be an impossible one. The search for the fact of death becomes displaced, and the narrator pursues instead a quest of adventure on the trapline with her father. The telling of the trapping is, then, a "substitutive turn," an act of troping.[51]

The trapline inscribes a metaphoric plot-line. Since the narrator's father "came back to us always, to my mother and me, from places where our judgement could not follow" (36), he is, in his reliable returns ("I never asked how far we were going, or if the trapline would ever end" [37]), connected with her mother's life: if he returns, then her mother survives. The animals killed by the mechanical traps represent death-as-fact, what the narrator "did not understand or care" about (36) but needed physically to touch to be able to recognize the fate her mother faces. Her quest is also an epistemological one, then, since she believes that knowledge can be acquired through factuality, through surface detail alone; as the narrator of "Boys and Girls" states, "It was not something I wanted to see; just the same, if a thing really happened, it was better to see it, and know" (121). These narrators, when young, equate seeing with knowing, perception with comprehension – but this view is undermined when, as adults, they re-evaluate the past.

The narrator almost welcomes her father's death when Joe Phippen, the scythe-carrying human figure of the grim reaper, appears to threaten her father's life: "This is the sign that does not surprise you, the thing you have always known was there that comes so naturally ... All my life I had known there was a man like this and he was behind doors, around the corner at the dark end of the hall ... The man slipped down through the bushes to my father. And I never thought, or even hoped for, anything but the worst" (38). The narrator, then a child, is "transfixed, as if struck by lightning," assuming that reality was fulfilling an imagined plan, a fiction. This epiphanic experience provides the narrator with knowledge that "fears are based on nothing but the truth" and makes her "powerful with secrets" (43). Suddenly she is "no longer afraid" of Mary McQuade, the symbol of death, either.

Of course, had Joe murdered her father, the narrator would have been partially responsible, since she did not warn him of the approaching man, so certain was she in her belief that a fiction was being enacted before her eyes. The outing with her father, then, narrated in the midst of a memory of her mother's illness, provides a new understanding of life and death, a new perspective on both. Commenting on the surrounding outdoors scene, she thinks: "It did not occur to me, not till long afterwards, that this was the same bush you could see from our yard" (37). Munro's moments of vision offer the reader a de-familiarization, a version of knowledge that both surprises and partially mollifies us by opening up a new field of vision.

The characters of "Memorial" have a similar need to have death contained as "fact," though they lack the necessary wider perspective on the significance of death. The events of this story allude to *A Death in the Family*, since it is suggested in the latter that Jay, killed in a senseless car accident, may have had the car fall on top of him – which is what happened to the boy in "Memorial." In Munro's story, however, we witness the apparent lack of grief in June and Ewart, whose son has been killed in a car accident. Of June, her sister thinks: "She preferred, did she, to see the fact of death set up whole and unavoidable, in front of everybody's eyes? Without religion, that could not be done" (172). One alternative exists for Munro: story-telling itself is able to combine the "fact of death" with an imaginative reconstruction of the work of mourning (in place of religion), as this story attests. The work thus produced resists "setting up" death "whole and unavoidable" and suggests that meaning is produced by resisting falsifying order and rationalistic explanations of the unknown.

In this story we question the parent's response to loss precisely because they refuse to enter into the work of mourning, whereby their emotions – as well as the boy's life – would be narrativized, signified, and given significance. Their "morality of consumerism" (169) extends into their grieving, which merely consists of acceptance of the fact of death and its assimilation (173), without a ceremonial re-evaluation of the significance of the death (or the life) of their son. The story, told from Elaine's point of view, provides the memorial for the boy by implicitly criticizing the lack of ceremony, both funereal and rhetorical, employed by his parents.

Similarly, the third-person narrator of "The Time of Death" describes questionable reactions to a child's accidental death by contrasting the thoughts and conversations of Leona, the mother, with those of a neighbour, Allie McGee. Mrs McGee's parenthetical, unspoken opinion of Leona and of Patricia, the daughter who is blamed for her brother's death, silently corrects the mother's account of events. She thinks "it was not a time for any sort of accuracy" (91) and allows Leona's story to stand, but her own description of the girl is so clearly biased that the reader does not believe what is seen through her eyes either. Since the story begins "afterwards" (89), the reader is given fragments of information with which to construct the plot. The neighbourhood women wear "the ritual masks of mourning and compassion" and use "tones of ritual soothing" (91), but since Leona is disliked, we question the level of sincerity in this reaction. The Salvation Army woman uses formulaic words of religious consolation: "In the garden of heaven the children bloom like flowers. God needed another flower and he took your child. Sister, you should thank him and be glad" (91). This imagined garden is juxtaposed in the reader's mind with the frozen cornstalks and cabbages that Leona and her husband failed to harvest (90) and the cold, empty street filled with puddles that "was all turned to ice and splintered up – but it didn't snow, did it, it hasn't snowed yet" (91).

The snow is connected to Patricia's reaction to her brother Benny's death by scalding. Her own responsibility in the accident is questioned – she had boiled water in order to scrub her mother's dirty kitchen clean. Leona blames the girl, refuses to see her, while Patricia (a nine-year-old singer, a "natural performer," according to Mrs McGee [90]) becomes emotionally frozen, dead: she behaves "as if nothing had happened" (97). The reader awaits her reaction to both the death and her mother's rejection of her as the characters await the coming of the snow. On the day of the funeral Allie McGee says, "I wouldn't be surprised if it snowed today, would you?" (96), but by November, the narrator tells us in syntax that repeats that used by Leona earlier, "the snow had not come, the snow had not come yet" (98).

The suspended seasonal state signifies not only Patricia's suspended emotional condition but that of the others who reacted insincerely, or not at all; it also represents the reader's condition, who sees the episode through a variety of inadequate eyes and has yet to find a workable model of mourning. Leona's "What's life? You gotta go on" (98), and the father who "was not equal" to the bereavement expected of him, provide an unsatisfying sense of life's going on unchanged by the event or by anyone's personal revelation about its meaning. Leona's choice of sheet music for Patricia's performance a short time after the funeral is ironic: "May the Circle Be Unbroken" and "It Is No Secret, What God Can Do" (98). Clearly the circle has been broken, and if Benny's death is an act of God, then the title of the second hymn must be read ironically. Munro questions the religious attitudes that these songs/hymns embody, since the consolation they might achieve cannot answer the questions raised in our minds when confronted with death.

It is only after Patricia's hysterical reaction to the sound of the scissors-man's "unintelligible chant, mournful and shrill" (98) – a metonymy that reminds her of Benny, since the man's name (Bram) is one of the only two words he knew how to say – that her pathological grieving process begins, and it is then that the narrator (in a manner reminiscent of Joyce in "The Dead")[52] tells us descriptively that

There was this house, and the other wooden houses that had never been painted ... Behind them there was the strip of earth, plowed in some places, run to grass in others, full of stones, and behind this the pine trees, not very tall. In front were the yards, the dead gardens, the grey highway running from town. The snow came, falling slowly, evenly, between the highway and the houses and the pine trees, falling in big flakes at first and then in smaller and smaller flakes that did not melt on the hard furrows, the rock of the earth.   (99)

The epiphanic moment for Patricia, evoked by the man's voice, provides a queer but not very bright moment for the reader. Though the snow falls, suggesting a normal continuation of the life-cycle and a release of repressed grief for Patricia, the lack of any acceptable adult reaction to the original accident or to Patricia's emotional condition eliminates any sense of consolation and places the reader in a continuing condition of suspended emotion, caught between different ways of seeing and of grieving.

"The Day of the Butterfly," originally titled "Good-by, Myra" (July 1956), is another story about repressed emotion, although the insight of Helen, the narrator, into her own limitations of feeling *is* made available to the reader. The story is the narrator's attempt to come to terms with life and survival in the social world.[53] The sentence "I start remembering her [Myra Sayla] in the last year" (100) implies that the remembering is an activity enacted periodically in the present and that the end of the relationship with Myra is significant in terms of Helen's emotional growth.

It is not grief that Helen comes to feel for the terminally ill Myra but a recognition of her ability to allow "the treachery of [her] own heart" to release her from grief and from the "barriers which now closed about Myra" (119) – impending death, the journey to the "other country." Helen admits her guilt for setting Myra apart "for legendary uses" (110) – for constructing a story about her and detaching herself from the girl by living according to its plot and not according to real life, real emotions. As a commentary on the act of elegizing, Munro's story indicates the necessity of maintaining both fact and fiction, known and unknown in any authentic version of the past. In telling this story, Helen – an unsuccessful elegist – cannot accommodate the unknown, and so invents an untruthful story to evade it.

Some of Munro's narrators learn to accomplish the telling of stories in more ethical ways than does Helen, who cannot accommodate the "other" in her reality and has the necessary insights but chooses not to allow them to surface.[54] Collected in *Something I've Been Meaning To Tell You*, "Winter Wind" is a story that compares knowledge to understanding, fact to fiction, and it explores the possibility of finding truth in story-telling. The family photograph in this story is both literal (of the narrator's grandmother, parents, and siblings) and figurative in that she provides a series of fictional snapshots of her relatives – including her sick mother (hence the story is closely connected to "Ottawa Valley" and "The Peace of Utrecht" as well as "Home").[55] Looking at the photograph, the narrator writes: "And how is anybody to know, I think as I put this down, how am I to know what I claim to know? I have used these people, not all of them, but some of them, before. I have tricked them out and altered them and shaped them any way at all, to suit my purposes. I am not doing that now, I am being as careful as I can, but I stop and wonder, I feel compunction."[56] The story is both about the work of mourning and an enactment of the same. The narrator admits that aside from "the facts" she has "said other things" that are not "invented" but believed "without any proof" (201). She articulates a

pure reality by transforming fact to fiction, and after her grandmother expresses grief angrily for a long-dead friend (and for herself), she is able to conclude: "I understand various things now"
(205).

What she now seems to understand is that her grandmother's
doctrine of "acceptance," of avoiding danger (something that the
girl's mother represented both in her terminal illness and in behaviour that went against conventional marital norms), is a fatalistic
philosophy. The grandmother is the one who has become emotionally "frozen to death," which is one of her fears if her granddaugh-
ter ventures homeward in what she thinks of as a winter storm
(204). The struggle that continues at her mother's house is a struggle
against death, against passive acceptance. This is analogous to the
writer's struggle to use the past carefully as a means of "get[ting]
messages another way" (201) – of accepting the unknowable, the
mysterious other world behind the world of fact alone.

We use our pasts in our effort to story our lives and ourselves, insists Munro, who has commented that "life is made into a story by
the people who live it"[57] and that "you edit your life as you go
along."[58] In "Material" this metafictional message is discovered and
rendered by the narrator, who is divorced from Hugo, a writer. The
story is in part an incomplete work of mourning for the loss of his
love; she addresses her apostrophe to his photograph on the back of
his most recent book (28), constructing a version of him from her
knowledge and by deconstructing the biographical blurb, full of lies,
beneath the photograph. Her second marriage is comfortable but
passionless. Gabriel has "forgotten the language of his childhood"
(25, 26), and thus seems without identity and remains "mysterious"
to her (26), while the Hugo that she knows is, as she states, still "in
my blood" (27). The narrator's story is about Hugo's fictional use of
the past, of a time that they shared, and about her own version of
that personal past with Hugo. Munro's story identifies the narrator
as a self-conscious elegist who, in writing her past, simultaneously
considers the responsibilities involved in the act of writing itself.

Margaret Osachoff states that "[the narrator's] story ... is partly
memoir and partly a meditation on the right use of the past as raw
material for art" in that the narrator offers "a corrective to Hugo's
faulty vision and misuse of Dotty [a neighbour] as material";[59] but in
fact, on one level the narrator is acknowledging the success of his
transformation of life into art, and envies it: "I was moved by Hugo's
story; I was, I am, glad of it, and I am not moved by tricks. Or if I
am, they have to be good tricks. Lovely tricks, honest tricks" (43).
The paradox of the honest trick – truthful fiction – is accomplished

by Hugo's use of realism as trope: in fiction "disguises would not do," notes the narrator (29).

Hugo's story provides the narrator with a queer, bright moment through his "act of magic" (43) – she learns that it is important to understand "how to ignore or use things" (44), to make "arrangements" so that one is not "*at the mercy*" (44). She needs to transform Hugo into "the marvelous clear jelly that Hugo has spent all his life learning how to make," to lift him "out of life and held in light, suspended," as he was able to do with his past via the character of Dotty (43). The narrator's inability to use the past honestly, her inability to use "the reality you *feel*" rather than the reality you see (as Munro describes her own strategy),[60] is the cause of her continued "unhappiness" (44). As a lesson in elegy, then, Munro suggests that elegiac writing involves the inclusion of the unresolvable qualities of life, of the fictional truth that, once captured, may be viewed epiphanically – "out of life" and embalmed in a "clear jelly."[61] And jelly, of course, is a flexible substance.

The narrator of "Tell Me Yes or No" takes this methodology of mourning to an extreme and prefigures Munro's later story, "Bardon Bus." The first-person story is like a dramatic monologue, a spoken letter addressed to "you," an ex-lover. Written in terse sentences that suggest, as does the epistle form, both "spontaneity and calculation,"[62] the discursive style interrupts the narrative and mimics the writer's emotional disturbance: "I persistently imagine you dead. You told me that you loved me years ago. Years ago. And I said that I too, I was in love with you in those days. An exaggeration," she begins (106). The construction of his death is an anti-prosopopoeic trope and an anti-elegiac figuration, an attempt to murder her own love for the man by eliminating his existence rather than remembering it.

The relationship existed for some time mainly in the form of letters written to each other, and then only those sent by the narrator to the man, unrequited. The epistolary form of the relationship, and of the story, allows the narrator to "simultaneously analyze [her] illusions about the beloved and create new ones by writing; the act of writing itself is one means of creating the illusion of presence," as Linda Kauffman writes of the genre (24). But in her letter to the metaphorically dead male, whose "permanent absence" has created a "hole [she] fall[s] into" (117), the narrator is attempting to believe in the illusion of absence, while it is Munro who attempts to instil in the reader the illusion of actual event, of presence.

In her letter the narrator invents a story about her actions following his death: she travels to the city of his home and seeks out his wife, who mistakes her for another mistress of her husband and presents her with love letters that had been sent to him after his death, begging for a response. The narrator invents this other woman in her fantasy in order to embody his betrayal of her and also to provide a displacement of herself; she thinks of the invented other woman in order to "see it, as something going on at a distance; a strange, not even pitiable, expenditure; unintelligible ceremony in an unknown faith" (124). The constructed self (which is a figure for the self-construction that takes place in any epistolary mode of writing) allows her to ask questions that make her vulnerable to his rejection, without actually risking that rejection herself: "*I could deal with my feelings if I had to and recover from loving you but I must know whether you love me and want me any more so please, please, tell me yes or no*" (122). She embeds fragments of these invented letters and apostrophes in her own invented letter, making her experience seem common and part of a pattern of "shopworn recognizable pain" (117), as the "betrayal" stories in women's magazines teach her that "one's case holds no particular agony" (117). As the grieving narrator of "The Spanish Lady" states, after tearing up two letters written to her husband and his mistress, "The banality will make you weep as much as anything else" (176).

By using the epistolary mode Munro tricks her reader, just as the narrator tricks herself: using the seeming factuality of the discourse, she constructs a plausible course of events that are really part of a fantasy, a fairy-tale written with the intent of recovery and knowledge. The letter is an apostrophe and counters the anti-prosopopoetic gesture of imagining him dead. She asks: "Am I right, am I getting close to you, is that true?" and "How are we to understand you?" (124) But love, the "unknown faith," is, like death, part of that "other country," that other mysterious and dangerous world that coexists with reality.[63] Letters to the dead are of course unanswerable, and the episteme of the epistle is fragmentary – as the relationship itself was only partially fulfilling.

While the narrator cannot allow herself to "understand [her tricks] at the present moment, but [has] to be careful" (124), the reader of this story understands that the version of events and emotions created by the narrator in her letter offers only a temporary and tenuous consolation for her. By inventing the death of her beloved, she evades the fact that, while he is still alive, he no longer loves her. Thus she grieves for a loss she did not experience in order to deny the real loss. The reader's queer, bright moment occurs when the model of mourning presented in the story is deemed inadequate, pathological, yet somehow perfectly understandable.

With these early stories Munro begins to explore both themes and fictional methods that contribute to a poetics of elegy. That is, what happens in these stories is inextricable from *how* the stories happen. In *Dance of the Happy Shades* and *Something I've Been Meaning to Tell You* Munro lays a foundation for her elegiac enterprise, one that has continued to dominate her entire *oeuvre*: it entails questions of how to revise the past into story and how to signify the significance of loss.

MODELS OF MOURNING IN *LIVES OF GIRLS AND WOMEN*

Lorraine York writes that in terms of form Munro's interconnected short-story collections "function on the same borderline between motion and stasis; each self-contained story is an image in itself."[64] *Lives of Girls and Women* (1971), Munro's first linked collection of short stories, is about the representation of personal histories and the various generic uses of such representations. The original title, *Real Life*,[65] raises questions about both subject-matter (life) and fictional aesthetics (realism). The generic multiplicity of the text produces a quality of self-consciousness, and though it contains a form of the word "life" in its title, the generic dominant is the elegy. The stories go "round and round and down to death," as Del says of her mother's tales.[66]

Robert Alter writes: "Perhaps the most basic paradox of this [self-conscious] mode of fiction which functions through the display of paradoxes is that as a kind of novel concentrating on art and the artist it should prove to be, even in many of its characteristically comic embodiments, a long meditation on death."[67] *Lives of Girls and Women* has such a focus. It is Munro's version of *A Portrait of the Artist as a Young Man*, as many critics have noted;[68] however, where Stephen achieves epiphanic consolation in the aesthetic, and apostrophizes Daedalus, Del Jordan questions the ethics involved in ordering reality with words. Her epiphanies are such that the truth achieved is located not in the pure order of the artifact but in ambiguity and paradox, in the dialectical juxtaposition of art and fact.[69]

Sontag's comments about photography as cultural ruins may be accurately applied to Munro's text: "Photographs are, of course, artifacts. But their appeal is that they also seem, in a world littered with photographic relics, to have the status of found objects – unpremeditated slices of the world. Thus, they trade simultaneously on the prestige of art and the magic of the real."[70] In an article on Munro and photography Deborah Bowen writes that "photographs are a product of both the realm of physical reality and the realm of artifice."[71] For Munro the photograph is a metaphor for her realistic fiction, which is an elegiac art, as is photography. The collection is therefore fiction-elegy as artifact in the form of Del's record and evaluation of responses to life, loss, and grief.

If, as Franco Rella writes, "reason develops through a reflection on grief, transforming it into a new and positive rapport with the world,"[72] then Lives charts Del Jordan's developing epistemology. Alternative philosophies and methods of mourning are appraised by Del, whose reflection of grief leads to the conclusion that a vision of life as order does not console, or protect one from death; rather, it limits life. Disorder, such as that symbolized by the life of Uncle Benny, is representative of the "truth about life," as Rae McCarthy Macdonald puts it.[73] Though clearly art creates imaginative order, in Munro's aesthetic of elegy that order must also account for the "other country" – disorder, death, mystery, the unknown – and not merely eliminate it, so that a truthful work of mourning is produced.

In "The Flats Road" Uncle Benny has accumulated "fifty years or so of family life," "people's throwaways," and "information about the outside world" (4–5). He is a collector-figure, as is Del; he "told stories, in which there was nearly always something happening that [her] mother would insist could not have happened" (9). He is part of the "other country," a world that Del positions "lying alongside our world ... like a troubling distorted reflection" (26). The word "lying" is ambiguous, and draws attention to the deceptive potential of fiction. Significantly, Benny is able to read but unable to write. Hence he can collect facts of the past but cannot transform them into any kind of legible order; he cannot elegize. Del's role as artist is to re-collect other people's unwritten, mysterious, and legendary tales; she must learn which facts and "revelations of evil" (5) she should value, and how to transform them into stories, into art that might provide comfort.

In "Heirs of the Living Body" Del begins to evaluate different methods of representation or "kinds of discourse," as E.D. Blodgett writes;[74] she also compares their potential value in rendering life truthfully and in consoling survivors for the ephemerality of that life. Uncle Craig's linear, historical discourse, accurate but unshaped and written unselectively, fails to provide Del with any sense of the real past. Fact is not truth, as Munro consistently reminds us. The family photograph of Uncle Craig with his siblings and parents is, by contrast, a *memento mori*, signifying his own future death. The story is not only an elegy for Craig but also an allegory of elegizing.

Craig's family tree lists the ancestral history of the Jordan family dating from 1670. Craig's version of the past, which Del describes as an "intricate structure of lives supporting us," is a relatively ineffectual one; while he collected "daily life" in the form of "newspaper clippings, letters, containing descriptions of the weather, an account of a runaway horse, lists of those present at funerals, a great accumulation of the most ordinary facts" (31), he did not transform any of these facts into art; nor did he take the extraordinary into account at all.

Craig left out the story from Del's family history, from the family tree (this genealogical metaphor is interesting in the context of elegy).[75] In the family history that is *Lives of Girls and Women* Del includes details about the unusual yet seemingly ordinary events in her memory of the past. For example, she describes witnessing her parents embracing their "unsupported selves" in a private moment of private grief (49) after Craig has died, a rare sight in her household. Thus the difference between "Uncle Craig's history" (60) and Del's written past is that the former seems "dead ... dull and useless" to Del – "a mistake" (62) – whereas Del's includes details of everyday life. Eventually (after the manuscript has been destroyed) Del becomes "greedy for Jubilee" (249) and has a "hope of accuracy" that recalls Uncle Craig's. But Del uses facts only as points of departure for her fictionalized family, and produces an artifact that is neither merely history nor a purely aesthetic object. Her relatives (parents, aunts, Mary Agnes) and her own experiences are transformed. At Uncle Craig's funeral she has "a vision which was, in a way, the very opposite of the mystic's incommunicable vision of order and light; a vision, also incommunicable, of confusion and obscenity – of helplessness, which is revealed as the most obscene thing there could be" (57). This epiphany, this recognition of the need not to evade but to *see* that which makes us helpless (the natural disorder epitomized by death), provides the basis for Del's aesthetic of fiction: pure, linear order is not a "true image" of life.

In "Heirs of the Living Body" Del confronts "death as we know it" (48). Her mother's humanistic philosophy, developed in part by reading a magazine article from which the story takes its title, is one of physical transformation and literalizes traditional pastoral consolation ("Uncle Craig is flowers!" [47]); Del's is an aesthetic version, wherein fiction does not "fix" fact, in either sense of the word, but transforms it. In "Princess Ida" and "Age of Faith" Addie Jordan's beliefs about life and death, as well as her stories, instruct Del further (indirectly) in the modes of mourning. Addie tells "stories of the past" that go "round and round and down to death" (77), and her daughter, in writing stories about these stories, places "scenes from the past" – scenes that "were liable to pop up any time, like lantern slides, against the cluttered fabric of the present" – in an aesthetic order that adds to the family fiction-tree.

"Princess Ida" reverses the usual order of genealogical story-telling in that it tells stories about deaths in the family rather than documenting the birth of successive generations. Its achronological pattern creates a narrative cycle that, in going "round and round," contains secrets not explicitly told. Addie's grief and anger at her mother are eventually located at the centre of this revision of Genesis: "In the beginning, the very beginning of everything, there was that house," Del writes of her mother's birthplace (73). This story is translated into Del's narrative from Addie's voice, which, "telling these things, is hard with her certainty of having been cheated, her undiminished feelings of anger and loss" (74).

The origin of the anger is told first: Addie's mother had been a religious fanatic; then, briefly, her unresolved grief is identified with the story of her mother's death due to breast cancer. Addie's attitudes against religion and its inadequacies are illuminated by this story of her mother, which, we are to understand, Del hears several times (the phrase "at this point in the story" [76] is one marker of this). Religion, rather than providing Addie with consolation, is seen as the source of her mother's destruction; it removed her mother from her own world and could not heal the wound of separation caused by fanaticism and death.

Del experiences an empathic epiphany after the story of her mother's escape from paternal tyranny: "And my mother could not help, could never help, being thrilled and tender, recalling this; she was full of wonder at her old, young self. Oh, if there could be a moment out of time, a moment when we could choose to be judged, naked as can be, beleaguered, triumphant, then that would have to be the moment for her" (77). This isolated picture of Addie, with her "luminous shadow" made clear to Del, is contrasted with another, confusing memory of Addie related to her Uncle Bill. His visit has been narrated after previous tales of death have been told (and tolled), and at the end of the story we learn that he is "a dying man" (88).[76] Addie will inherit a much-needed three hundred dollars from her brother upon his death, and this fact recalls the entire narrative of pain and loss that she experienced with her mother's religious fanaticism: when she had come into a similar sum (two hundred fifty dollars), she spent it on bibles rather than on food and clothing for Addie and her brothers. With the recollection, which is not narrated, Del tells us that "there was something in the room like the down-

flash of a wing or knife, a sense of hurt so strong, but quick and isolated, vanishing" (89). The "downflash" is an embodiment of the vision of her mother's "luminous shadow," which she experiences at
the same moment.

Uncle Bill's visit provides not only a human embodiment of death;
his perspective also complicates the plot of the past, as Del juxtaposes his and Addie's stories about their mother to demonstrate different versions of the past and different uses of its material. Where
Addie's stories go "down to death," Uncle Bill's memories have a
resurrectional quality: the story of the caterpillar, saved by his
mother who allowed it to transform itself into a butterfly (87–8), is,
ironically, an allegory of individuation – of the natural process of
maturation and independence that Addie was not allowed to experience. The comparison between Bill's and Addie's childhood memories surprises Del: "That was in the same house. The same house
where my mother used to find the fire out and her mother at prayer
and where she [Addie] took milk and cucumbers in the hope of getting to heaven" (88). Such variations on a single story prove to be a
recurring interest in Munro's later stories because they demonstrate
the way in which the mind revises or edits different versions or editions of life, and they emphasize the importance of interpreting
those editions.

Del is able to absorb both versions of her mother's past since she is
at a distance from it, as her mother can never be. In rendering these
tales about her mother, "Princess Ida," she raises questions about
grief and about how one "works away" at finding consolation – as
the butterfly "works away on one [wing] … Works away on the
other … takes a little fly," as Bill describes it (88). "Age of Faith" is a
record of Del's effort to work away at understanding religion and its
potential for consolation during times of grief, and enacts the process in its form. The epistemological potential of elegy thus comes to
the fore in Del's evaluation of models of mourning, and the story
represents another of her quests for knowledge: "How could people
rest, how could they even go on breathing and existing, until they
were sure of this [security in faith]?" she thinks (99).

The story is riddled with such rhetorical questions. Others include
"How about my mother?" (99); "But did I really, *did I really want it*
[being saved] *to happen to me?*" (99); "that proved something, didn't
it?" (106); "*Were Christ's sufferings really that bad?*" (107); "But why – I
could not stop thinking though I knew it could bring me no happiness – why should God hate anything that He had made?" (108) The
ultimate rhetorical question is, to Del, a "vulgar" act (101), in the
form of a question posed to God himself: "I asked God to prove him-

self by answering a prayer." To ask God a question is to ascribe a prosopopoetic identity that not only gives voice but demands that that voice be used to answer her question.

Del initially thinks that God's existence would eliminate "the strange, anxious pain that just seeing things could create" (99) – which, she thinks, is "the only way the world could be borne, *the only way it could be borne*" (99). But this trope of prosopopoeia is a trick of fiction that inadequately simplifies the emotional needs of Del. In a sense Munro aestheticizes Addie's rejection of religion: "God was made by man! Not the other way around! God was made by *man* ... Man made God in his own image" (105–6). Man *stories* his world, then, a familiar Munrovian message, and Del sees her own need for another version of life-as-story, one that includes a God *"not contained in the church's net at all, not made manageable by any spells and crosses, God real, and really in the world, and alien and unacceptable as death"* (114).

Appropriately, the story ends with another question – "Do missionaries ever have these times, of astonishment and shame?" (114) – because Del's religion is really an aesthetic of wonder and of wondering, of rendering mysteries that are "beyond faith" (114), so that the reader might ponder the paradoxes for herself. As Barbara Godard writes of *Lives of Girls and Women*, "It is this possibility for action which is at the basis of Munro's revision of Joyce."[77] Munro does not advocate a modernist's religion of art but rather uses the "unavoidable collision ... of religion and life" (113), of fiction and fact, to question the consoling ability and ethics of an ordering faith, be it religious or aesthetic.[78]

"Epilogue: The Photographer" is a commentary on the preceding stories, which are photographic portraits of Del and other people in her life. The emphasis on the photograph (as opposed to Joyce's on the portrait) is at the centre of Munro's difference from her modern predecessor. Rather than fix life in an aesthetic artifact that claims truth because of its very separation from life, Munro's aesthetic of elegy is such that reality is rendered realistically, providing epiphanic recognition of truth in the paradoxes of "dull, simple, amazing and unfathomable" reality itself (249).

Del's initial attempt to fictionalize her life and people in it is recognized, in this story, as an unethical, untruthful account of reality. "I did not pay much attention to the real Sherriffs, once I had transformed them for fictional purposes," she notes (244). Her translation of the real mysteries into stereotypical gothic romance buries the more interesting reality, and Del loses faith in her novel (247) since it is so clearly divided from real life. Instead she finds that real life offers an "odd consolation" ("Baptizing" 236), and acquires skill in using the trope of realism, as demonstrated throughout the stories, to capture "every last thing, every layer of speech and thought, stroke of light on bark or walls, every smell, pothole, pain, crack, delusion, held still and held together – radiant, everlasting" (249).

The photographer in the story took the picture of Marion Sherriff (whose suicide is mentioned in "Age of Faith" [101]).[79] He is described as being "shrouded" (242), and his photographs are said to distort his subjects: "The pictures he took are said to be unusual, even frightening. People saw that in his pictures they had aged twenty or thirty years. Middle-aged people saw in their own features the terrible, growing, inescapable likeness of their dead parents; young fresh girls and men showed what gaunt or dulled or stupid faces they would have when they were fifty ... He was not a popular photographer, though cheap" (242–3). This man is a photographic artist, a profession Barthes associates with death: "All those young photographers who are at work in the world, determined upon the capture of actuality, do not know that they are agents of Death" (92). He provides realistic photographs, and it is the unretouched and therefore aesthetically unfamiliar quality that frightens viewers. His photos, like Munro's fiction-elegies, reveal the strange, the mysterious, the unknown that does exist in reality but that we do not often recognize in or for ourselves.

Barthes writes that "Death must be somewhere in a society; if it is no longer (or less intensely) in religion, it must be elsewhere; perhaps in this image which produces Death while trying to preserve life."[80] Perhaps, too, Death is captured in Munro's short stories. If so, by analogy Munro would be considered an agent of Death, but it is more accurate to say that in *Lives of Girls and Women* she is a self-conscious agent of both art and (the fact of) death combined – in other words, an agent of the elegy.

5 Munrovian Melancholy

I have been arguing that Munro's fiction, with its emphasis on loss and on the importance of story-telling as a method of gaining knowledge of the past, reveals and enacts a poetics of elegy. Munro, like Gallant, insists that the past must be evaluated and re-evaluated and that memory – though not equivalent to truth – is the most important source of knowledge, of a necessarily fictional truth. Gallant's characters often learn very little of the lessons she urges her readers to learn; we acquire insights about memory, history, truth, and writing by interpreting the ironic narrative stance employed in her fiction. Self-knowledge is the aim of most Munrovian narrators and characters, however, and the structure of each of Munro's performative fiction-elegies is as telling of the quest as is the tale.

Despite the differences in narrative strategies, Munro also shares with Gallant an interest in child-parent relationships.[1] After the creation of Del in *Lives of Girls and Women* the child's *perspective* is not often used by Munro, but her characters and narrators are often portrayed in the midst of working through a relationship with one or both parents (Gallant's are usually abandoned in one way or another as children and, as adults, need to recover retrospectively and independently). In *The Moons of Jupiter* elegiac themes include parental deaths and lost loves, themes that serve as points of departure for the metafictive constructs that result from Munro's double concern: for both the representation of responses to loss and the role that stories or fictions play in the grieving process.

The work of mourning, then, is a specific example of the ways in which we use stories to shape our lives, our experiences, and this collection contains stories that render diverted, diverse, and even perverse griefs in a metafictional framework. This frame*work* includes fram*ing* stories – "The Stone in the Field" opens the collection as part 2 of "Chaddeleys and Flemings"; "The Moons of Jupiter" closes it, and together the stories enact a Freudian work of mourning for a deceased father. Munro states that "the title story has something to do with my father's death ... But if I were to write, even for my own satisfaction, an account of my father's death ... the result would be quite different, not just in factual detail, in incident, but in feeling."[2]

Though a real death in the family may have provided the impetus for "The Moons of Jupiter," Munro is not writing autobiography; rather, she is writing fiction about the process of coming to terms with loss, in both senses of that phrase. Similarly, in many stories ("Images," "Winter Wind," "The Peace of Utrecht," and "Friend of My Youth" are examples) the recurring figure of the mother inflicted with Parkinson's disease is clearly based on the author's own mother (Munro has stated that "Images," "The Peace of Utrecht," and "Ottawa Valley" are autobiographical);[3] yet in her fiction-elegies Munro's use of autobiography is tropological, not generic, a use that paradoxically distances Munro as implied author from the real story and allows the reader to move closer to the mind and the story of the narrator.

MOURNING THE MOTHER: MUNRO
AND ELEGIAC EPIPHANY

The narrator of "The Peace of Utrecht" embarks on a retrospective retracing of her relationship with and attitude towards her mother, now dead. Cathartic disclosures of her own past behaviour, of which she is ashamed, break down the fictive façades she has constructed in the past. The differences between fictive truth, which is attainable in fiction-elegy, and distortions of the past are explored in this story. The narrator realizes that both she and her sister Maddy have preserved versions of their childhood in "anecdote, as in a kind of mental cellophane,"[4] which is mistaken by a friend as "good memories" (193). The irony in the pun on the word "good" (meaning both "accurate" and "pleasant") is evident: their memories are distorted, and they are also painful, recalling "continuing disaster" (191). Her think-act is effective in producing a self-judgment on the ethics of remembering, of reconstructing the past, in this manner:

"Now I listen to them speak of her [their mother], so gently and cere-
moniously, and I realize that she became one of the town's posses-
sions and oddities, its brief legends" (194), she thinks, concluding
that "we should have let the town have her; it would have treated
her better" (195).

The narrator edges towards an acknowledgment of her emotional
irresponsibility; upon returning to the empty house, she thinks: "I
was allowing myself to hear – as if I had not dared before – the cry
for help – undisguised, oh, shamefully undisguised and raw and
supplicating – that sounded in her voice" (198). This is the narrator's
exorcism – not of her mother's ghost, but of her repressed emotional
response to her mother's prolonged suffering. It is an exorcism that
Maddy will not allow herself (191, 202). Maddy's method of mourning is clearly inadequate; the story ends with her mournful cry, in
response to her sister's suggestion that she leave the town and begin
to live: "But why can't I, Helen? *Why can't I?*" (210) Neither sister is
capable of working through her guilt or loss; the narrator envies
their aunt, who seems to be "an old hand at grief and self-control"
(209). But it is her own self-control that the narrator must re-view,
and revise.

We are witness to the narrator's delayed self-confrontation in the
course of the story. The death of her mother is connected to the
"rhythm of life in Jubilee," which "is primitively seasonal": "Deaths
occur in the winter; marriages are celebrated in the summer. There is
good reason for this; the winters are long and full of hardship and
the old and weak cannot always get through them. Last winter was
a catastrophe, such as may be expected every ten or twelve years;
you can see how the pavement in the streets is broken up, as if the
town had survived a minor bombardment. A death is dealt with
then in the middle of great difficulties; there comes time now in the
summer to think about it, and talk" (194). This passage clearly presents a communal and pastoral parallel to her personal situation: ten
years ago, her mother died during the winter (a blizzard prevented
the narrator from attending the funeral [195]), and now, in the summer, she is able to "unbury the catastrophe" of her mother's death,[5]
to think about it, to *talk*. Recalling that she and her sister "took all
emotion away from [their] dealings with her, as you might take
away meat from a prisoner to weaken him, till he died" (199), she
admits that she "can, but will not, imagine" her mother's struggle to
continue living (199).

The ethics of her past actions, and of her selective memory in the
"now" of the narrative, are presented to the reader for questioning.
Though the sisters "make their memories bearable and manageable"

by making "their mother into a 'character' in a story," as Margaret Osachoff notes,[6] this *story* – a defence mechanism rather than a method of mourning – is now questioned by the narrator, who "felt the beginnings of a secret, guilty estrangement" from the believed truth of the story. The "picture of her [mother's] face which I carried in my mind seemed too terrible, unreal ... [The story] now began to seem partly imaginary" (201). Upon finding a high-school essay in which she had written "The Peace of Utrecht, 1713, brought an end to the War of the Spanish Succession" (201), the narrator is able to recognize "only then for a few moments" that her "old life was lying around [her], waiting to be picked up again" (201). The confrontation with the versions of her past, and an acknowledgment of the partially understandable, partially cruel reaction to her mother's disease and death, similarly brings an end to the "war of succession" that is the survivor's guilty legacy – though peace is yet to be found.

Part 1 of the story is, then, a double prosopopoeia, a brief resurrection of both her mother and the narrator's youthful self, as well as an evaluation of the prosopopoetic figuration she has imagined. In reading her own past (figuratively, in terms of memory and of the constructed legend of her mother), fragments of her adolescence "had been transformed into something curiously meaningful for me, and complete ... it spread over the whole town ... under an immense pale wash of sky" (202). This epiphanic moment is followed by another admission: italicized so as to differentiate the thought-process from the rest of the story, the text tells us that the narrator sometimes remembers their mother *"before,"* which is her attempt at *"cowardly tender nostalgia, trying to get back to a gentler truth"* (202). This gentler truth, which the narrator has used to assuage her guilt, is peeled away in her retelling of the past, and she thereby "transforms" the narrative into "something curiously meaningful," though the specific meaning she has found remains vague for the reader.

In *Something I've Been Meaning To Tell You* the "something" that is meaningful again is withheld from the reader, as the title suggests. The idea that there is danger in telling permeates the stories in the collection. Yet the show must go on, so to speak, and the power of the performance – the power of performatives, since think-acts are indeed such – is in the effect it has on the absent addressee, a role that is sometimes assumed by the reader. "Ottawa Valley" is also "about the death of a mother," as Munro has stated.[7] Further, it is about elegizing the mother, about the connection between fact and fiction, and the power of that fiction to provide a vision of life that is both acceptable and accommodating, true and transformed. The story begins: "I think of my mother sometimes in department stores. I don't know why, I was never in one with her; their plenitude, their sober bustle, it seems to me, would have satisfied her" (227). The metaphoric association of "sober bustle" with her mother produces a think-act that is translated to a speech-act, a performance that is explicitly an attempt "to mark her off, to describe, to illumine, to celebrate, to *get rid* of, her" (246). The activities are narrated during the summer spent in the Ottawa Valley, another version of that "other country,"[8] described as "blackness on either side of us" (229). During this time her mother's illness was becoming visibly noticeable, when she "would have been forty-one, or forty-two years old" – approximately the age that the narrator is in the "now" of the telling (237). This psychological connection to her mother is reinforced when the narrator is told that people see her mother in her own children (241).

The mother is never to be gotten rid of, then, which is a curse rather than a consolation. The narrator is unable to find the ironic distance that the elegist requires to distance herself from the loss, to interpret, to evaluate and to *tell*. The "journey ... undertaken" (246) has the potential to make the narrator, in metaphoric terms, an under*taker*: one who embalms, or fixes, the past. As a writer of one such fiction, which is a failed elegy, the narrator notes that her mother is "heavy as always, she weighs everything down ... [She] refused to fall away, and I could go on, and on, applying what skills I have, using what tricks I know, and it would always be the same" (246). To mix my Greek and Latin, it is a case of *katharsis interruptus*.

The daughter, through writing, produces a narrative that is "like a series of snapshots" – elegiac photographs – where the entire family "come[s] out clear enough;" but her mother, whose "edges melt and flow" (246),[9] is more difficult to visualize. The narrator has not captured the Barthean "luminous shadow" of her mother, that which "accompanies the body" and represents the "value," the "truth," the "true image" of the deceased.[10] The lack of a truthful effigy may preclude a release from the daughter's guilt, but the photographs (and the self-conscious story) none the less induce an epiphany, a re-evaluation of her past methods of transforming the past.

Munro often pluralizes the concept of the past and thereby complicates the fictional model of truth achieved in writing the past, and in elegizing. In the title story of *The Progress of Love* the narrator performs a meditative think-act, also occasioned by recalling the death of her mother, and which ends epiphanically. Munro's narrative is broken into fragments, which are arranged achronologically, as if to imitate a mind spontaneously recollecting different but related parts of the past in unconnected moments. But Munro embeds story within story, leading the reader to the "truth" at the labyrinthine core. There rests a suggested truth about the truth of interpretation. The convoluted shape of the story, then, forces the reader to "get straight with" the text, as the narrator attempts to "get straight with" her mother[11] – who "was another *story*," according to (Aunt) Beryl (21, emphasis mine).

The story of Beryl's visit to her sister Marietta and her family is introduced after several memory-scenes are presented to us, and it provides clues about their mother and about their parents' relationship. The narrator first states: "All these things I remember" (7), but the next sentence – "All the things I know, or have been told, about people I never even saw" – is puzzling in its fragmentary syntax and in the riddle that it establishes for the reader. The connection between knowledge and story-telling, between truth and perspective, is put into question. Munro's story creates in verbal form a disjunction between appearance and intent, as figured by the joker who keeps a "straight face" (21). (Of course Munro has consistently referred to fiction itself as a "trick"). This ironic disjunction makes readerly deciphering more difficult, and it draws attention to the teller, whose apparent detachment may be deceptive.

Narratologically, "The Progress of Love" enacts "the stories, and griefs, the old puzzles you can't resist or solve" (14). Its layered structure is also imaged metaphorically in the wallpaper that the narrator peels in the farmhouse of her childhood; she can see her mother's chosen design of "cornflowers on a white ground" underneath the paper that covered it, but in trying to get to the original, she damages it, ripping it away with plaster as well. The story of Beryl (which spans twenty-two pages) is punctuated with two "layered" stories about her mother: one about their mother Marietta's half-attempted suicide, and one about Marietta's act of burning the money she inherited from her father. Each of these is told twice, from two different perspectives. The first story is told the first time in the narrator's voice, it seems, since she refers to her mother as "Marietta," someone who "was separate, not swallowed up in [her] mother's grownup body" (9). But the information and details provided in this telling are those that would be available only to Marietta herself; hence the first telling is performed in Marietta's own voice, partially heard by the narrator, though no quotation marks indicate where hearing ends and invention begins.

This version of the story is open-ended: "Her heart was broken. That was what I always heard my mother say. That was the end of it. Those words lifted up the story and sealed it shut" (13). Marietta's traumatic experience of seeing her mother stand on a chair, noosed, remains a mystery to the reader, and to the narrator, who "never asked" the questions we ourselves ask. Her stories, like her life, are immersed in a "cloud, a poison" that "you couldn't see through, or get to the end of" (13). Munro clouds her story with conundrums, with unanswered and unanswerable questions that are only exacerbated by the story retold.

For example, Beryl's version of the same event (narrated several pages later) is a combination of her own perceptions and of her father's retellings of events. The clouded narratorial authority serves to confuse the reader and makes Marietta's mother's horrific act sound like a practical joke, a puzzle for the father to figure out. For the narrator this creates an interpretive problem; her aunt's story "stayed sealed off for years" (23), and though we know that her mother's version "held, for a time," we are not told what conclusions have been drawn. Her father's statement comes to mind: "People are dead now … It isn't up to us to judge" (22). But surely it *is* the judgment of both character and reader that is at stake in the quest for fictional truth.

The narrator's re-evaluation of her judgment provides her with an epiphanic moment: belief can console, and her fiction is "so much the truth that it is the truth," she thinks (30). Yet she decides to stop telling the story to others, realizing that she "had to give up expecting people to see it the way [she] did" (30), to approve of her version of and judgment on the past. In denying her readers closure and conclusions, Munro is similarly "giving up" the urge to moralize. But she is also suggesting that stories that recover the past, while fictional, are of potential value in terms of consolation. Her concession to plurality allows certain "moments of kindness and reconciliation" (30) between survivors, whose private reconstructions of the past may certainly differ.

Munro's fictional explorations of the past often involve multiple reconstructions of a single story. In the title story of *Friend of My Youth* (1990) the narrator tells a layered story about the Grieves sisters, with whom her mother once lived. The mother told her daughter about the sisters, and the story proper is thus a retelling, another performance of the original narrative act. In a 1936 essay Walter Benjamin writes that the "evolution of the 'short story' … no longer permits that slow piling one on top of the other of thin, transparent layers which constitutes the most appropriate picture of the way in which the perfect narrative is revealed through the layers of a variety of retellings";[12] but Munro's layers of retelling precisely locate her in the kind of tradition of which Benjamin speaks. "Friend of My

Youth" uses a modified elegiac-romance structure in that the biographical story about the Grieves thinly disguises the biography of
and elegy for the narrator's mother. The narrating daughter grieves
her mother, who is the muse of the story, the phantom friend who
haunts her dreams. The phrase "Friend of My Youth" is an epistolary address used by the mother in an unfinished letter, possibly
written to Flora Grieves years after their friendship ended and
shortly before the mother's death. It also refers to the mother herself, who was a friend of the narrator before her debilitating illness
altered the emotions of her daughter.

In the framing dreams that are described for the reader, the narrator retrieves her "real" mother as she had been "before her throat
muscles stiffened and a woeful, impersonal mask fastened itself
over her features."[13] The analeptic retrieval is made possible
through the mother's surprising performance of a speech-act in the
dream: she forgives her daughter for her resentment and emotional
withdrawal. This makes the narrator feel "tricked" (26) and surprised, however, since she had been deceived by the physical deterioration into believing that the woman herself had changed, when
really it was only a mask, the disease given face.

By telling the story of the Grieveses, the narrator approaches her
mother's history through a displacement. She constructs her mother's self as she might have been before the birth of the narrator,
though obviously the mother is seen through the daughter's eyes.
Flora's forgiveness of Robert's betrayal, "not once but twice" (19), is
the apparent interest of the narrator's (and Munro's) story; however,
the posthumous forgiveness that the mother bestows upon the narrating daughter is the co-textual[14] fiction-elegy in "Friend of My
Youth." The daughter imagines finding Flora, who has been "dead a
long time now" (25), in a department store in the textual present;
but the parenthetically acknowledged dream is the end-frame version of the dream at the beginning of the story, and Flora – the
friend of her mother's youth – is conflated with the dead mother,
friend of her daughter's youth.

The retrieval is a reprieve as well (26), a qualified happy ending of
the story-within-the-story, which has a "once upon a time quality,"
as Peter Buitenhuis notes.[15] Munro is what Benjamin would call a
"true storyteller" (102), one of those tellers of fairy tales who employ
their "liberating magic," as Benjamin describes it, to de-mythologize
that which has become overly familiar – to "shake off the night-
mare" of myth that causes us passively to "act dumb" towards myth
(102). In some ways Munro is trying to make her readers "happy,"

as the child is made happy with a fairy tale; but the route towards this happiness is also criticized in "Friend of My Youth."

The narrator questions her mother's improper use of Flora's life when she speaks of turning the morality-story into a novel with the possible title *The Maiden Lady*. Similarly, the ethics of the elegy for her mother – the mortality-story – are questioned here: the narrator appropriates the mother's life and stories in order to write about that life and about the effect that the *end* of that life has had on herself. This need of an elegist to appropriate another's story for one's own use in the work of mourning is exemplified more pointedly in "Goodness and Mercy." The title is taken from Psalm 23: "Surely goodness and mercy shall follow me all the days of my life: and I will dwell in the house of the Lord for ever." The ironic twist is that the unethical think-actions of Averill, who, we learn, has imagined herself neglecting her terminally ill mother's medical needs in order to expedite her death, are the basis of the story. These thoughts are turned into a story by the observant captain of the ship on which they are travelling. The displaced tale of morality and mortality serves to set Averill free from the guilt of inventing such a scenario. The captain, in adopting the tale under the guise of a true story and telling it himself, literalizes the need of the mourner to displace the experience and to transform the experience into story; Averill, as the captain's audience, listens to and transforms the tale, and enacts a work of mourning in the process.

It is a relief to Averill that such stories of questionable morality could be told, and told "safely."[16] This story is a gift from the captain (an ambiguous figure who, in his professional capacity, is able both to marry and to bury people at sea). It is an offering that absolves Averill (179), but it raises uncomfortable questions in the reader's mind about private and sometimes disturbing reactions to loss – reactions such as relief. Munro, like the captain telling Averill's story, has "left off the finale" (178) to "Goodness and Mercy." In this and other stories the reader is "left" to "finalize" the "accidental clarity"[17] that is the moral of the story, the morality of mourning, or the ethics of elegy. The reader of Munro's fiction is implicated in her gestures of interpreting and inventing the past and in the creation of a vision of the past in the present. Consolation acquired in the reconstructive process is a kind of knowledge or truth, modelled on the epiphanic moment(s) of the fictional text. The truth thus attained is not absolute but is, rather, an understanding of narrative ritual or story-telling as a potentially useful method of mourning. The epiphanic, queer, bright moments of Munro's texts thus serve to illumi-

nate the emotional and intellectual capacity of the reader and invite
us to recognize the underlying ethics and efficacy of elegy.

TELLING TALES: THE TERMS OF LOSS IN *THE MOONS OF JUPITER*

The framing stories of *The Moons of Jupiter* are about loss and lineage,
tracing the genealogy of the Chaddeleys and the Flemings; but they
are also about the potential of art to console the mourning mind.
They constitute a work in terms of both the emotional and aesthetic
connotations of the phrase "work of mourning"; the narrator works
through the grieving process and also produces the textual versions
of the experience in the form of the narrative itself. They are self-
conscious in their focus on themselves as fictive constructs and in
the narrator's search for an appropriate form within which to fulfil
both artistic and psychological purposes. Psychopoesis is foregrounded, then. The focus of these stories is on both the behaviour of the
human mind and the language of mourning, and Munro experiments with methods of rendering aesthetically that mourning mind.

The title story, which is the open-ended end-frame of the book (in
terms of closure and structure, respectively), opens with the line "I
found my father in the heart wing, on the eighth floor of Toronto
General Hospital."[18] This speaker finds her father in more ways
than one; that he is in the heart wing suggests metaphorically that
an emotional quest is being undertaken, despite the flat, detached
tone of the narration. "The behaviour of his heart was on display,"
she reports clinically, though the behaviour of *her* heart is displayed
in more subtle terms through the form of her elegy. Thinking of her
father's physical condition becomes analogous to meditating upon
"issues of the human condition."[19] The meditation on the universality of death and loss, often a trope of consolation in elegy, serves to
divert the narrator's attention from the immediate crisis. Ildikó de
Papp Carrington states that "the story is not so much about what
Janet gains in perspective as about what she loses from her life,"[20]
and while loss does form the focus of the story, the narrator-elegist
meditates on her own mortality too, since her father is not only her
predecessor but her "pre-deceasor," so to speak.

He is her predecessor in another way as well: she is his appren-
tice, inheriting his interest in story, his pleasure in poetry – though
that pleasure is somehow shameful and needs to be "excuse[d]"
(225); it is implied that decorum must be upheld, and the narrator
adopts this tenet in her own story-telling as well. Her father quotes
poetry and remembers the phrase "shoreless seas" (from Joacquin

Miller's "Columbus") only when his daughter walks into his room. It is suggested implicitly that he has the need to understand his situation in poetic terms, as does his daughter; though "shoreless seas" are indeed what lie ahead, the refrain of the poem is an affirmative "Sail on! Sail on! and on!"

The father becomes a raconteur while in hospital, relating details of his life to his daughter by way of family anecdotes. When he mentions a "fact" about his father (220), she is reminded of his history as "the escaped child, the survivor" (220), the story he told of himself in "The Stone in the Field" (29). This story-telling makes the narrator "less resigned to his dying" (219), since she identifies with him at these moments more than any other. We hear his voice, posthumously, in the narrator's version of the story; since she has inherited her gift from her father, he is given voice again in her act of telling his tales again.

Munro suggests proleptically that the living voice of the dead might literally exist when the father himself discusses patients who survived an operation after their hearts had stopped. He says that "there was a series running [in the paper] on personal experiences of people who had died, medically speaking – heart arrest, mostly – and had been brought back to life. It was what they remembered of the time when they were dead. Their experiences" (226). But he resists the "great temptation to – well, to make a mystery" out of the unexplainable. This is Janet's dilemma as well: what balance between fact and fiction, explanation and mystery is needed in order to arrive at peace of mind? Her father detaches himself from the subject and from his daughter by turning to fact, saying, "There's a few practical details we ought to get straight on," including his will, the house, and the cemetery plot (226–7). Emotional responses to the thoughts of his own death obviously make both him and his daughter uncomfortable, and the after-life alluded to is so tenuous a form of consolation that the issue is abandoned before it is explored.

The narrator-elegist does bring her father back to life analeptically, and draws closer to him, with the telling of the story; she gives him a voice again. In "Connection" ("Chaddeleys and Flemings," part 1), Janet finds that "life is transformed by th[e] voices, th[e] presences" of her mother's cousins (18), and here too, by recalling her father's voice (a metonymy of presence) and voicing it herself in the telling of the story, the narrator transforms her understanding of him and of her relationship to him. In the process of telling she is able to get over *her* heart failure, her "hardened" heart (219), which prevented her from listening to the stories of regret her father had told her over the years. She took care with her father "not to feel anything much ... because you have to survive," which is how she describes her reaction to her infant daughter's suspected leukemia years before (230). This blunt statement about the instinct to survive disturbs a perhaps commonly held belief that a mother (or daughter) should not be capable of such a reaction, but Munro dismantles such pretensions by showing us very human, very real situations and by disallowing her characters sentiment and false consolation.

This is a necessarily retrospective story, and Munro has ordered the anecdotes and revelations in a seemingly haphazard way. But this textual organization is an imitation of the mind of the narrator, who makes connections between past and present experiences and emotions. The repetition of the tale of her father's childhood escape (first told in the first framing story [29–30]) limits the linear progression of the story-line; his death is deferred, delayed, and the elegy becomes cyclical, without closure. It is through the structure of the story that Munro allows grief to emanate from the detached, recitative voice that needs to speak in order to console herself for a still-unspoken loss. The reader, perhaps, is as unprepared for the emotional response of the narrator when she does listen to her father, and feels "an appalling rush of love and recognition" (226). The cathartic experience allows her to compare the man who had always been "the survivor" to the "old man trapped here by his leaky heart" (220).

The telling of this story about her father and her father's family background is an example of the general human need to comprehend the world through story. Personal myth-making parallels a culture's efforts to name and to mythologize its experience. And in "The Moons of Jupiter" the solar system – named for mythological gods – figures prominently as both the title and several scenes suggest. The trip to the planetarium, which involves the narrator's own "brief death" (233), foreshadows her father's death and prompts her to ask him in a child-like voice, "Tell me the moons of Jupiter." "The moons of Jupiter were the first heavenly bodies discovered with the telescope," her father begins (232). His genealogical list of the planets is a gift to his daughter, who is a writer, just as the detail of the lace curtains had been a gift in "The Stone in the Field" (32).

Her father is Jupiter in the narrator's elegiac reconstruction of their relationship: the god of all men, father of all. The "heavenly bodies" are, perhaps, a parody of the traditional consoling trope of apotheosis. The list includes, importantly, a confusion over the role of Ganymede in the lunar system: "A shepherd?" he offers at first (and Munro may here be evoking the pastoral elegy); he corrects himself, however, and in his last words to his daughter he calls out, "Ganymede wasn't any shepherd. He was Jove's cupbearer." The daughter too is Jove's "cupbearer," the inheritor, the one to continue the family "line" both bodily and in terms of her writing the lines of the story. The story is figured in "the line his heart was writing" on the electrocardiogram equipment he was hooked up to (228); the elegy is a translation of his heart-lines and her own, demarcating her bloodline both figuratively and literally in the form of a text.

The narrator plays the role of Saturn, with its "icy rings," as she describes her vision of it in the planetarium. The star of Saturn (the god is turned into a star in ancient Roman mythology) has been associated with melancholy since the later Middle Ages;[21] in the pathology of humours the colour associated with it is black, and the element is earth, which is "cold and dry" (128). In this astrological allegory, which parallels her father's elegy, Saturn is quite literally situated next to Jupiter. Saturn is also the god of agriculture – of fertility, of produce, of creativity (134). Saturn is the poetic inheritor, then, the lunar equivalent of Pan the pipe god and his pastoral descendants. As the pattern of the melancholic story unfolds, it imitates the "innumerable repetitions, innumerable variations" within the *mise en abyme* of galaxies ("The Moons of Jupiter" 231).

But this *mise en abyme* structure of the universe disconcerts the narrator, who feels more comfortable when "realism [is] abandoned, for familiar artifice" (231) – in the form of a model for the solar system at the planetarium. Though the narrator distrusts its potential to falsify reality, to "play tricks" on us (she prefers the children's perspective of focusing on surfaces to the planetarium voice explaining the "horrible immensities" of the universe), she also depends on story-telling as a process that might lead us to truths about the human condition. In Munro's poetics realism alone is deemed an inaccurate method for representing the world and our experiences in it; she suggests that the quest for absolute precision may actually falsify reality, whereas artifice may serve to clarify or illuminate to a greater extent. A consoling mental fiction or model – one that parallels that of the solar system she admires – is inscribed in the narrator's story. The story is her artifact, based on memory but transformed to fiction. Pure fact is abandoned as an artistic dead-end in terms of elegiac consolation: it cannot explain the unknown that is death.

In its place the art Munro strives for is what Blodgett describes as "a mode of discourse that demonstrates that the problem of life, death, loss and recuperation must pass into the telling. This suggests," he continues, "that fiction itself might be a kind of fraud, a magic act and an act of faith that obscures a truth."[22] But for Munro this magic act does not obscure truth; rather, it is revelatory. The re-membered past may be always a "blur," as the narrator of the title story notes (and as the rendering of her own past suggests), but the truths of our necessary fictions may be retained and contained within that blur once memory is turned to story.

In Munro's fiction-elegies the attempt to provide consolation through artifice is an attempt to supersede the limitations of the world of fact – the world to which death does not quite belong. The narrator of "The Turkey Season" states: "I would still like to know things. Never mind facts," (74), implying that fact will only provide the desired knowledge when transformed to that *other* kind of knowledge: story. In some ways any form of consolation (whether religious, philosophical or artistic) is a fiction and the comfort found therein is an imagined knowledge. So the narrator discovers in "The Stone in the Field." Her desire to see the stone,[23] the absent grave-marker for a strange family neighbour, is stronger than the desire to see gravestones of her paternal aunts (who lived all their lives in their childhood home near, significantly, Mount Hebron – the namesake of the location of Jacob's family burial ground in the Old Testament). While the latter marker is relatively uninteresting, "a modest pillar with all their names and dates on it, a couple of dates of death filled in" (31), the mysterious stone in the corner of the field across the road from her father's family – an object unconnected with fact – becomes a source of fascination that develops, signifi-cantly, only after her father has died (32).

The narrator reads (in a microfilmed newspaper) that the farm's hermit, Mr Black, took "the mystery of his life with him" (33). His life and death stand contiguously for the life and death of her father, who remains mysterious, unknowable. On finding the stone absent, the narrator realizes that it would have been a marker to which only she would impart meaning; that as an absence it is an even more ap-propriate sign, signifying the ultimate absence: death. If the stone is an emblem of melancholy and a heavy heart, as Walter Benjamin writes,[24] then the absent stone is an even more "readable ruin" – a *rune* – because it allows and requires her to "figure out" a story from the remains, from reminders and remainders of people including Mr Black and her relatives. The narrator distinguishes between different kinds of stories she might have told about the man: she rejects the romantic invention of a relationship between Mr Black and an aunt; she rejects the opposite extreme of finding "a horrible, plausible" explanation for his history; and "now," she tells us, "I no longer be-lieve that people's secrets are defined and communicable." The truth is found somewhere between these extremes of fantasy and fact, then, in fiction. The telling of "The Stone in the Field" itself is the model of mourning provided for the reader as well, who figures grief in the process of reconstructing the events in the narrative.

In fiction-elegy such as "The Moons of Jupiter" and "The Stone in the Field" Munro writes testaments to the impossibility and undesirability of writing factually about the past. But even though "the boulder is gone,"[25] as is her father, the narrator is still able to "carry something" of her dead relatives with her (35).[26] What she carries is memory, recorded in a digressive, open-ended narrative structure; though memory is unreliable, the story-telling that it produces is as close to truth – and to reconstructing (or re-presenting) both the past and her father's presence – as possible.

In "Connection" (part 1 of "Chaddeleys and Flemings") the narrator tells a story about her story-telling "mother and her cousins" (2). Despite the importance of connections in this and its companion story ("The Stone in the Field"), Munro writes in the vein of Benjamin's story-teller: "The most extraordinary things, marvelous things, are related with the greatest accuracy, but the psychological connection of the events is not forced on the reader."[27]

The story begins with a list of names and identities and a narrative version of a map marking the route taken to arrive in Dalgleish; it proceeds to list the "unpacking of presents," the thought of which seems to be a Proustian remembrance of things past: "In the wintertime I would sometimes go into the cold dining room and sniff at the cups, inhaling their smell of artifice and luxury" (3). Though Proust divided memory into voluntary and involuntary types and claimed that "recovery of the past [was] a matter of chance," as Ackbar Abbas notes, Benjamin's notion that the ritual of story-telling summons involuntary recollection is applicable to the narrator's act in "Connection."[28]

Abbas also discusses Benjamin's notions of *Erlebnis*, experience that the consciousness holds in a specific time, and *Erfahrung*, experience that is not located specifically in time. In Munro's queer, bright moments, it could be argued, her narrators translate the former to the latter form of "memory," making them epiphanically eternal, atemporal, and repeatable. The ambiguity of these moments creates what Benjamin would call "the pictorial image of dialectics, the law of dialectics seen at a standstill. This standstill is utopia and the dialectic image therefore a dream image."[29]

In "Connection" the narrative that contains details of the cousins' visit and of their family history is punctuated with "queer, bright moments" of varying degree, which put the story in temporal disarray. The story is a matriarchal map (of the Chaddeley line), as

"The Stone in the Field" and "The Moons of Jupiter" are, I have argued, fictive versions of the patriarchal line. This genealogical focus is emphasized by the embedded stories about Janet's great-grandfather. Her mother and the cousins who visit talk about their grandfather with great pleasure, and the narrator – in retelling their tellings and in revealing the true history of the family tree – comes to her own conclusions: "at one time," she admits, she would have refused to believe the facts; later she would have been "triumphant" to have torn away all illusions; at the time of the news she did not care (10). What she thinks at the time of the telling is understood only implicitly: she is telling a story about her family history, and is interpreting as she tells.

Both parts of "Chaddeleys and Flemings" are fiction-elegies for relatives to whom the narrator is physically and emotionally "connected," and both test the limits of the ability of story to console by connecting life and art in a version of the "real truth" (6). This "real truth" is most often found by the retrospective re-evaluation of interpretations of personal history, which produces surprising revisions of the past. These moments of surprise have a cumulative effect. The first is induced by the mere report that "once they decided to sing a round" followed by the lyrics to "Row, row, row your boat" (4). The second is the narrator's recognition that stories about the cousins' "selfish and wilful grandfather" (8) gave them a sense of "possession," which "continued to delight them" (9), though this recognition is a retrospective one: "I couldn't understand this, at the time or later," we are told (9). But clearly the narrator understands the paradoxical sense of both shame and pride in one's family at the time of writing this story.

The third bright moment is evoked for the narrator upon the visit of cousin Iris to the house she lives in with her husband Richard; it is achieved by recollecting "that memorable visit" with which the story begins (13), and it leads to a *mise en abyme* of memory, through which the narrator recollects her *mother* recollecting that visit. The centre of this epiphany provides the narrator with a picture of her mother's "bright shadow," as Barthes would say.[30] Her question, "What did I do?" (13), allows the narrator to remind her mother of the stunt that she performed with the cousins – she stood on her head.

The narrator's stunt is the written progression from the position of not understanding the necessity of story-telling, to one of disbelief in the banality of the truth, to one where "all false notions, all illusions" had to be torn away so that she could be "triumphant" in such banality (10), and finally to one where "life is transformed, by these voices" in her memory, by "these presences" (18). First, and symbolically, she throws a pie plate – lemon meringue, like her mother made for the cousins – at her critical husband, who wanted his wife to be "amputated" from her past altogether. In throwing her past *at* Richard, Janet is also reclaiming it for herself. The story ends with the queerest, brightest moment of all, as the narrator writes in the present tense: "I lie in bed beside my little sister, listening to the singing in the yard" (18). The lyrics to "Row, row, row your boat" are again embedded in the narrative, but this time the words *are* the voices of her dead mother's dead cousins, providing her with an insight, just as their personalities had provided her with another window on the world (16):

The mixture of voices and words is so complicated and varied it seems that such confusion, such jolly rivalry, will go on forever, and then to my surprise ... the song is thinning out, you can hear the two voices striving.
    Merrily, merrily, merrily, merrily,
    Life is but a dream.
    Then the one voice alone, one of them singing on, gamely, to the finish.   (18)

In this "dream image" the last voice – surviving after the mother's death – is that of Iris.[31] The epiphanic moment is produced by this remembered confusion and its subsequent surprise as it is re-experienced in the "mixture of voices and words." This is the narrator's mixture of memory and song, which parallels Munro's mixture of narrative and elegiac lyric.

The reader is directed in responding to this epiphany: "*Life is*. Wait. *But a*. Now, wait. *Dream*" (18). The last word is almost an order: we are to "dream," to transform life, so that it might "go on forever" as, it seems to the narrator, the song itself might. The descending notes of this song counter the meaning of the word "merrily" – the last line, especially with the musical pauses inscribed in the narrative, sounds like a sigh; the aesthetic consolation in the queer, bright moment contains, like the song, "an unexpected note of entreaty, of warning" (18). Indeed, the warning "*hangs* the five separate words on the air" (18, emphasis mine). Munro entreats us not to separate life and art, not to reject the real in favour of the aesthetic, but instead to use one to illuminate the other. Those queer, bright moments – born of recognizing both the relation *and* the differences between art and life, and the importance of envisioning a dialectical relation between them – transform our experience of both.

In "Visitors" Wilfred is a writer-figure, someone who transforms reality into story; his brother Albert, in contrast, can neither tell a story nor recognize the difference between story and fact. Wilfred and Mildred are visited by Wilfred's brother Albert (who, it is implied, is dying), Albert's wife, and her sister. The two brothers do not share a common past, since Wilfred was raised (until age twelve) by an aunt after their mother's death; they take opposite approaches to the past as well. Mildred thinks: "In Wilfred's stories you could always be sure that the gloomy parts would give way to something better, and if somebody behaved in a peculiar way there was an explanation for it. If Wilfred figured in his own stories, as he usually did, there was always a stroke of luck for him somewhere" (215). Wilfred tells versions of the past – he "figures" it, and therefore invents some of it, though he believes in this past (212).

Albert, on the other hand, refuses story-telling – he is unaware that the facts he tells about Lloyd Sallows, the swamp-dweller, compose a story: "It's not a story. It's something that happened," he insists (215). Albert cannot figure the past, nor read its necessarily "figured" accounts in any way, except by taking the figurative literally. His method of writing the past is uninteresting to Mildred, since it lacks "some kind of ending" (215); she requires that an enlightening "turn," a trope of consolation, be provided. During a road trip in search of the brothers' birthplace (209) her imperative statement, "Watch for the turn, Wilfred" (209), is a direction to the reader as well. Albert knows precisely where the turn is – he can even trace "the outline of the house" where it used to stand (212) – but he fails to "turn" facts of the past into any kind of narrative with fictional truth. His memory, for example, of taking his mother's coffin through the front door is told in flat statements, evidently devoid of any emotion (212).

Munro does not always provide consoling turns in her fiction, and "Visitors" ends without an ending; Wilfred cries about the unlikelihood of ever seeing his brother again (216) – at least this is the reason he gives Mildred. Though Mildred thinks (to herself) that this is "only distantly connected to the real reason," Wilfred's stated reason is "as close as he could get" to the truth – perhaps because the deeper grief – one that is connected somehow to Albert and the loss of each other as children in the past – is too painful to approach except from a distance. A figuration of the past, a narrativized version or story, produces the necessary distance and allows the "gloomy parts [to] give way to something better," as Wilfred's stories do. Wilfred, too, has yet to distance himself from his childhood loss of

Albert to the extent of being able to "story" or figure the past in a work of mourning.

With her elegiac rhetoric Munro juxtaposes past and present, providing the reader with an image of the past and indicating the importance of its translation into story in the present. For example, the characters, in their dialogue, combine comments about the past with ordinary conversation in the present: Wilfred does this in telling his Soo story (the past) amidst questions about and responses to directions he is given on the drive (the present, 210); Mildred identifies a lilac bush on the site of the ancestral home (the present) and asks a question about the original location of its front door (the past, 212). Albert does not see these connections and will not confuse past and present in this way, and the reader, in contrasting the two brothers (who seem to have "no connection" [212]), clearly is aligned with Mildred's wish for a happy ending. Munro suggests that we take this "direction," this "turn" down the road, but she also questions the limits of this act of troping, ending the story with a queer, sad moment.

The ability of art to console is also a central issue in "Dulse." Klaus P. Stich relates Munro's title to D.C. Scott's poem "Dulse Gathering."[32] For Scott dulse "holds the soul of the tide" and "brings the sea into the pulse," allowing "memories lone on the heart [to be] hurled" (13–17). Similarly, for Lydia the image of dulse provokes memories that take the form of story, the telling of which brings her "into the pulse" of life again after a period of mourning. Munro has said that "Dulse" is "about the ways people discover for getting through life."[33] Lydia, a poet, is learning to read events in her life, and compares her reaction to those events and griefs to the "durable shelter" that Mr Stanley constructs (59).

Mr Stanley does not "do any reading or writing beyond what is necessary," he tells Lydia (40). Since he is a non-reader, then, his vision and version of life are immediately suspect. He values what he believes is an artist's knowledge, which is inherently separate from the real world: "She [Willa Cather] knew things as an artist knows them. Not necessarily by experience," he states (57), an attitude that Lydia immediately calls into question: "But what if they don't know them? ... What if they don't?" (57) Lydia sees the relation between fact and fiction to be much less clear than does Mr Stanley. Since Lydia is an artist and has very few answers herself, she rejects the "durable shelter" of "layers of dull knowledge, well protected" (50); she recognizes the limits of Mr Stanley's perceptions yet admits that "the day *may* come when [she] will count herself lucky to do the same" – to believe in false fictions (59, emphasis mine). This self-revelation – that, for now at least, being "up and down" is preferable to building a consoling, stable, yet false fiction – occurs in Lydia's queer, bright moment.

Munro's narrative techniques imitate Lydia's mental highs and lows, leading the reader up and down in a quest for the epiphanic answer to such questions as "whose reality is real?" and "whose fictions are consoling?" The story also contains a great many interrogatives, indicating the difficulty of arriving at the (perhaps multiple) answers as well as suggesting the value of the process of questioning itself.[34] The many questions Lydia asks of herself[35] also parallel the questions her psychiatrist asks her, some of which are embedded in a segment of the story about Lydia's past (53–6). Lydia explicitly questions the value of questioning: "Do you think it helps to ask these questions?" (55) – a rhetorical remark that the form of the story itself answers in the affirmative.

The story demonstrates Lydia's reaction to the loss of her relationship with Duncan, who is an historical writer (43) facetiously named "the Tin Wood-man" by a friend of Lydia's (49).[36] His matter-of-fact way of reading life and of writing the past contrasts with Lydia's emotional roller-coaster ride. The gaps between segments of the story also take the reader back and forth between Lydia's recent past and narrative present. Munro images Lydia's ways of "getting through life"[37] as metonymic segments: "She set little blocks on top of one another and she had a day" (36); by connecting the blocks of narrative that portray these days, Munro represents Lydia's work of mourning.

Ironically, Lydia arrives at consolation by accepting the condition of *not* knowing, of living adventurously. Explanations have become mere habit for her, and though they may provide what seem to be answers, in fact "what she says [early in the story] ... doesn't help her. She might just as well cover her head and sit wailing on the ground" (50). In mourning for Duncan, she gradually works through memories of her relationship in order to achieve a more trustworthy understanding of what has happened to her. Her first memory of Duncan is of his asking a question in a bookstore: "Lydia heard him saying that it must be difficult to know where to shelve *The Persian Letters*. Should it be classed as fiction or as a political essay? Lydia felt that he revealed something, saying this. He revealed a need that she supposed was common to customers in the bookstore, a need to distinguish himself, appear knowledgeable" (49). Though arrogant, Duncan is at least aware of the problems involved in differentiating between fact and fiction, whereas Lydia, at this point in the story, is not.

Lydia is a sceptical mourner; she is unclear about the power and the limits of knowledge acquired through fictional constructs. "The worst thing is not knowing what is true about any of this. I spend all my waking hours trying to *figure out* about him and me and I get nowhere. I make wishes. I even pray. I throw money into those wishing wells," she admits to her therapist before breaking up with Duncan (55, emphasis mine). Her own "figur[ing] out" of their relationship, however, had been based on "an idea of love which is ruinous" (55) – on a false fiction, on a love that had been too much invention and reinvention (52) and not on "the truth about what she wanted and needed," on more "tender-hearted fantasies" (52). It is this balance of truth and fiction, and the possibility of a fictional truth, that interests Munro in these stories of loss.

Lydia is learning to read signs and signals both from Duncan and within herself, so that her figuration is an imaginative revision of the past that rings true in the present. A character less capable of such change is Prue, in the story named for her. In "Prue" the kleptomaniacal protagonist is completely incapable of reading signs; Prue cannot even read her own motives, and "more or less forgets" about the objects she has stolen from various people. To her, we are told, they are "not sentimental keepsakes" and "don't have ritualistic significance" (133) – they do not signify anything, in other words. Clearly, Munro is demonstrating that these objects *do* have some kind of talismanic quality, though Prue, on one level, will not allow herself to read them as such. Her denial of language is accomplished in terms of both memory and signs, and as a result she does not need to confront the potential pain involved in interpreting the actions of others – especially those of her lover, who rejects her. In Munro's poetics of elegy a non-reader such as Prue is also a non-mourner in that she is incapable of coming to terms with loss.

Lydia, also rejected by her lover, does interpret and find significance in words as well as in objects or tokens, and she becomes a better reader by the end of the story. At the end of "Dulse" the reader is told that the gift (of dulse) from a man named Vincent has a literal effect on Lydia: the "present slyly warmed her, from a distance" (59). By talking with Mr Stanley of Willa Cather's life, Lydia consolidates what she has been gradually learning throughout her working-through[38] of grief: that false fictions, such as the one she had constructed and believed in regarding herself and Duncan, are inadequate and potentially destructive.

Vincent, the dulse-eater, is connected to those "tender-hearted fantasies" in Lydia's mind because he is the one person who offers her a gift. As a displacement of Duncan (whose rejection of love closes doors and damages Lydia), Vincent allows Lydia to "foresee doors opening, to what she knew and had forgotten; rooms and landscapes opening; *there*" (52). Her consolation arrives from a distance, then, since Vincent is a fantasy figure for her, but also because he evokes distant truths about the potential of love that will sustain Lydia during her recovery. Munro's aesthetic of elegy consists of this careful use of fictions that have the potential for an inherent, consoling truth.

"Bardon Bus" both names a thirteen-part fragmented work of memory, variously painful and consoling, and evokes, for the unnamed narrator, "a whole succession of scenes" (112) of a time she has spent with *her* ex-lover, "X." The narrator states that "using just the letter, not needing a name, is in line with a system I often employ these days," (112), a system that produces variously useful epiphanies. A think-act such as this provides a form of consolation by analeptically resurrecting the absent figure. The use of a letter in place of the man's name also contributes to the impression that "Bardon Bus" is a puzzle for the reader to piece together.

The story opens with an unusual flash-forward fantasy of a "lifelong dream-life" based on an unsatisfied need for love. The fantasy presents the reader with the narrator's secret imagination; yet it is set in a *past* time – "I think of being an old maid, in another generation. There were plenty of old maids in my family" (110) – such that Munro implicitly compares the function of fantasy with that of memory and thereby demonstrates that both are fictive constructs. But for a contemporary woman such as the narrator this kind of dream-life or pure illusion could not provide adequate consolation for lost love, and in the process of telling the story she is released from her painful illusions about her ex-lover.

Munro contrasts this fantasy with the textual present in the next section of the story; though most sections begin with a statement in the present tense, in charting the movement of the narrator's mind they do not stay there. Temporally, the sections of "Bardon Bus" move in and out of the narrative present, which is set in "this summer" (111), as the unnamed narrator reconstructs different scenes of the past, a reconstruction that initially provides consolation: "I filled the space quickly with memories of his voice, looks, warmth, our scenes together. I was swimming in memories, at first. Those detailed, repetitive scenes were what buoyed me up" (123).

The narrator, in the act of thinking through these scenes, pieces them together in a story about herself and X that is an attempt to resurrect "the story of their days," to paraphrase the poem by Sir Walter Raleigh that "go[es] through" her head (122). But the story, like Lydia's early fictional perception of her relationship with Duncan, is based on the "lie" that "it's been perfect," as she begins to realize (123). Her friend Kay describes a scene she has read about that is written in the journals of (she guesses) Victor Hugo's daughter; the woman, obsessed with a man for years, "passes him in the street and she either doesn't recognize him or she does but she can't connect the real man any more with the person she loves, in her head" (117).[39]

This analogy between love and art – both of which are fictional constructs, to a certain extent at least – is one often drawn by Munro. The narrator's belief that "misplacement is the clue, in love, the heart of the problem" (128) is an acknowledgment of the fictive element in relationships, and in recognizing this truth (near the end of the story), the narrator performs a think-act that produces a kind of consolation. The difference between our need for fictions of "permanent vistas" and our knowledge that life is instead "contradictory and persistent and unaccommodating" (128) – the two forces that are "at war" within us – is finally understood by the narrator. In recovering, the re-placement of the narrator's "misplacement" is required. It is a kind of renaming of her relationship in the light of an epiphanic understanding of her experience.

The final think-act induces a partially consoling epiphany because it is a revelation about the perception of reality and the fictions that misplace it:

When you start really letting go this is what it's like. A lick of pain, furtive, darting up where you don't expect it. Then a lightness. The lightness is something to think about. It isn't just relief. There's a queer kind of pleasure in it, not a self-wounding or malicious pleasure, nothing personal at all. It's an uncalled-for pleasure in seeing how the design wouldn't fit and the structure wouldn't stand, a pleasure in taking into account, all over again, everything that is contradictory and persistent and unaccommodating about life. I think so.   (128)

This queer, bright moment for the narrator is also a commentary on the structure of this kind of fiction-elegy: though there is "a limit to the amount of misery and disarray you will put up with, for love" (127), the attempt to arrange the past in a story that is structured on only a fantasy level merely contributes to the disarray.

This revelation regarding the use and abuse of fiction is similar to the epiphany of the narrator in "Hard-Luck Stories," who is "stumped by a truth about [her]self" (197): "I felt something go over me – a shadow, a chastening. I heard the silly sound of my own voice against the truth of the lives laid down here [in the grave-yard]" (196). Fiction-elegy must accommodate the truth of our lives, then, in order to enable us to build a structure that *will* hold, and console.

Though her fiction involves "the fight against death," Munro's approach is not to sentimentalize the subject(s) of loss and mourning; rather, she figures grief in the form of fiction-elegy and suggests that "the fact of death" might be accommodated within life and within our fictions without false consolation. The reader is invited to participate in this fight and to evaluate various reconstructions of the past for their capacity both to achieve a fictional truth and to provide a model of mourning that might find a place in "real life."[40] Munro charts the movements of a mind in mourning, a mind in motion, reconsidering the past and its relation to the present so that memory is not a trap but something that can be learned from. Her narrators and characters perform their "figuring out" in the act of story-telling.

Of the significance of this process Munro states: "There are just flashes of things we know and find out ... We think we've got things figured out and then they turn around on us. No state of mind is permanent."[41] And like Gallant's "light of imagination," Munro's works of mourning are figured such that the reader sees a series of "flashes" and acquires consoling insights that are intermittent and impermanent. Thus her stories contain not a single epiphanic consolation but what Munro refers to as "lots of periods of happiness," the source of which, she insists, is "curiosity" – the desire to learn from and about both life and death. "Absences," she notes in this context, "certainly interest me a lot. Loss, which everyone experiences all the time ... we keep losing ourselves and the worlds we used to live in. Whether this is more a factor in modern life, I don't know. But I think maybe it is."[42]

6 Forms of Loss: Contemporary Fiction-Elegy

In this study I have argued that Mavis Gallant and Alice Munro have adapted conventions of elegy within fictional frameworks, a practice refined by modernist fiction-elegists such as Virginia Woolf and James Joyce. A digressive structure, the focus on the self (on the narrator-elegist or character-elegist as survivor), and a tendency towards self-reflexivity are characteristics of both modern and late modern fiction-elegies. But where Woolf and Joyce employ self-reflexivity as a trope of consolation and suggest that the work of art is an immortal and idealized product achieved at the end of the work of mourning, Gallant and Munro use that trope as a point of departure for the exploration of the *process* of writing and of mourning. Thus in the late modern development of the fiction-elegy from its modernist predecessors, the emphasis in Freud's phrase "the work of mourning" shifts from the idea of a work (an object) to that of work as a narrative act.

In the course of studying the fiction-elegies of Gallant and Munro I have also theorized the sub-genre of fiction-elegy. Consequently, I have not only offered readings of the works of these two authors but also suggested that the reading process – through which the mourning process is enacted or performed – is figured in the very form and language of the fiction-elegies themselves. The mourners within the texts narrativize the process, one that is repeated by the reader in reconstructive acts. Gallant places the reader in a position of judgment to review the past with an eye to the ethical use of memory; Munro invites a collusive reading, a participatory witnessing that involves an "ethics of seeing." In some ways, then, the aims of modernist elegists would fall into category of the aesthetic realm, the late modernists into the ethical, wherein the reader is directed to assume a moral perspective on the model of mourning presented within and by the text.

The reader of fiction-elegy creates a mental model of mourning, thereby transforming the text into a parallel plausible text through an effort of mimpathic engagement. The consolation acquired in the reconstructive process is a kind of knowledge or truth modelled on the epiphanic moment(s) of the fictional text. The truth thus attained is not absolute but is, rather, an understanding of narrative ritual as a potentially useful method of mourning. Both authors seem to seek what might be called a fictional truth, one that acknowledges the difference between fact and fiction but also the impossibility of achieving pure truth in the medium of language. But neither Gallant nor Munro is willing to abandon the attempt, either, and in this sense they are quite different from their postmodern contemporaries whose frequent aim is to subvert the conventions of writing, often in parodic ways, in order to expose as illusory the differences between fiction and truth (or fiction and history), language and reality. Though a study of postmodern elegy is not feasible here, it might be suggested that postmodern elegists mourn not only our political and social conditions but also realism (in metafictive terms); a linguistic consolation or alternative is often found in versions of fantasy, in other worlds that critique our own.

These worlds of language – "tropological worlds," as Brian McHale describes them[1] – constitute the thematic and structuring principles of postmodern texts, and thus the models of mourning as developed by modern and late modern writers are often abandoned for what Julia Kristeva calls "the heartrending distraction of parody."[2] E.L. Doctorow's *The Book of Daniel*, Donald Barthelme's *The Dead Father*, Thomas Pynchon's *The Crying of Lot 49*, John Barth's *The Sot-Weed Factor* all might be considered variations of postmodern fiction-elegy. (*Finnegans Wake*, though chronologically a modernist text, would also fall into this category of the postmodern elegy.[3]) These texts subvert realist conventions while also admitting to what Linda Hutcheon calls "the important postmodern concept of 'the presence of the past.' " Central to that concept is "a critical reworking [of the past], never a nostalgic 'return,' "[4] and this reworking involves recalling the past through parody as well as irony – techniques that implicitly question the very past they evoke as well as the discourses that are used to accomplish such evocations.

The "presence of the past" is a defining characteristic of all fiction-elegies; but the modern and late modern narrative models of mourning – like all narrative models, systems, and structures – are subject to revision and even rejection by postmodern writers, who tend critically to disclaim the potential for any consoling truth to be found in fiction. My theoretical argument concerning the efficacy of late modern elegy provides a working model for the interpretation of Gallant's and Munro's revisions of the past, and of their visions of the past in the present. It also offers a framework for the interpretation of other late modern contemporary fiction-elegies, of which there is a considerable corpus.

As Peter Sacks notes in his epilogue to *The English Elegy*, there is an abundance of elegies in contemporary letters. Sacks concludes that ours is "a distinctly elegiac age."[5] Kristeva attributes the cause of this literary condition to the events of the Second World War, the spectacles of which, she argues, damaged "our systems of perception and representation."[6] The agenda of elegiac fiction includes the attempt to find an appropriate mode of mourning, an appropriate language with which to conduct the work of mourning, whether it be for a personal or a public loss.

Analysis of three other contemporary late (as opposed to post-) modern writers from three different countries – Marguerite Duras, Edmund White, and Edna O'Brien – will serve both to re-emphasize the theoretical premises of fiction-elegy and to extend the usefulness of my interpretive framework. Though esteemed, these three authors have been, it seems, critically neglected. Their work shares many of the elements of elegy exhibited by the work of Gallant and Munro. The novels of Marguerite Duras and the novel of Edmund White considered here are brief, novella-like, and the thematic and linguistic parallels between these texts and those of Gallant will become evident. The short stories of Edna O'Brien institute epiphanic, queer, bright moments as do those of Munro. My intent here, as in the introductory chapter, is not to develop an argument of influence nor to provide a detailed comparative study, but to demonstrate with close readings of three exemplary authors the prevalence of fiction-elegy in late modern writing.

WRITING AND RECOVERY: MARGUERITE DURAS, EDMUND WHITE, AND EDNA O'BRIEN

In *Black Sun: Depression and Melancholia* Julia Kristeva writes that "the practice of Marguerite Duras" constitutes "a confrontation with Valery's 'nothing' – a 'nothing' that is thrust upon a perturbed consciousness by the horror of the Second World War and independently but in similar fashion by the individual's psychic unease due to the secret impacts of biology, the family, the others."[7] Kristeva's chapter on Duras originally appeared as an article, and its translation suggests that "the others" are "interpersonal calamities."[8] Thus Duras's agenda is, it would seem, very similar to Gallant's elegiac project. Both authors are interested in the relationship between (historical) political and personal issues, and in the effects of abandonment on the psyche; both seek a form of representation in which the "unsayable" may be signified.

Sharon Willis states that, for Duras, separation and death are the unrepresentable.[9] Abandonment and death are thematically paralleled in the fiction-elegies that Duras writes, and *The Ravishing of Lol V. Stein* in particular exemplifies this parallel. Lol's loss, suffered through abandonment and a witnessed, public betrayal by her fiancé, is the cause of her interminable mourning, her "split subjectivity." Jacques Lacan provides an interesting word-play in suggesting that Lol must at some level say "Je me deux," which is an archaic form of "I feel sorrow" as well as, literally, "I two myself."[10] Her traumatic experience remains untranslatable into words, as if Duras were asking "How can loss and absence be signified?" as well as "How does one represent a fragmented subjectivity?"

Lol's answer to the signification of loss (usually accomplished through the narrativization of the work of mourning) leads to an impossible grieving, one that is tendentious or perverted on many levels. Since (as a split subjectivity) she cannot narrate her own story – Duras uses a male narrator to do so – Lol seeks reconstitution of self by viewing the non-verbal staging of a sexual scene, a spectacle of narcissistic sexuality that she recreates with other people as actors who substitute for her fiancé and the "other woman" – and, simultaneously, for her fiancé and herself.[11] Duras's narrative strategy in representing Lol's work of mourning – in literalizing her "perverted" think-act, her incorporation[12] – is to indicate that visual signifiers may seem to represent trauma but also cover or evade the "malady of death" (a phrase that titles another of Duras's books), the invisible and unrepresentable grief that requires narrativization in a completed work of mourning.

Lol's mourning evades this process, then, and the repetition of the moment in which her metaphoric death occurred is a repetition of the death scene, not a narrative attempt to represent it and consequently recover. The re-enactment immobilizes the text, producing a frozen moment (which is a kind of self-portrait) that fragments the narrative temporally and spatially; Lol's model of mourning is seen to produce a death of narration rather than a consoling construct within a narrative form. Jacques Hold, the male narrator of Lol's story, also seeks consolation for his alleged loss (or lack) of Lol in the process of the telling. But Duras disallows this consolation as well, since the only way that Jacques knows Lol is in her fragmented form; hence he is unable to narrate the loss of a loss.

Kristeva claims that Duras's work is without catharsis, that it "confin[es] itself to baring the malady": "Lacking catharsis, such a literature encounters, recognizes, but also spreads the pain that summons it."[13] Lol V. Stein is like many of Gallant's characters, those who seem unaware of their own need and/or inability to come to terms with loss. Flor Harris would be the closest analogy here in terms both of her psychic numbness and of the semiotic silence that Gallant employs to represent that absence. Both characters lack the ability to recover from loss; however, the reader of Durassian fiction-elegies reconstructs another model of mourning from the structure that, in Lol V. Stein, Jacques Hold tries to make work for him.

As readers of Duras's fiction-elegy we "bear witness to the neutralization of our own distress," to the "psychic numbness ... [as] the ultimate sign of grief," as Kristeva writes of the reader's complicity.[14] The texts are disturbing because consolation, for Duras, is prevented by negative repetition and by the refusal of the elegist to recover using the work of mourning. While many of Gallant's characters, too, refuse the work of mourning, Gallant guides the reader, using ironic narration, towards a potential model of mourning that might work, at least in part. But Duras offers no such hope. "There is no purification in store for us at the conclusion of those novels written on the brink of illness, no improvement, no promise of a beyond, not even the enchanting beauty of style or irony that might provide a bonus of pleasure in addition to the revealed evil," states Kristeva.[15]

Duras's semi-autobiographical fiction-elegies The Lover and The War (an interpretive translation of La Douleur, meaning "The Grief," "The Pain," "The Sorrow," or "The Sadness"),[16] involve the reader in their narrative strategies of resistance to the grieving process, then, in that pain is dramatized but alleviation not permitted. Recovery requires thinking, interpreting, understanding in narrative terms – all of which is resisted by Duras's grievers, who remain immersed in their suffering. But understanding is denied the reader, too. In her recent book of transcribed conversations, Duras states of her fiction: "You can't understand these books anyway. That's not the right word. It's a matter of a private relationship between the book and the reader. They weep and grieve together."[17] And there is no recovery for either; it is as if the repetition of loss is the only insurance that falsely comforting consolation will be resisted.

The Lover, which Duras describes as a "very difficult" book,[18] consists of a story of a fifteen and one-half-year-old girl from the point of view of herself as an old woman with a "ravaged" face.[19] This narrator-elegist repeatedly describes "the image" of herself at her first meeting with her first lover, and the recall of this image (which, like Lol's repeated "scene," fragments the text) evokes think-act narratives that substitute for "the story of [her] life," which "doesn't exist. There's never any centre to it" (8). The narrator self-consciously states: "What I'm doing now is both different and the same [as narrating the 'image']. Before, I spoke of clear periods, those on which the light fell. Now I'm talking about the hidden stretches of that same youth, of certain facts, feelings, events that I buried" (8).[20]

The fiction-elegy serves as a work of mourning not only for the narrator's lost love but also for those family members who are literally buried – her dead mother and brothers: "I've written a good deal about the members of my family, but then they were still alive, my mother and my brothers. And I skirted around them, skirted around all these things without really tackling them" (7). "Tackling" these things requires a confrontation with the past, and the present-tense descriptions of the "image" function as think-acts that immerse the narrator-elegist and reader (addressed as "you") in that earlier time period: "I'm wearing a dress of real silk, but it's threadbare, almost transparent. It used to belong to my mother ... I can't see any others [shoes] I could have been wearing, so I'm wearing them" (11). The image is potentially consoling in that it has "the virtue of representing, of being the creator of, an absolute" (10). It is also the representation of an absence – of the forced separation of the girl and her lover, and of the deaths that separate her from her relatives.

Duras alternates between first- and third-person points of view. The distancing effect of the third-person narration when used (the narrator refers to herself as "the girl") provides a semblance of objectivity and makes the story a representation of her emotional experience rather than an expressive discourse, but it also demonstrates her need to separate herself from the emotions and experience, to dissipate or neutralize the pain. The narrator is able both to represent the work of mourning and to witness it at the same time, as she would a photograph. Comments about photographs of her mother permeate the text, and it is this kind of displaced approach to the woman's death that the fiction-elegy requires and enacts. The memory of the image of the lover and memories of the mother are intertwined; the first time the girl makes love with "the man from Cholon," as he is called, she tells him "I couldn't yet leave my mother without dying of grief" (40) and thinks that her "mother's approaching death, too, must be connected with what has happened to [her] today" (40). Their physical relationship seems to offer the narrator a kind of consolation for her mother's unhappiness and her own: "Kisses on the body bring tears. Almost like a consolation. At home I don't cry. But that day in that room, tears console both for the past and for the future" (46).

The mother's death is doubled in the novel: first, she dies a figurative death through madness, wherein a "substitution took place ... that identity irreplaceable by any other had disappeared and I was powerless to make it come back, make it start to come back. There was no longer anything there to inhabit her image" (85–6); and second, she literally dies. It is only after the actual death that the narrator "can write about her so easily now, so long, so fully. She's become just something you write without difficulty, cursive writing" (29). But the form of the fiction-elegy betrays the real difficulty that the narrator faces in writing of her mother – a difficulty that Munro's narrators, too, often face – and the real need she has to narrativize her own life and her mother's death. Memories of the family's life, especially of the elder brother's cruelty to his siblings and their mother, erupt and disrupt the text: "Let me tell you what he did, too, what it was like," she says to the reader (76).

It is the death of the younger brother, though, that caused the narrator-elegist to "die" as well. His death teaches her that "immortality is mortal, that it can die" (105). The narration of her own grief at his death evokes her "wild love" for him, which "remains an unfathomable mystery" (106) and contradicts her own earlier statement that "for memories too it's too late. Now I don't love them [her family] any more" (28). In this alinear novel Duras's narrator-elegist performs the work of mourning for her family and for her lost lover using methods of psychological realism; the think-acts produced by the repeated image constitute a consolation in that they represent that "absolute" to which the narrator refers early in the text. That absolute is literalized for the elegist at the close of the novel, when the lover contacts the narrator by phone "years after the war, after marriages, children, divorces, books," and provides her with the knowledge that "it was as before, that he still loved her, he could never stop loving her, that he'd love her until death" (117). If we assume that his words have a consoling effect on the narrator-elegist, then his statement functions as a speech act that ameliorates her long-term grief at his absence. Interestingly, the end of the novel is narrated in the third person, perhaps indicating that the necessary emotional distance finally exists between the two people and that her grief has become dissipated in the course of telling the "hidden stretches" of her past.

The narrator-elegist of *The War / The Grief* is the same "she" of *The Lover*, who here records in a journal the experience of waiting for her husband Robert L. to return from a German concentration camp at the end of the Second World War. "War is a generality, so are the inevitabilities of war, including death," the elegist writes (8). Duras points to the banality of death and also to the human ability to act against humanity – to the "great levellers, the crematoriums at Buchenwald, hunger, the common graves at Bergen-Belsen" (47). The elegist and her husband share the belief that responsibility for the Holocaust must be placed on everyone: "He didn't accuse any person, any race, any people. He accused man ... the governments that come and go in the history of nations" (52). According to the narrator, "in order to bear it, to tolerate the idea of it, we must share the crime" (50). Duras makes explicit the issue of social responsibility, an issue that Gallant explores in a much more subtle and ironic manner in exposing the "seed" of fascism in "everyday living," in its "small possibilities in people."[21]

Duras's historiographic concerns in this novel are similar to those of Gallant in her political fiction-elegies, though Duras's insistence that all "share the blame" runs counter to Gallant's belief that such generalizations allow no blame to be placed anywhere, no judgments to be made. Responsibility for the events of the war is examined in *The War / The Grief*, as is the narrator's personal grief for what she thinks is the certainty of her husband's death. The text is both a personal fiction-elegy and a public one; since "no national mourning for the deportees" was declared (34), the narrator's work is doubly imperative. Like *Hiroshima Mon Amour*, Duras's well-known screenplay, the text addresses historical and personal pasts and draws attention to the difficulty of narrating what is in many ways an unrepresentable history. (Duras's statement that "all one can do is talk about the impossibility of talking about Hiroshima"[22] recalls Gallant's refusal to use adjectives in captions for the first photographs of concentration camps printed by the Montreal *Star*; however, Duras is much more explicit in voicing her position on this issue.) *The War / The Grief* "can't really be called 'writing,' " according to Duras, since she "still can't put a name" to it[23] (though Duras does, in fact, "talk about" the effects of the Second World War on individuals and on society directly at times in this text); rather, it is a performance of the mind's quest to find words and names for the pain it endlessly endures.

While the narrator waits for Robert L.'s return, she equates her experience to "the vanguard of a nameless battle, a battle without arms or bloodshed or glory" (35). Her suffering is unnameable, and therefore not understood by her close friend D., who says "When you think about it later on you'll be ashamed" (23). But it is the attempt to name the grief that drives the fiction-elegy and the narrator. The waiting prevents her from entering into a work of mourning that would allow the elegist to distance herself from the pain, and thereby recover.

The narrator writes most of the fiction-elegy in the present tense; it is only after the return of her husband, when the waiting and the anguish it entailed has ended, that the past tense is employed to complete the story. The mourning that the narrator performs is for the assumed death of her husband, and his return would seem to eliminate the cause of that particular mourning. But it does not; it is as though the emotional energy invested in Robert's absence is too great for his presence to satisfy, and the elimination of the need for grief upon his return and recovery precipitates a new, inverted work of mourning: the narrator grieves for the loss of grief.

Initially she believes that until she is able to "record" his name on one of the lists of returning prisoners, which she compiles for the paper *Libres*, she cannot alleviate her grief. But well after Robert L.'s recovery the narrator is provoked to tears at the sound of his name: "At the name, Robert L., I weep. I still weep. I shall weep all my life" (67). The metonymy of the name figures the grief she experiences in reaction to Robert's horror. It is as if the name signifies "all the inexpressible things of all the days" (68), and perhaps even the death of her love for Robert L. – she decides to leave him, and tells him so while he convalesces. No reasons are given for the separation she chooses, just as no reasons or answers are available to Duras or the reader for the events of the war; but by leaving Robert L., the narrator perpetuates his absence and allows herself to continue an interminable mourning.

Such constant proximity to loss permits both an ahistorical suspension of event (Robert L.'s imprisonment) and a prolongation of affect (the emotional intensity and self-involvement of the narrator's response). Again, the characteristically static movement of Duras's text, so similar to the rhythm of obsession in its refusal to terminate, circles about a single median, though irremediable, point. Temporal progression is replaced by mental regression to the extent that the textual focus remains fixated not on the grieved but on the griever. Accordingly, the reality of Robert L.'s return must be revoked in order that the narrator may invoke, repetitively, the voice of her own mourning, thus guaranteeing the fictive and protecting identity as she who grieves eternally. But ironically, the compulsion to mourn, to share the blame for wartime atrocities, obviates the necessity for the judgment of history and for the narrator's *self*-judgment in terms of her relationship with Robert L.

This novel, like many of Duras's other works, performs what Kristeva calls "the drama of our times, a drama that imprints the malady of death at the heart of the psychic experience of most of us."[24] Profoundly political but also highly personal, Duras's fiction-elegies work to demonstrate the human mind in the process of failing or refusing to come to terms with private and public losses. The fiction-elegy, then, is crucial to Duras's aesthetic not because of any hope of reconciliation it might offer but in that it provides the most useful method and form of exploring, with literary means, the failure of consciousness to recoup itself whole from the loss that wounds it.

Edmund White, too, alters paradigmatic structures of elegy to suggest that resistance to consolation is a necessary stage, if not a perversely desirable prolongation, of an impossible work of mourning. Writing in a personal vein, the first-person narrator-elegist of White's novel *Nocturnes for the King of Naples* self-consciously reconstructs his relationship with "you," the pronomially identified lover, by remembering the past, "the wreckage of adult passion," which he figures metaphorically as "leaf-mold and the arms and shoulders of tree roots or men."[25] The reconstruction of the past is also a fictive resurrection of the lover – "from these scatterings I fashion you" (49), who, we learn at the end of the novel, is dead. White deceives the reader in this fiction-elegy (a strategy reminiscent of Munro in "Tell Me Yes or No"): we believe that the apostrophe is an address to an abandoned or abandoning lover, that the loss mourned is the relationship between two living people, while the narrator is actually mourning the death of this lover using another narrative form: the epistle.

The book-length address to this "you" is an extended apostrophe, an extended think-act that brings the "you" back to life: "The answer to the riddle – what's preserved but moves? what existed only in the past but rustles, flickers brilliantly into sunlight, then soars? – is you, your presence, thoughts of you" (22). The resurrection is not conventionally prosopopoetic since the dead lover is never given voice but only spoken *to* in an extended apostrophe. In *The Post Card* Jacques Derrida writes of this trope: "Thus I apostrophize. This too is a genre one can afford oneself, the apostrophe. A genre and a tone. The word – apostrophizes – speaks of the words addressed to the singular one, a live interpellation (the man of discourse or writing interrupts the continuous development of the sequence, abruptly turns toward someone, that is, something, addresses himself to you), but the word also speaks of the address to be detoured."[26] For White's narrator, the address that is detoured is not only a literal (street) address but the address to the lover as a *dead* person. The monologuic epistle, which is sent to "you" as if "you" were still alive and able to read the letter, is really more of a disguised soliloquy, then. But the speaker will not relinquish the apostrophic rapport with the lover; in fact he explicitly refers to his "tale that lies coiled, messy but alive, in the hot hollows of memory" and tells "you" to "take your stick and poke the steaming entrails. Read them; read me" (53–4). The "me" is figured in the convoluted autobiographical discourse of the apostrophized letter, of which the entrails are a figuration (the reading of entrails is a ritualistic method of prophesying, of "seeing" the truth.) The present "I" details his "amorous history" in the desire to "anticipate your laughter at my method," as he tells "you" (43), in the full expectation that his words indeed will be read by the dead lover.

White's epistolary elegy, which is alinear, achronological and digressive ("I've wandered so far from my subject, my dear, which is you" [63]), produces a necessary condition for the elegist: distance from the loss. This distance is inscribed in the very genre that White has adapted in this fiction-elegy. As Derrida remarks in one of his own amorous epistles, "[I must] distance myself *in order* to write to you" (*The Post Card* 28). The letter thus serves not only as a resurrectional fiction but as a seductive discourse, one in which desire – which itself signifies distance implicitly – is coded into the very being of the text in the continually deferred desire to close the gap between the writer-elegist and the addressee.

What I have not yet established is that the love relationship mourned by White's narrator is a homosexual one. While Linda Kauffman argues in *Discourses of Desire* that heroines of epistolary fiction use the letter form to "challenge not just men's representation of them but – particularly as it relates to gender – the fundamental tenets of representation itself,"[27] and while the content of White's novel might suggest that stereotypical representations of homosexual love need to be challenged, White's use of the epistle is more generally a function of the flexibility it provides for the psychonarration of a mourning mind, regardless of the gender of the mourner or the mourned.

This mode of writing fiction-elegy has been employed by Gallant and Munro, as we have seen (Gallant's *A Fairly Good Time* and "An Autobiography" and Munro's "Friend of My Youth" and "Tell Me Yes or No" are obvious examples), and seems to function in a particularly satisfactory manner for the elegist seeking a consoling mode of narration. For White's narrator, though, seduction plays a more important role than it does in these other works; the constant detailing of seduction scenes between himself and other men parallels the structural strategy whereby he might seduce the addressee with his apostrophized discourse. The deliberately excessive language, the rhythmical poetics, and the layers of metaphor produce a compensatory tease that covers and distances the pain of loss. Since most of these seductions end or begin with the narrator and his new lover talking about "you," they therefore perform two functions of the text.

The reader, the other "you" to which the discourse is addressed, is also seduced into believing in the power of the performance. We "plot" the novel (in much the same way that we plot the achronological and relatively plotless stories by Gallant) and, in plotting, produce a model of mourning from our reconstruction of White's text. The narrator provides a model of this plotting activity for the reader: while we are told that the face of "you" watches the narrator even after he is "away" from his "gravitational pull" (74), the narrator's need to revivify the dead lover is made even more immediate to the reader when the "you" is re-created not only in memory and words but in a theatrical staging of a memorable, significant scene. In the dramatization the narrator "impersonates" the "you" figure, and his then-lover plays the role of the narrator (84–6). Like Lol V. Stein's staged scene, it is as if a representation of the two lovers might offer some kind of vision, an anamnesis produced by a literalized acting-out of the narrator's past self and the lover's self in that past time. Yet, as is the case for Lol, this acted-out think-act provides no release from the "grip of the past," to use Kenneth Bruffee's term.[28]

The narrative, composed of scattered "miniatures of memory" (141), also explores the relation between the autobiographical and the elegiac. The text performs other unmourned losses: the abandonment by and death of his father, and the suicide of his mother (his beloved childhood dog also suffocates in the gas-filled garage). The "heavy pages of my childhood" are turned, revealing a "fractured pastoral" (55), and these traumatic losses of the narrator's youth are intertwined with the loss of "you"; the mother's suicide (she is unable to recover from being abandoned by her husband) is referred to intermittently and especially seems connected to the narrator's mourning over his lost lover.

The allusions to and intertextual uses of pastoral myths both establish and subvert the elegiac tradition within which the ritualized narrative of mourning is enacted. For example, when overtaken by grief, the narrator fantasizes a pastoral scene that recalls Arcady of the pastoral elegy: in the scene his mother "pictures lovers in that garden saying, each to each, 'Happy are we within our sacred grove, two forms, perhaps, but one soul, one love" (144). This fantasy also constitutes the closing scene of the fiction-elegy, though the addition of the narrator and the "you," figured in the form of "two lost dogs" (figures that represent his childhood pet and a lover's abandoned animal, as well as the two lovers themselves), leads to a "fractured pastoral" after all.

Just prior to his narration of the fact of "you' "s death, he thinks of the Pan and Syrinx myth, taking the role of the transformed nymph rather than that of the poet-figure. He writes: "I felt my body becoming a reed, piping two notes, the mournful dyad. When I lived here the city was full of your absence. My longing played over everything I saw. But now even that loss has been lost" (127). The traditional elegiac apotheosis is also alluded to: "Nothing will come of my pleas and protestations, the outcome is in the stars, never more radiant than when they die, tyrannical novae" (134) – a statement of fate and fatality that is recalled when the dead "you" is thought to have "put in a star appearance" as friends gather in remembrance of him (145). If any consolation is found in this epistolary fiction-elegy it is in the narrator's ability to perform an autobiographical think-act that enables him to mimpathize with the "incomprehensible, disturbing" figure of "you," to admit that his emotions towards this lover whom he had abandoned were authentic and loving, and to recognize in his own feelings a parallel with his mother's incurable grief.

Mieke Bal describes autobiography as that which "gives a representation and leaves the model to be constructed."[29] Clearly White's narrator-elegist provides a representation of his life as well as his grief, from which the reader is able to recognize a model of mourning. Bal's suggestion that "katharsis is an aspect of mimesis in its effect on the recipient" (175) is also an appropriate way to describe the behabitational aspect of elegy with its potential perlocutionary effect on both the elegist and the reader.[30] In Edna O'Brien's works of short fiction, critically noted for their elements of "abjection,"[31] consolation is quite often absent; in this sense her fiction-elegies, like those of Gallant, often fall short of catharsis for the narrator- or character-elegist, though in constructing the model the reader is able to mimpathize and recognize its limitations. In his foreword to *A Fanatic Heart: Stories of Edna O'Brien* Philip Roth writes: "The words themselves are chiseled. The welter of emotion is rendered so sparsely that the effect is merciless, like an autopsy."[32] In Roth's analogy O'Brien is a coroner; but if her stories are interpreted in terms of the poetics of elegy – a "thanatopoetics," perhaps[33] – then her work is more "thanato-anatomy" (or thanatomy) than autopsy.[34]

Where Gallant portrays the after-effects of loss (often by abandonment), O'Brien renders her sufferers in the midst of despair over literal deaths or broken hearts. Her most recent collection, *Lantern Slides*, contains many stories that might be read as fiction-elegies: "Long Distance," "Epitaph," "Widow," "What a Sky," and the title story, which seems to be O'Brien's version of Joyce's "The Dead," with evening festivities and a character named Conroy.[35] Like Gallant, O'Brien also employs a characteristically detached narrating voice and therefore is able to suggest emotion rather than directly (or sentimentally) express it. The plot of "Baby Blue," for example, is nearly absent in that the story renders a woman's reaction to the prophesied death of her love relationship: "Three short quick death knocks resounded in her bedroom the night before they met."[36] The narrative is composed of a series of anecdotal scenes, which act as photographic depictions of moments that, taken together, chart the progressive decline of the bond between the lovers. Even one of O'Brien's harshest critics, Peggy O'Brien, concedes that there is a "subtle interaction of emotion and description" in her work.[37]

In "Baby Blue" the female mourner-figure is said to be "maudlinly recalling dead friends, those in the grave and those who were still walking around" on a New Year's Eve spent alone, apart from her married lover (324). This narrated memory also foreshadows the soon-dead relationship, as do the artificial lake and black swans at a mutual friend's country home (329) – which contribute to a sense of an inverted pastoral, a figure for grief rather than its consolation. The double sense of an expected and a delayed end is inscribed as well in the monotony of the plotless story; the reader both waits for the separation to occur and experiences the tension that the prolonged suffering creates.

The end of the affair changes the narrator's perceptions of everyday objects into signs of death: "The swivel chair was like a corpse in the room and she threw the paperweight at it ... for a moment she saw those Christmas roses, a sea of them, pale and unassuming in a damp incline from the opposite side, and he eerily still" (334). The

think-act presents the absent lover to the narrator's vision, suspended ("eerily still") in an atemporal moment. But this image fails
to console the woman, and O'Brien's use of metaphoric language to
figure the work of mourning suggests that her character is possibly
incapable of confronting the truth of her loss. Indeed, her last act in
the story is to pray for her lover as if he were dead, as she seeks a
tombstone in an anonymous graveyard "with Jay's name on it"; she
specifies that it must be Jay's because another tombstone nearby carries "his daughter's name" (337). She accepts the false epitaph as a
marker of her lover's absence, and in so doing she demonstrates that
the need to figure loss goes beyond reason.

The last paragraph recalls that of Joyce's "The Dead": "It will pass,
she thought, going from grave to grave, and unconsciously and almost mundanely she prayed for the living, prayed for the dead,
then prayed for the living again, went back to find the tomb where
his name was, and prayed for all those who were in boxes alone or
together above or below ground, all those unable to escape their afflicted selves" (338). The image of the coffin as box is also an image
of the character-mourner's thanatopoetic incorporation of the lost
lover, one that prevents her from escaping *her* afflicted self. Of an
artwork composed of coffins, Derrida writes: "In the *mise en boîte* as
putting-to-death of the model, the body has disappeared but it is not
absent. Once pocketed or boxed, incorporated, it makes the labor of
mourning impossible, it makes it do the impossible. And the ghost
takes its revenge, multiplies its apparitions."[38] O'Brien's story consists of a series of box-like segments, though *les boîtes* are sequential
and not framed in a structure of infinite regress, as is the woman's
grief. Thus the reader is able to open the crypt and to construct a
work of mourning from the narrative that renders a woman's boxed-
up (cryptic and encrypted) grief.

"Long Distance" presents another female character in mourning
for the loss of a love relationship; she too incorporates an image of
the man and remains in a melancholic state, weeping "for life, its
heartlessness and her qualms about losing something incarnate in
herself."[39] A series of flashbacks and imagined future scenarios is
evoked as the two people meet some years after the end of the affair.
In this story O'Brien's narrator records a rather superficial dialogue
between the man and the woman but counterpoints the text with
"what they were thinking" (45). The realistic prose shifts, though, at
the end of the story, to a pastoral style wherein nature mourns: the
woman's grief is mirrored in "a drizzle that pattered onto the leaves
and onto her face, and the fallen leaves rustled like taffeta as she
stepped over them" (46).

O'Brien provides a melancholy closure for the story, linking the love story to the pastoral elegy: "Love, she thought, is like nature, but in reverse; first it fruits, then it flowers, then it seems to wither, then it goes deep, deep down into its burrow, where no one sees it, where it is lost from sight, and ultimately people die with that secret buried inside their souls" (46). With this depiction of the woman's "thought" O'Brien inverts traditional pastoral consolation and institutes in its place an image of enclosure and burial. The incorporation is thus figured in the reversed analogy of nature, equating love with eventual grief and death. Love cannot "console" this mourner, then, but as "that bulwark between life and death" (46) it can partake only in the course of nature – in other words, in death. Surprisingly, perhaps, O'Brien's fiction-elegies are less consoling than those of Duras, where even incorporated scenes tend to console by displacing the need for the work of mourning.

"A Rose in the Heart of the Country" might be aligned with such works by Gallant as *Green Water, Green Sky, A Fairly Good Time*, and "Its Image on the Mirror" (and with Duras's *The Lover*) in that a mother/child relationship necessitates or perpetuates the daughter's work of mourning for a vaguely defined loss. An omniscient narrator describes the house where the daughter is born using a simile that borders on prosopopoeia: "A solemn house, set in its own grounds, away from the lazy bustle of the village. A lonesome house, it would prove to be, and with a strange lifelikeness, as if it were not a house at all but a person observing and breathing, a presence amid a cluster of trees and sturdy wind-shorn hedges."[40] The simile (the "as if" construction that qualifies the prosopopoetic figure) contributes to the tentativeness with which the story is told and to the hesitancy of the text – a hesitancy that is reflected in the daughter's fear of becoming too close to her mother and in O'Brien's reluctance to use direct methods of rendering the "welter of emotion" to which Roth refers. Similarly, the narrator uses the conditional tense to state that the details of the scene of the birth "would become part of the remembered story" (375). Here O'Brien's syntactical strategy indicates that the relationship between the mother and her child already has been transformed into a text, one that is "read" by the narrator, as the interpretation of the life-like house suggests. The life of the house ends when the mother dies: "[it was] as if the house itself had died or had been carefully put down to sleep" (404).

O'Brien's use of metaphor and indirect representation of the work of mourning forces the reader to give voice to her character-elegists, to vivify the emotion that lies beneath the surface of the text and is contained in its figurations. Peggy O'Brien writes of her "seductive" fiction: "The prose unquestionably makes this powerful gesture of appeal to us, demanding reaction."[41] In this particular story what is demanded is the reconstruction of the mother's life-line, which includes her death at its end. The story-version of this life-line includes parable-like descriptions of the idealized mother/daughter bond, wherein the adult idolizes the child (379). The daughter's response to her mother's death and to what she perceived as an earlier emotional betrayal and abandonment by her mother are also reconstructed by the reader. The younger woman's perceptions are narrated (more precisely, "focalized"), causing the reader to mimpathize with her point of view. When she was a baby, her "eyes [would] star[e] out at whatever happened to loom in" (379), and the narrator's focalization through this adult character-mourner continues to project an immediacy of experience that is, paradoxically, narrated indirectly, such that a representation of the work of mourning is left to the reader to construct.

Prior to the mother's death, and after her own marriage ended, the daughter is afflicted with "assaults of memory" though her wish is to "wipe out the previous life" (393). But since the relationship between mother and daughter had at one time been so integral to each of their lives, the "figure of the mother, who was responsible for each and every one of these facets" of the past (393), must also be wiped out. Thus the think-act the daughter proposes is a metaphoric murder, one that would reverse the incorporation of the mother by expelling her from the younger woman's mind: "They [the memories] were more than thoughts, they were the presence of this woman whom she resolved to kill" (393). The mother's desire to "be buried together" with her daughter (394) is resisted by the latter, who dreams that the mother, while dying from giving birth to the girl, states: "all there is, is yourself and this little insect that you're trying to kill" (394).

The dream is prefigured by the narrator's biblical description early in the story of the mother's condition during the actual birth: "Her womb was sick unto death" (376), a phrase that connects the themes of life and death in a cycle and implies that the relationship between mother and child will prove to be unhealthy. The connected images of womb and tomb also indicate that a *mise en boîte* type of structure might be imposed on the life-stories narrated in the text; but the daughter's resistance to the mother's desire for a double tomb is also an insistence on another shape for her own life and for the story of that life. O'Brien's use of focalization (instead of framed points of view in a *mise en abyme* narrative structure) also suggests to the reader that an alternate model of mourning might be derived from the text.

The daughter's perception of her mother's motives prevents a mourning for her death, and her apostrophic attempt fails: "She tried to speak to her mother, but found the words artificial" (401). It is this inability to come to terms with her mother – to find a language that will permit communication (in life and after the death) – that eventually she does mourn: "It is emptiness more than grief. It is a grief at not being able to be wholehearted again. It is not a false grief, but it is unyielding, it is blood from a stone" (402). O'Brien's use of figurative language, not false but not true either, is necessary to represent this lack of mourning, this suppressed, silent cry for "some communiqué" (404).

The mother does leave an envelope with her daughter's name addressed "in her mother's hand" (404), and this metonymic figuration – the "hand" (an abbreviation of "handwriting") representing the mother herself – seems to promise a consoling memento. Yet there is no letter inside. The absent letter is a sign of the mother's absence, although the daughter is able to use both this absence and the tokens of money and jewelry in the envelope to "concoc[t] little tendernesses that her mother might have written." The daughter, then, finally begins to confront her loss by literalizing the figure of prosopopoeia – by giving voice to the woman whose death has created a "silence [that] filled the room" (404).

Giving voice, which is the function and effect of prosopopoeia, is a fundamental trope of elegy, one that writers of fiction-elegy often employ in conventional and/or subversive ways to culminate the work of mourning. Alice Munro, for instance, tends to give voice to those who are mourned in her fiction-elegies, which are often "written" by an elegist/writer-figure in the story; for Mavis Gallant, remembered voice is impossible to represent accurately in words. Hence Gallant parodies prosopopoetic constructs in some of her fiction-elegies and disallows the function of prosopopoeia as an unquestioned consolation. Giving voice for Duras often means instituting present-tense narration, evoked by think-acts on the part of her elegist-figures; for Lol V. Stein, for instance, this entails acting out the think-act itself. Edmund White's narrator think-acts his epistolary elegy, and voice is denied the dead lover only because the elegist maintains the fiction, at least till the end, that his voice has not been lost, that "you" has not died at all. The extended think-act none the less gives voice to his own grief and a structure to his work of mourning.

Fiction-elegists also cause the reader to be given voice by using narrativized think-acts. These internal experiences evoke images and resurrect the past through memory, but it is memory transformed and interpreted. Paul Hernadi discusses the relationship between thinking and discourse in "Doing, Making, Meaning: Toward a Theory of Verbal Practice": "we should conceive of the thinking person not only as silently speaking or invisibly writing but also as inwardly listening to the silent messages that come to each of us, in part at least, through the internalized voices of other human beings ... Whatever occurs to me (in both the external and the mental senses of *occur*) awaits transformation, through a kind of internal reading, into meaningful messages."[42] The think-act of fiction-elegy thus figures grief in that it gives voice to those absent "other human beings" for whom the elegist mourns; it gives voice to the character-elegist who reads or interprets the think-act, and thereby becomes what Hernadi would call a "transformed self" (752); and it gives voice to the reader, who figures grief in the model of mourning – itself a figuration, a representation – using his or her own internalized speech.

Thus the development of the fiction-elegy sub-genre, which I have traced in occasionally diachronic, predominantly synchronic form, might be understood to parallel the twentieth-century's concern with and complication of the act of reading. Understood in this way, and in spite of the inevitable reductiveness such a broad categorization entails, "reading" may stand as a useful code-word indicating the reconciliation of a wide variety of theoretical discourses within a general identity of critical focus. The relation of reader to text has been aestheticized in the sense that any interpretation of the word, any close exegesis or discursive analysis, is now considered to be just that – an interpretation, a version of textual truth, to some degree subject to the creative interaction of what is read and who reads it, and why.

It also seems logical that in an era that, through war, technology, and psychology, has so radically altered our perceptions of death and traditional philosophical and religious consolations, the elegiac component of this reading project is accentuated in current aesthetic and historical representations. More specifically, that the narrative version of the work of mourning has become so prevalent in contemporary literature indicates both the endurance of the elegiac answer to loss and, in the exemplary works studied here, the extent to which those answers must be questioned in order to effect the possibility – whether rejected or embraced – of a true reading of ourselves.

Notes

PREFACE

1 To date, books by single authors on Munro include E.D. Blodgett's *Alice Munro*; Ildó de Papp Carrington's *Controlling the Uncontrollable*; and W.R. Martin's *Alice Munro: Paradox and Parallel*. Three single-authored books on Gallant have been written: Grazia Merler's *Mavis Gallant: Narrative Patterns and Techniques*; Neil Besner, *The Light of the Imagination: Mavis Gallant's Fiction*; and Janice Kulyk Keefer's *Reading Mavis Gallant*.
2 A wealth of scholarship has been done on the genre of the poetic elegy (from its classical origins to the Victorian period), and rather than review the critical literature to date I will draw on relevant sources throughout the study.
3 Sontag, *On Photography*, 3.
4 Miller, *Versions of Pygmalion*, 46–7.

CHAPTER ONE

1 Kristeva, "On the Melancholic Imaginary," 107.
2 Frye, *Anatomy of Criticism*, 66.
3 Cairns, *Generic Composition*, 70, 34.
4 Müller, "Bemerkungen zur Gattungspoetik," 2.
5 My use of the term "late modern" refers to the period of literature that falls between high modernism (which ends roughly after the Second World War) and postmodernism. However, "late modern" is

also a descriptive term for a style of writing still engaged in by many contemporary writers. Brian McHale makes the distinction between modern and late modern texts in *Postmodern Fiction,* claiming that the former is predominantly concerned with epistemological issues and that these concerns contrast with the ontological issues central in postmodern texts. Late modern texts are thus concerned with both of these broadly defined issues, placing varying degrees of emphasis on one extreme or the other.

6 Fowler, *Kinds of Literature,* 210–11.

7 WATT, *The Rise of the Novel,* 13.

8 Engelberg, *Elegiac Fictions,* 2.

9 Robert Langbaum's *The Mysteries of Identity* also situates modern literature within the themes of loss and reconstitution of "self."

10 The name of this sub-genre was devised by Kenneth A. Bruffee in articles preceding his study *Elegiac Romance.*

11 Bruffee, *Elegiac Romance,* 134.

12 Smith, *By Mourning Tongues,* 21.

13 This term is Hans Robert Jauss's. See "Genres and Medieval Literature" in *Toward an Aesthetic of Reception,* 81.

14 Fowler, *Kinds of Literature,* 107.

15 T.P. Harrison and H.J. Leon, introduction to *The Pastoral Elegy,* 1.

16 See James Hanford, "Pastoral Elegy and 'Lycidas,' " 407.

17 See Patricia Merivale's study *Pan the Goat-God* for detailed analyses of the story.

18 Poggioli, "The Oaten Flute," 167. This study was expanded into *The Oaten Flute.*

19 Celeste Schenck has written an extensive study of poetic apprenticeship in pastoral elegy. See *Mourning and Panegyric.*

20 The term is Claudio Guillèn's. See *Literature as System,* 146, 155.

21 It must be emphasized that the autobiographical is used as a *trope* and is a rhetorical device used by the narrator-elegist; it does not involve an incorporation of the author's (or even implied author's) autobiography into the fiction-elegy.

22 Mieke Bal defines "psychopoetics" as "a body of language about literature, used as knowledge, characterized by a relation of information with psychoanalysis ... [It is] one part of a general poetics that will always interact with others." See "Introduction: Delimiting Psychopoetics," 280.

23 Sacks, *The English Elegy,* 19.

24 Bloomfield, "The Elegy and the Elegiac Mode: Praise and Alienation," 148.

25 Todorov, "The Origin of Genres," 169.

26 Schleifer, *The Rhetoric of Death,* 220, 221.

27 See de Man, *The Rhetoric of Romanticism*, 76.

28 Miller, *Versions of Pygmalion*, 4.

29 Holman, *A Handbook of Literature*, 513.

30 See Squires, *The Pastoral Novel*, and Empson, *Some Versions of Pastoral*.

31 Harold Toliver, *Pastoral Forms and Attitudes*, 18.

32 Schleifer traces the historical conditions that produced changes in modes of apprehension and representation in the West in "Historicizing the Modernist Rhetoric," chap. 2 of *Rhetoric and Death*.

33 Tolchin, *Mourning, Gender and Creativity in the Art of Herman Melville*, xiii.

34 Woolf, "A Sketch of the Past," 129.

35 Woolf, "The Narrow Bridge of Art," 226.

36 Woolf, "A Sketch of the Past," 122.

37 Kristeva, "On the Melancholic Imaginary," 107.

38 The term is Dorrit Cohn's. See *Transparent Minds*, 11.

39 Reinhard and Lupton, "Shapes of Grief: Freud, *Hamlet* and Mourning," 61.

40 Bruffee, *Elegiac Romance*, 112.

41 Friedman, "Narrative Is to Death as Death Is to the Dying: Funerals and Stories," 67.

42 Potts, *The Elegiac Mode*, 36.

43 Woolf, "A Sketch of the Past," 72.

44 Munro, introduction to *The Moons of Jupiter*, xiv.

45 Besner, *The Light of Imagination*, 153.

46 The phrases "image-event" and "work of figuration" are Flieger's ("Proust, Freud, and the Art of Forgetting," 69).

47 Abel, *Virginia Woolf and the Fictions of Psychoanalysis*, 3.

48 Harding, "Psychological Processes in the Reading of Fiction," 313–14.

49 "The Metaphorical Process as Cognition, Imagination, and Feeling," 148.

50 Jacques Derrida develops his argument that "representation is death" in "Freud and the Scene of Writing," *Writing and Difference*.

51 Schleifer, *Rhetoric and Death*, 6.

52 Mills-Courts, *Poetry as Epitaph*, 8.

53 Spacks, "The Novel as Ethical Paradigm," 182.

54 Woolf, *The Diary of Virginia Woolf*, 2:13.

55 *Jacob's Room* is often thought of as Woolf's elegy for her brother Thoby; *The Waves*, too, is described by John Mepham in "Mourning and Modernism" as "a kind of shrine to Thoby's memory" (142). In this study I do not consider any of the fiction-elegies from a biographical perspective (such as that adopted by Mark Spilka, Helen Corsa, and Thomas Caramagno), since in my theory elegy is a paradigmatic representation of the work of mourning, a form that is

accessible to the reader and not limited to a specific personal loss of the author.

56 Woolf, *Diary*, 3:34.
57 Beer, *Arguing With the Past*, 147.
58 Woolf, *Jacob's Room*, 168.
59 Ibid., 6–7.
60 Abel, *Virginia Woolf and the Fictions of Psychoanalysis*, 3.
61 Williams, "Virginia Woolf's Rhetoric of Enclosure," 50.
62 Woolf, *Mrs Dalloway*, 106.
63 Stewart, *Death Sentences*, 309.
64 Ibid.
65 Woolf, *Mrs Dalloway*, 282.
66 Woolf, *To the Lighthouse*, 241, 269, 300.
67 Abel, *Virginia Woolf*, 69.
68 Mieke Bal discusses autobiography in a similar manner: "autobiography gives a representation and leaves the model to be constructed." See "Mimesis and Genre Theory," 176.
69 Iser, *Prospecting*, 244.
70 Woolf, "A Sketch of the Past," 72.
71 Stanislaus Joyce, *My Brother's Keeper*, 104.
72 Hartman, *Saving the Text*, 123.
73 Ibid., 127–8.
74 Although the term "thought-act" is more precisely analogous to that of "speech-act," I have chosen to use "think-act" in order to emphasize the activity involved in the process.
75 Dix, *The Shape of Liturgy*, 161.
76 Austin, *How To Do Things with Words*, 83.
77 Derrida, *Memoires for Paul de Man*, 65.
78 Austin, *How To Do Things with Words*, 101.
79 Woolf, "A Sketch of the Past," 72.
80 Munich, " 'Dear, Dead Women,' or Why Gabriel Conroy Reviews Robert Browning," 127.
81 Frank, *The Widening Gyre*, 60n.
82 Ibid., 59.
83 This word refers to the pastoral noonhour, the time of day set aside for self-reflection and peace. See Rosenmeyer, *The Green Cabinet*, 89.
84 Culler, "On Apostrophe," 67.
85 Pound, "A Retrospect," *Literary Essays of Ezra Pound*, 4.
86 Morris Beja notes a historical basis of this apparent relationship between Imagism and epiphany. See *Epiphany in the Modern Novel*, 64, where he discusses the influence of Bergson's *An Introduction to Metaphysics* on the poetry of T.E. Hulme.

CHAPTER TWO

1 Keith, *A Sense of Style*, 101.
2 Murray, "Canada, Canonicity, the Uncanny," 114, 119; emphasis mine.
3 Blodgett, "Heresy and Other Arts," 4; emphasis mine.
4 Gallant, "What Is Style?" in *Paris Notebooks*, 177.
5 Bouson, *The Empathic Reader*, 171.
6 Dagobert, *Dictionary of Philosophy*.
7 Donald Jewison, "Speaking of Mirrors," 94; Robertson Davies, "The Novels of Mavis Gallant," 69.
8 Borklund, "Mavis Gallant," 324.
9 Ronald Hatch, "The Three Stages of Mavis Gallant's Short Fiction," 94; Lorna Irvine, "Starting from the Beginning Every Time," 246.
10 Woolf, *Diary*, 2:56.
11 Keefer, *Reading Mavis Gallant*, 207. Keefer's quote is from her (unpublished) interview with Gallant, conducted in Paris, June 1987, and quoted in her "Mavis Gallant: A Profile," 205. The emendation and the ellipses are Keefer's.
12 Wilde, *Horizons of Assent*, 120–1, 109.
13 As used by Freud in "Remembering, Repeating and Working-Through," 1914, the phrase "working-through" implies a "work of remembering" through an "acting out" (151). Late modern writers "work through" modernism via repetition with a difference.
14 Kristeva, "On the Melancholic Imaginary," 107.
15 Roudiez, introduction to Kristeva's *Desire in Language*, 18.
16 Kristeva, "On the Melancholy Imaginary," 108.
17 Iser, *Prospecting*, 282.
18 Iser, "The Reality of Fiction," 21.
19 Iser, *Prospecting*, 244.
20 Ibid., 270.
21 Riffaterre, *Fictional Truth*, 4.
22 Rooke, "Fear of the Open Heart," 267.
23 Ricoeur, "The Metaphorical Process as Cognition," 141, 155.
24 Bruner, "The Narrative Construction of Reality," 6.
25 Iser, *Prospecting*, 244.
26 Ricoeur, "The Metaphorical Process," 155.
27 Riffaterre, *Fictional Truth*, xiv.
28 Freud, "Remembering, Repeating, Working-Through," 154. Freud also indicates that transference is a "first-order" experience of reality, and *not* a representation, by insisting that transference could not successfully destroy neuroses "*in absentia* or *in effigie.*" See "The Dynamics of Transference," 108.

29 Freud, "Remembering," 154–5.
30 Hatch, "Mavis Gallant and the Fascism of Everyday Life," 21.
   Though Hatch's comparison is interesting, Gallant's aesthetic and
   political stances are, of course, vastly different from those of Brecht.
31 Brooks, "The Idea of a Psychoanalytic Literary Criticism," 10.
32 See Peter Brooks, "Psychoanalytic Constructions and Narrative
   Meanings," 57.
33 Schleifer, *Rhetoric and Death*, 58.
34 Chase, " 'Transference' as Trope," 214.
35 Ibid., 217.
36 Brooks, *Reading for the Plot*, 35.
37 Iser, *Prospecting*, 247.
38 Keefer, *Reading Mavis Gallant*, 163.
39 Gallant, "What is Style?" 177.
40 Hancock, "An Interview with Mavis Gallant," 45.
41 Woolf, introduction to *Mrs Dalloway*, vii–viii.
42 Munro, too, describes the structure of fiction as a house that
   "presents what is outside in a new way." See "What Is Real?" 224.
43 Hancock, "An Interview with Mavis Gallant," 48.
44 Gallant, "What Is Style?" 177.
45 Keith, *Canadian Literature in English*, 158.
46 Brooks, *Reading for the Plot*, 22.
47 Ricoeur, "Narrative Time," 167.
48 Gallant, "Wing's Chips," in *The Other Paris*, 141.
49 Freud, *The Psychopathology of Everyday Life*, 22, 2.
50 Riffaterre, *Fictional Truth*, 20.
51 Derrida, *Memoires for Paul de Man*, 73.
52 Ibid., 73.
53 Riffaterre, *Fictional Truth*, xv.
54 De Man, "Sign and Symbol in Hegel's *Aesthetics*," 773.
55 Similarly, "Rose" (Dec. 1960), an uncollected story, prefigures these
   continuing concerns with childhood, betrayal, memory, and
   recovery, which are explicitly thematized in the story. Interestingly,
   the protagonist of "Rose" is named Irmgard, as is the child in
   "Jorinda and Jorindel," a later story (Sept. 1959), collected in *Home
   Truths* (1981).
56 Besner, *The Light of the Imagination*, 24.
57 Gallant, "About Geneva," in *The Other Paris*, 196.
58 Freud's thesis, which equates writing with fantasy, is similar to this
   theory of think-act evocation: "Mental work is linked to some current
   impression, some provoking occasion in the present which has been
   able to arouse one of the subject's major wishes." See "Creative
   Writers and Day-Dreaming," 147.

59 Keefer, *Reading Mavis Gallant*, 46.

60 Deutsch, "Absence of Grief," 228.

61 Keefer, *Reading Mavis Gallant*, 109.

62 Gallant, "The End of the World," in *The End of the World and Other Stories*, 88.

63 Helmut Bonheim comments that in "Acceptance of their Ways" (Jan. 1960) the "ratio of story to discourse time gives Gallant's narrative a distinctly modernist flavour." Bonheim states that the technique of alternating perception and apperception is "that of James Joyce" in *Ulysses*. Gallant uses the technique to a greater extent in her longer fictions. See Bonheim's "The Aporias of Lily Little," 75.

64 Schrank, "Popular Culture," 57.

65 Besner, *The Light of the Imagination*, 27.

66 Gallant, "Bernadette," in *My Heart Is Broken*, 24.

67 Schrank, "Popular Culture," 61.

68 Gallant, "The Moabitess," in *My Heart Is Broken*, 42.

69 O'Rourke, "Exiles in Time," 101.

70 The story was also published in *Home Truths*, 1981.

71 Gallant, "The Ice Wagon Going down the Street," in *My Heart Is Broken*, 256.

72 Derrida, *Memoires*, 49.

73 Peter Stevens claims that "a full revelation" is not possible for the reader of Gallant's novels "until all the pieces can be placed together when the reader reaches the last page" ("Perils of Compassion," 68); but it is doubtful whether the reader indeed reaches a "full revelation" even then.

74 Besner, *The Light of the Imagination*, 27.

75 Gallant, "Its Image on the Mirror" in *My Heart Is Broken*, 60.

76 Jewison, "Speaking of Mirrors," 103.

77 Gallant, "Its Image on the Mirror," 101, 103.

78 Moss, *A Reader's Guide*, 84.

79 Besner, *The Light*, 29.

80 Foster, *Confession and Complicity*, 7, 16.

81 Derrida, "Fors," 67–68.

82 Murray, "Canada, Canonicity, and the Uncanny," 115.

83 Derrida, "Fors," 68.

84 Besner, *The Light of the Imagination*, 38.

85 Keefer, *Reading Mavis Gallant*, 63.

86 Besner, *The Light of the Imagination*, 31.

87 Ibid., 37.

88 Derrida, "Fors," 78.

89 The first three parts of the novel were published separately in the

New Yorker in June, July, and August of 1959. Part 4 was previously unpublished.

90 Jewison, "Speaking of Mirrors," 109.

91 Gallant, *Green Water, Green Sky*, 67.

92 Woolf, *The Voyage Out*, 262.

93 Keefer, *Reading Mavis Gallant*, 79.

94 Smythe, "*Green Water, Green Sky*: Gallant's Discourse of Dislocation," 74.

95 Moss, *A Reader's Guide to the Canadian Novel*, 85.

96 Gallant, *Green Water, Green Sky*, 52.

97 The title of the novel describes how Flor perceives the world: "Everything was so clear and green, green water, even the sky looked green to me," she says to George (17). Interior worlds are indistinguishable from reality for Flor.

98 Hatch, "Mavis Gallant and the Creation of Consciousness," 52.

99 Kristeva, *Black Sun*, 42.

100 This is Kristeva's term for the stage of psychic life that precedes the entrance into "symbolic" language, where words and signs replace the severed relationship with the mother and negate that loss. See *Desire in Language*, 133.

101 Lacan, "The Mirror Stage," 2.

102 Neil Besner, *The Light of the Imagination*, 57.

103 Early in the novel Flor's green eyes cause George to remember falling in a mossy pond as a very young child: "The most oppressive part of the memory was that he had lain there, passive, with the mossy water over his mouth" (6–7). He then contradicts this memory with the memory of being "fished" out, "not on his back at all, but on his face, splashing and floundering" (7).

104 Keith, *A Sense of Style*, 108.

105 Lorna Irvine states that "the novel is culturally allegorical, and Gallant's attention focuses on patriarchal systems, as opposed to matriarchal ones." See "Starting from the Beginning Every Time," 249 n 7.

106 Linda Leith, "The Scream," 215.

107 See Besner, *The Light of the Imagination*, 58, and Hatch, "The Creation of Consciousness," 57.

108 Northrop Frye writes that in Old Comedy there is a catharsis of sympathy and ridicule that parallels the pity and fear of tragedy; comedy and elegy do seem to intersect at such points of sympathetic release. See *Anatomy of Criticism*, 43.

109 Gabriel, "Fairly Good Times," 24.

110 In Gallant's more overtly political fiction the case is not quite so

simple: narrating and forgetting of the past constitute an amoral refusal of history.

111 Blodgett, "The Letter and Its Gloss," 187.
112 Ibid., 184.
113 Riffaterre, *Fictional Truth*, 28.
114 Blodgett, "The Letter and Its Gloss," 188.
115 Moss, *A Reader's Guide*, 87.
116 Borklund, "Mavis Gallant," 324.
117 Keefer, *Reading Mavis Gallant*, 86.
118 Gallant, *A Fairly Good Time*, 208.
119 Nietzsche, "The Use and Abuse of History," 2, 8.
120 Blodgett, "The Letter and Its Gloss," 174.
121 Nietzsche, "The Use and Abuse of History," 8.
122 This section of the novel is a revision of the previously published story "The Accident" (Oct. 1967), collected in *The End of the World and Other Stories* as well.
123 Mavis Gallant, *In Transit*, 157.
124 Kauffman, *Discourses of Desire*, 26.
125 The address is written/thought during "the dead period of daylight, midafternoon – the time of day when she always felt slightly nauseated," we are told (211); the conventional hour of the pastoral *otium* is thus used but subverted in Shirley's elegiac epistle.
126 Blodgett, "The Letter and Its Gloss," 188.
127 Hatch, "Mavis Gallant and the Creation of Consciousness," 64.
128 Blodgett, "Heresy and Other Arts," 8.
129 Keith, *A Sense of Style*, 108.
130 Ibid., 115.
131 Blodgett, "The Letter and Its Gloss," 184.
132 Besner, *The Light of the Imagination*, 66.
133 Irvine, "Starting from the Beginning," 248.

CHAPTER THREE

1 Robinson and Hawpe, "Narrative Thinking," 111.
2 Kenneth A. Bruffee writes that the narrator of the elegiac romance is "cast in the role of a highly conventional, highly traditional, hence a highly reliable figure," (*Elegiac Romance*, 45); but Gallant tends to preclude her relatively *un*reliable mourner-figures from arriving at a revelatory insight or consolation, since they conventionally evade the significance of the "truths" that the story points to.
3 de Man, *Allegories of Reading*, 205.
4 Interestingly, Walter Benjamin states that "mourning … is at once

the mother of the allegories and their content." See *The Origin of German Tragic Drama*, 230.

5 de Man stresses the sequential structure of allegory, and writes that "allegory is sequential and narrative, yet the topic of its narration is not necessarily temporal at all." See "Pascal's Allegory of Persuasion," 1.

6 Benjamin, *The Origin of German Tragic Drama*, 230, 185.

7 Martens, "The Past Projected," 41.

8 In "The Three Stages of Mavis Gallant's Short Fiction" Ronald Hatch states that "in the series of Montreal stories" readers learn "something about Gallant's own early life in Montreal" (107). George Woodcock also discusses the Montreal setting and similarities between Linnet's life and Gallant's, though he does stress that "everything has been reshaped and transmuted in the imagination so that what emerges is a work of fiction on several levels"; see his article "Memory, Imagination, Artifice," 88. Lorna Irvine, in "Starting from the Beginning Every Time," discusses the autobiography of "a woman writer" with alternating references to Linnet and Gallant (252–5). As Michelle Gadpaille writes in *The Canadian Short Story*, "it is to these stories that readers and critics look for the autobiographical material that Gallant so continually denies her public" (52). Neil Besner clearly differentiates between author proper and author-character in *The Light of Imagination* (131).

9 Hancock, "Interview with Mavis Gallant," 28.

10 Woolf, *A Room of One's Own*, 78.

11 See Godard, "Stretching the Story," 27–71. Godard discusses Laurence's *A Bird in the House*, a story sequence that is structurally similar to the Linnet series.

12 Keith, *A Sense of Style*, 110.

13 Flieger, "Proust, Freud, and the Art of Forgetting," 69.

14 Jaeck, *Marcel Proust and the Text as Macrometaphor*, 21.

15 Gallant, *Home Truths*, 260.

16 Gallant, introduction to *Home Truths*, xxii.

17 The term *Künstlerroman* could also be used to describe this sequence of stories. The relationship of this form to the prose elegy is significant since the elegist is self-consciously an artist-figure, and makes use of the autobiographical as well.

18 Gallant, *Home Truths*, 285.

19 Laurence, Munro, and Atwood have all written similarly elegiac works mourning the loss of a father. In the interview with Geoff Hancock, Gallant notes the thematic importance of fathers in Canadian fiction (Hancock, "Interview," 25).

20 See Peter Sacks, *The English Elegy*, 15, for a Freudian reading of this aspect of elegy; see also Celeste M. Schenck, "Feminism and Deconstruction," for an interesting perspective on elegy, patriarchy, and poetic inheritance.

21 On this elegiac convention see Edward Honig, *Dark Conceit*, 163. Linnet *does* long for one aspect of childhood, though – intuitive knowledge: "everyone under the age of ten knows everything ... It is part of the clairvoyant immunity to hypocrisy we are born with and that vanishes just before puberty" (304).

22 See Malcolm Ross, "Mavis Gallant and Thea Astley on Home Truths, Home Folk."

23 Zeiger, "Lilacs Out of the Dead Land," 17.

24 Freud, "The Uncanny," 241.

25 Kermode, "Secrets and Narrative Sequence," 81.

26 de Man discusses these issues at length in *The Rhetoric of Romanticism*. See especially "Autobiography as De-Facement" and "Anthropomorphism and Trope in the Lyric." I am equating aesthetics with writing and the epistemological with memory in the formulation of my theory of elegy.

27 "Varieties of Exile" is a story-length digression that is like an allegory of the sequential elegy. In the story Frank Cairns takes on the roles of both Linnet *and* her father – he is depressed and homesick like Angus, but he also suffered a "childhood of secret grieving" as did Linnet (269).

28 Culler, "On Apostrophe," 66.

29 Ricoeur, "Narrative Time," 167.

30 Keefer, *Reading Mavis Gallant*, 75.

31 Angus's death had been kept from Linnet for years. Her elegy is not written until several more years have passed, after she learns of the manner of his death.

32 Benjamin, *The Origin*, 175.

33 Eric Smith suggests that elegy is basically a dramatic form. See *By Mourning Tongues*, 15.

34 Peter Sacks, *The English Elegy*, 19.

35 For a definition of the term "critical nostalgia," see Michael Squires, *The Pastoral Novel*, 14. Squires suggests that the "critical nostalgia" employed by authors such as Faulkner involves the interplay between the past and the present, noting that this perspective is available "only when the fantasy of returning home is surrendered." Linnet has definitely surrendered this fantasy, if indeed she ever entertained it.

36 Derrida, *Memoires*, 37.

37 Peter Sacks, *The English Elegy*, 5.

38 de Man, *The Rhetoric of Romanticism*, 262. Linnet is aware of the anthropomorphic potential in her own thinking and writing and is usually careful to reject the tendency: "The house he came to remained for a long time enormous in memory, though the few like it still standing – 'still *living*,' I *nearly* say – are narrow, with thin, steep staircases and close, high-ceilinged rooms" (302, emphasis mine).

39 Derrida, *Memoires*, 31.

40 Neil Besner notes that Linnet writes in a "historical framework" after recognizing that memory "makes necessary fictions." See *The Light of Imagination*, 133.

41 See Derrida on the *pharmakon* in *Dissemination*, 70; see also Paul de Man's "Sign and Symbol in Hegel's *Aesthetics*."

42 Derrida, *Dissemination*, 107.

43 This again is a reversal of the tendency in much elegiac literature to write about the past in order to release oneself from its grip. See Kenneth Bruffee, "Elegiac Romance," for a discussion of this convention.

44 Derrida, *Memoires*, 38.

45 On inheritance of the poetic vocation in pastoral elegy, see Celeste M. Schenck, *Mourning and Panegyric: The Poetics of Pastoral Ceremony*.

46 Ricoeur, "Narrative Time," 186.

47 Kermode, "Secrets and Narrative Sequence," 81.

48 Derrida, *Memoires*, 34, 35.

49 Sacks, *The English Elegy*, 23.

50 See Lorna Irvine, "Starting from the Beginning Every Time," 252.

51 Gallant, *Home Truths*, 237; my emphasis.

52 Gallant, *Overhead*, 157.

53 Keefer, *Reading Mavis Gallant*, 186, 187.

54 Besner, *The Light*, 151.

55 Ricoeur, "Narrative Time," 174.

56 Keefer, *Reading Mavis Gallant*, 187.

57 Smith, "The Will to Allegory," 107.

58 The name "Sandor" could be an allusion to the German photographer August Sandor, who was arrested because his pre–Second World War portraits of Germans contradicted the Nazi fiction of German superior beauty.

59 Besner, *The Light*, 141, 143.

60 Besner writes that "Speck owes all of his success and his prospects as a cultural middleman to the modern expropriation of art from its former position as an expression, distillation, or crystallization of beauty, grace, inspiration, or spiritual values, and to its relocation as a medium of purely material value to the consumer" (*Light of the*

Imagination, 143). I assume that Besner's use of the word "modern" is meant to be synonymous with "contemporary" in this statement, and not a reference to the aesthetic period of "modernism."

61 Iser, "The Play of the Text," 331.

62 R.P. Bilan writes that some of the stories in *From the Fifteenth District* represent "the fag-end of modernism: they belong to the world of Eliot's early poems and of Joyce's 'The Dead,' and it seems late in the day for this kind of writing" ("Letters in Canada, 1979: Fiction," 326). However I am arguing that Gallant's stories, though similar to modernist elegiac literature, work to subvert certain conventions and revise the fiction-elegy in a "late modern" framework.

63 Ghosts haunt several of Gallant's characters and stories. Another example of the haunted is Jean Price, who confronts the ghosts of her brother, her house, and herself in "Its Image on the Mirror."

64 Benjamin, *The Origin of German Tragic Drama*, 193.

65 Freud, "The Uncanny," 241.

66 Borklund, "Mavis Gallant," 325.

67 Gallant, *From the Fifteenth District*, 163.

68 Ibid., 167.

69 Keefer cites Benjamin's description of the angel of history in *Reading Mavis Gallant*, 157; the relevant passage is in Benjamin, *Illuminations*, 257–8 (Keefer cites another edition).

70 Gallant, *From the Fifteenth District*, 27.

71 Keefer, *Reading Mavis Gallant*, 184.

72 This is how Besner refers to Netta's memory (*The Light of Imagination*, 109 and 114), since we are told that Netta, upon hearing "some deeply alien music," has a memory that "automatically gave her a composer's name" ("The Moslem Wife," 38).

73 Besner, *The Light of the Imagination*, 104.

74 Keefer, *Reading Mavis Gallant*, 94.

75 Besner, *The Light*, 104.

76 Gallant, "What is Style?" 176.

77 Gallant, introduction to *Home Truths*, xv.

78 Derrida, *Memoires*, 48.

79 Miller, *The Ethics of Reading*, 43.

80 Besner, *The Light*, 153.

81 de Man, *Allegories of Reading*, 206.

82 Gallant comments on the meaning of the word in an interview with Pleuke Boyce. See Boyce, "Image and Memory," 31.

83 Hatch, "Mavis Gallant and the Fascism of Everyday Life," 37.

84 Besner, *The Light*, 82.

85 White, "The Value of Narrativity," 14.

86 Ibid., 21; author's emphasis.

87 Benjamin, *The Origin*, 178.
88 Ibid., 166.
89 Gallant, *The Pegnitz Junction*, 70.
90 Gallant, "Things Overlooked Before," 85.
91 Arendt, *Eichmann in Jerusalem*.
92 Hancock, "An Interview with Mavis Gallant," 40.
93 Nietzsche, "The Use and Abuse of History," 10.
94 Ibid., 9.
95 Keefer, *Reading Mavis Gallant*, 173.
96 White, "The Value of Narrativity," 2.
97 Nietzsche, "The Use and Abuse of History," 28.
98 Hancock, "Interview with Mavis Gallant," 39.
99 de Man, "Anthropomorphism and Trope in the Lyric," 262.
100 I am alluding to Linda Hutcheon's term "historiographic metafiction," which she uses in her article "The Pastime of Past Time" and elsewhere.
101 In "The Old Friends" the commissioner is a good example of someone who employs intentional forgetfulness and distortion in order to invent a version of events during the war and to protect himself from taking any personal responsibility for his participation.
102 Gabriel, "Fairly Good Times," 24.
103 Gallant states that "the castle of Kafka" appears in this scene (Gabriel, "Fairly Good Times," 24); Keefer states that the entire novella is a "parody of Kafka's *The Castle*" (*Reading Mavis Gallant*, 172).
104 Woodcock, "Memory, Imagination, Artifice," 86.
105 Gabriel, "Fairly Good Times," 24.
106 Benjamin, *Illuminations*, 264–5.
107 White, "The Value of Narrativity," 20.
108 Besner, *The Light*, 67.
109 White, "The Narrativization of Real Events," 254.
110 Keefer, *Reading Mavis Gallant*, 181.
111 Benjamin, *Illuminations*, 94.
112 Bruffee, *Elegiac Romance*, 62.
113 Freud, "Creative Writers and Day-dreaming," 151.
114 This is another use of the metaphor of the worm that Gallant discusses in the Hancock interview, as previously noted.
115 Irvine, "Starting at the Beginning," 249.
116 Buck-Morss, *The Dialectics of Seeing*, 168.
117 Gabriel, "A Fairly Good Time," 23.
118 Ricoeur, "The Metaphorical Process," 155.

CHAPTER FOUR

1 Twigg, "What Is: Alice Munro," 15–16.
2 Woodcock, "The Plots of Life," 239.
3 Schleifer, *Rhetoric and Death*, 50.
4 Gold, "Our Feelings Exactly," 6.
5 Hoy, "Alice Munro," 7, 15.
6 Struthers, "Alice Munro's Fictive Imagination," 103.
7 Keefer, "Mavis Gallant," 196.
8 In an interview Munro states that "as a writer, I don't think that [political] way at all." See Hancock, "An Interview with Alice Munro," 85–6.
9 Gibson, "Alice Munro," 243; emphasis mine.
10 Derrida, *The Post Card*, 363.
11 Lamont-Stewart, "Order from Chaos," 114.
12 Derrida, *The Post Card*, 363.
13 Dombrowski, "Down to Death," 21.
14 Hoffman, *The Mortal No*, 163.
15 Barthes, "The Reality Effect," 16.
16 Hoy, "Alice Munro," 9.
17 Sontag, *On Photography*, 15.
18 Barthes, *Camera Lucida*, 110.
19 Munro mentions an interest in magic-realist painters when asked by John Metcalf about their "magic of the ordinary." See Metcalf, "A Conversation with Alice Munro," 58; also Gibson, "Alice Munro," 256.
20 Munro, introduction to *The Moons of Jupiter*, xv.
21 I am indebted to Alan Bewell for suggesting this term.
22 Slopen, "PW Interviews Alice Munro," 76.
23 Carscallen, "Alice Munro," *Profiles in Canadian Literature*, 2:74.
24 Munro, *The Moons of Jupiter*, 197.
25 Barthes, *Camera Lucida*, 82.
26 Ibid., 32.
27 Ibid., 26.
28 Benjamin, *Illuminations*, 262.
29 Ibid., 161. Here Benjamin refers to Freud's stimulation/protection model of consciousness and memory (from *Beyond the Pleasure Principle*).
30 Ibid., 237.
31 Carscallen, "Alice Munro," 74.
32 Blodgett, "Prisms and Arcs: Structures in Hébert and Munro," 115.
33 Munro, "What is Real?" 225.
34 Bouson, *The Empathic Reader*, 28.

35 Keith, "The Ethics of Fiction," 16–17.

36 Martin, "The Strange and the Familiar," 219, 226.

37 Keefer, "Strange Fashions of Forsaking," 727.

38 Barthes, *Camera Lucida*, 70.

39 Fitzpatrick, " 'Projection' in Alice Munro's *Something I've Been Meaning To Tell You*," 20.

40 Sontag, *On Photography*, 3.

41 Ibid., 4.

42 Hoy, "Alice Munro," 20.

43 Lamont-Stewart, "Order from Chaos," 114. Lamont-Stewart also applies this description to Clarke Blaise's work. Ildikó de Papp Carrington calls some of the narrating "watchers" in Munro "witnesses," who are produced via her strategic "psychological distance," in *Controlling the Uncontrollable*, 7.

44 Munro, "Author's Commentary," 125.

45 York, "The Other Side of Dailiness," 59.

46 See John Metcalf, "A Conversation With Alice Munro," 57; see also J.R. Struthers, "The Real Material," 6.

47 Struthers, "Alice Munro's Fictive Imagination," 110.

48 Alice Munro, *Dance of the Happy Shades*, 7.

49 Orange, "Alice Munro and a Maze of Time," 84.

50 This phrase alludes to one of Hamlet's soliloquies: "But that the dread of something after death, / The undiscovered country, from whose bourn / No traveler returns, puzzles the will" (III. i).

51 This phrase of Peter Sacks (*The English Elegy*, 5) has been cited in my discussion of Gallant's Linnet Muir stories.

52 W.R. Martin has also recognized the similarity between the last passage of Munro's story and that of Joyce's. See "The Strange and the Familiar in Alice Munro," 124.

53 See Rae McCarthy Macdonald, "A Madman Loose in the World," 367–8, for discussion of Helen's "survivor's intuition."

54 "Dance of the Happy Shades" relates similar emotional perceptions about social survival and ceremonies, and the inability to assimilate painful discoveries in an empathic reading of other people and their mysterious situations, their existence in the "other country" (224). It is elegiac in the sense that it is about the seeming gradual deterioration of an elderly woman's life, but it is more importantly about other people's values as reflected in their view *of* that woman.

55 In "Home" the narrator remembers her dead mother as she tells the story of visiting her sick father. She self-consciously attempts to create what she calls, in the last of the italicized passages, "prosaic safety" for herself and for the reader. See Munro, "Home," *74 New Canadian Stories*, 153. In terms of theme, structure, and style "Home"

resembles the other stories about a dead or dying mother, as well as "Bardon Bus."

56 Munro, *Something I've Been Meaning To Tell You*, 201.
57 Struthers, "The Real Material," 33.
58 Hancock, "An Interview with Alice Munro," 94.
59 Osachoff, "Treacheries of the Heart," 77.
60 Struthers, "The Real Material," 7.
61 As Douglas Barbour writes, "you" (the reader) must "grant it [life's unresolvability] its place in *your* schema as well" ("The Extraordinary Ordinary," 110).
62 Kauffman, *Discourses of Desire*, 26.
63 Both can evoke "a howl" of "amazing protest" ("The Spanish Lady," *Something I've Been Meaning to Tell You*, 181), a cry "full of terrible grievances" (189–90).
64 York, "The Other Side of Dailiness," 54.
65 Munro discusses this title in Stainsby, "Alice Munro Talks with Mari Stainsby," 30.
66 Munro, *Lives of Girls and Women*, 77.
67 Alter, *Partial Magic*, 243.
68 See, for example, W.R. Martin, "Alice Munro and James Joyce," and J.R. Struthers, "Reality and Ordering."
69 Lorna Irvine writes that Munro's fiction "refuse[s] epiphany, stasis, closure," and that "Del assiduously avoids epiphany" ("Changing Is the Word I Want," 100). But the fact that Del's mind, and Munro's fiction, oscillate "between secrecy and revelation" (110) does not contradict the definition of epiphany, wherein a transcendent atemporal experience is achieved in the transformation of life into art; rather, I would argue that this oscillation schematizes and thematizes the temporality of the epiphanic moment.
70 Sontag, *On Photography*, 69.
71 Bowen, "In Camera," 22.
72 Rella, "Melancholy and the Labyrinthine World of Things," 30.
73 McDonald, "A Madman Loose in the World," 372.
74 Blodgett, *Alice Munro*, 42.
75 See Mark Turner's *Death Is the Mother of Beauty* for a discussion of what he calls "kinship metaphors" (191).
76 The death of Addie's mother is followed by the deaths of three people, two of whom she met in a boarding-house – Grandma Seeley, a married Miss Rush, and her baby (77). Blodgett perceptively states that the Miss Rush passage is written in an *ubi sunt* design (*Alice Munro*, 45).
77 Godard, "Heirs of the Living Body," 68.

78 These questions of reality, religion, and art are also raised and explored in the context of sexuality in "Baptizing," where Del's love affair with Garnet French ends in a struggle in the river (235). This directly alludes to two of the three suicides in the story – Miss Farris and Marion Sherriff both drowned in the Wawanash River. The other attempt was made by Addie in her youth (75).

79 The story of Miss Farris's suicide is relayed in "Changes and Ceremonies"; she is a figure of "universal sorrow and hurt," according to Macdonald (371). Both suicides are committed because of the pain of loss through unrequited love, which Munro uses in her fiction as a kind of death. In "Lives of Girls and Women" Fern is abandoned by Art Chamberlain (whose radio show is called *In Memoriam*), and in this story Munro explores themes of love, loss, and self-fulfilment.

80 Barthes, *Camera Lucida*, 92.

CHAPTER FIVE

1 Interestingly, *The Moons of Jupiter* is dedicated to Munro's literary "father," Robert Weaver, while *Dance of the Happy Shades* is dedicated to her real father, Robert Laidlaw; *Friend of My Youth* is dedicated to her mother.

2 Munro, introduction to *The Moons of Jupiter*, xiv.

3 Metcalf, "A Conversation with Alice Munro," 58; Hancock, "An Interview with Alice Munro," 104.

4 Munro, "The Peace of Utrecht," *Dance of the Happy Shades*, 193.

5 Here I paraphrase a line from "An Ounce of Cure" in *Dance of the Happy Shades*, 88.

6 Osachoff, "Treacheries of the Heart," 75.

7 Hancock, "An Interview with Alice Munro," 104.

8 This phrase is first used by Munro in "Dance of the Happy Shades," and refers to the unknown, the mysterious.

9 This phrase recalls Sontag's statement that "photographs testify to time's relentless melt." See *On Photography*, 15.

10 Barthes, *Camera Lucida*, 110.

11 Munro, "The Progress of Love," *The Progress of Love*, 13.

12 Benjamin, *Illuminations*, 93.

13 Munro, "Friend of My Youth," *Friend of My Youth*, 4.

14 This term resists the hierarchical positioning of one story above the other, a structure that is implied by the term "subtextual."

15 Buitenhuis, "The Wilds of the Past," 22.

16 Munro, "Goodness and Mercy," in *Friend of My Youth*, 178.

17 These are the final words of "Differently," in *Friend of My Youth*, 243.

18 Munro, "The Moons of Jupiter," *The Moons of Jupiter*, 217.

19 Blodgett, *Alice Munro*, 177.

20 Carrington, *Controlling the Uncontrollable*, 203.

21 Klibansky, Panofsky, and Saxl, *Saturn and Melancholy*, 127.

22 Blodgett, *Alice Munro*, 72.

23 The stone is also an emblem of Saturn in that it is synecdochic of the "cold, dry earth."

24 Benjamin, *The Origin of German Tragic Drama*, 155.

25 This may be an allusion to the resurrection of Christ from the tomb: the stone had been moved, and since his body was absent, he must therefore have been reborn in spirit.

26 This notion echoes Vanessa's idea of inheriting the past in Laurence's *A Bird in the House* (another elegiac short-story cycle).

27 Benjamin, *Illuminations*, 89.

28 Abbas, "Walter Benjamin's Collector," 228.

29 Benjamin, *Reflections*, 157.

30 Barthes, *Camera Lucida*, 110.

31 Benjamin uses the phrase "profane illumination" to describe knowledge that is acquired in the act of reading (*Reflections*, 190).

32 Stich, "The Cather Connection in Alice Munro's "Dulse.' "

33 Hancock, "An Interview with Alice Munro," 108.

34 Stich draws a parallel between the Lydia of Acts 16:14, "the seller of purple," and the Lydia of the story. He notes that this section of the Bible "refers to problems of truth" (107); Munro's story also probes such problems in connection with the act of story-telling.

35 See pages 37, 41, 42, 44, 50, 52, 53, 55, 57, 58, for example.

36 This may be an allusion to "The Wizard of Oz," where the Tin Man is in search of a heart.

37 Hancock, "An Interview with Alice Munro," 108.

38 This phrase of Freud's implies a "work of remembering" through an "acting out," as explained in "Remembering, Repeating and Working-Through," 151.

39 Certain clues seem to lead us to the conclusion that the narrator's friend, Kay, becomes involved with the same man ("X") – his name is Alex (containing the letter X, as we are told his name does); he is an anthropologist; and he makes an oddly attractive gesture (which is seemingly his seductive trademark), putting his head in Kay's lap, taking her by surprise. There are also connections to the narrator Janet of the title story and related stories: references to the spinster aunts, the black-eyed Susans, for example.

40 This was Munro's original title for *Lives of Girls and Women*. See "Alice Munro Talks with Mari Stainsby," 30.

41 Hancock, "An Interview with Alice Munro," 108.
42 Wachtel, "An Interview with Alice Munro," 52.

CHAPTER SIX

1 This phrase titles chapter 9 of McHale's *Postmodern Fiction*.
2 Kristeva, "The Malady of Grief," in *Black Sun*, 259.
3 Julia Kristeva writes that *Finnegans Wake* is "a single catharsis: the rhetoric of the pure signifier, of music in letters," in *Powers of Horror*, 23.
4 Hutcheon, *A Poetics of Postmodernism*, 4.
5 Sacks, *The English Elegy*, 325.
6 Kristeva, *Black Sun*, 223.
7 Ibid., 225.
8 Kristeva, "The Pain of Sorrow in the Modern World," 140.
9 Willis, *Marguerite Duras*, 28.
10 Lacan, "Homage to Marguerite Duras, on *Le Ravissement de Lol V. Stein*," in Marguerite Duras, *Duras by Duras*, 123.
11 See my article, "The Scene of Seeing," for a more detailed discussion of the relationship between Lol's sexuality and her subjectivity.
12 According to Nicolas Abraham and Maria Torok in "Introjection–Incorporation," the term "incorporation" refers to a fantasy that "preserves the intrapsychic situation" (4). Incorporation leads to melancholia, whereby a mental crypt (filled with memories, words, and images) creates an objective counterpart to the loss, in the form of a complete person (8). This complete "other" then fuses with the mourner's ego, producing "interminable mourning" (14). The procedure is analogous to swallowing an object in order to deny a loss and reject both mourning and its necessary "introjection," a term coined by Ferenczi that refers to a process of enlarging the ego: "To introject a wish, or grief, is to dispose of it through language," since the void is filled with words; "language represents presence," write Abraham and Torok.
13 Kristeva, *Black Sun*, 229.
14 Ibid., 228.
15 Ibid., 228–9.
16 Leon S. Roudiez translates *La Doleur* as *The Grief* and titles the novel as such in his translation of *Black Sun*. Barbara Bray's translation for Pantheon Books provides the English title *The War*.
17 Duras, *Practicalities*, 107.
18 Ibid., 107.
19 Duras, *The Lover*, 3.

20 The publisher of this edition of *The Lover* includes passages "from the reviews for *The Lover*," one of which states: "An elegiac memoir ... written in compressed, emotionally charged language that conjures up mood, time, and place with resonating effect" (*Publishers Weekly*).

21 Hancock, "An Interview with Mavis Gallant," 41.

22 Duras, *Hiroshima Mon Amour*, 9.

23 Duras includes a prefatorial note with this novel, from which this comment is cited. See Duras, *The War*, 4.

24 Kristeva, *Black Sun*, 238.

25 White, *Nocturnes for the King of Naples*, 49.

26 Derrida, *The Post Card*, 4.

27 Kauffman, *Discourses of Desire*, 22.

28 Bruffee, *Elegiac Romance*, 62.

29 Bal, "Mimesis and Genre Theory in Aristotle's *Poetics*," 176.

30 The term "behabitive" is used by J.L. Austin in his discussion of performative language to denote "a kind of performative concerned roughly with reactions to behaviour and with behaviour towards others and designed to exhibit attitudes and feelings," as noted earlier in this study.

31 For example, see Carriker, "Edna O'Brien's 'The Doll.' "

32 Roth, foreword to *A Fanatic Heart*, viii.

33 Derrida cites this term from a passage in his own "Fors" in *Truth in Painting*, 228. He uses the word "thanatographer" as well in his study of an exhibition of Gérard Titus-Carmel's work entitled *The Pocket Size Tlingit Coffin and the 61 Ensuing Drawings* (*Truth in Painting*, 198).

34 My coinage of "thanatomy" combines the word "thanatology" with "anatomy." My thanks to Gregory Betts for his contribution to this term to my thinking.

35 O'Brien's apt epigraph is taken from Thomas Mann: "Each human life must work through all the joys and sorrows, gains and losses, which make up the history of the world."

36 O'Brien, "Baby Blue," in *A Fanatic Heart*, 321.

37 O'Brien, "The Silly and the Serious," 482.

38 Derrida, *The Truth in Painting*, 224–5.

39 O'Brien, "Long Distance," in *Harper's*, 44. This story has also been published in *Lantern Slides* (New York: Farrar Straus Giroux 1990).

40 O'Brien, "A Rose in the Heart of New York," *A Fanatic Heart*, 375.

41 O'Brien, "The Silly and the Serious," 488.

42 Hernadi, "Doing, Making, Meaning," 752.

Works Cited

Abbas, Ackbar. "Walter Benjamin's Collector: The Fate of Modern Experience." In *Modernity and the Text: Revisions of German Modernism*, ed. A. Huyssen and D. Bathrick. New York: Columbia University Press 1989. 216–39.

Abel, Elizabeth. *Virginia Woolf and the Fictions of Psychoanalysis*. Chicago: University of Chicago Press 1989.

Abraham, Nicolas, and Maria Torok. "Introjection–Incorporation: Mourning *or* Melancholia." In *Psychoanalysis in France*, ed. Serge Lebovici and Daniel Widlocher. New York: International Universities Press 1980.

Adams, Robert Martin. "Hades." In *James Joyce's Ulysses: Critical Essays*, ed. Clive Hart and David Hayman. Berkeley: University of California Press 1974. 91–114.

Alter, Robert. *Partial Magic: The Novel as a Self-Conscious Genre*. Berkeley and Los Angeles: University of California Press 1975.

Arendt, Hannah. *Eichmann in Jerusalem: A Report on the Banality of Evil*. New York: Viking 1965.

Austin, J.L. *How To Do Things with Words*. Ed. J.O. Urmson and Marina Sbisa. Oxford: Clarendon Press 1975.

Bal, Mieke. "Mimesis and Genre Theory in Aristotle's *Poetics*." *Poetics Today* 3, no. 1 (1982): 171–80.

– "Introduction: Delimiting Psychopoetics." *Poetics* 13 (1984): 279–98.

Barbour, Douglas. "The Extraordinary Ordinary." Review of *Something I've Been Meaning To Tell You*, *Open Letter* 3, no. 3 (Fall 1975): 107–10.

Barthes, Roland. *Camera Lucida: Reflections on Photography*. Trans. Richard Howard. New York: Hill and Wang 1981.

– "The Reality Effect." In *French Literary Theory Today: A Reader*, ed. Tzvetan Todorov. Cambridge: Cambridge University Press 1982. 11–17.

Beer, Gillian. "Hume, Stephen and Elegy in *To the Lighthouse.*" *Essays in Criticism* 34, no. 1 (Jan. 1984): 33–55.

– *Arguing with the Past: Essays in Narrative from Woolf to Sidney.* New York: Routledge 1989.

Beja, Morris. *Epiphany in the Modern Novel: Revelation As Art.* London: Peter Owen 1971.

Benjamin, Walter. *Illuminations: Essays and Reflections.* Ed. Hannah Arendt; trans. Harry Zohn. New York: Schocken Books 1969.

– *The Origin of German Tragic Drama.* Trans. John Osborne. London: NLB 1977.

– *Reflections: Essays, Aphorisms, Autobiographical Writings.* Ed. Peter Demetz; trans. Edmund Jephcott. New York: Schocken Books 1986.

Besner, Neil. *The Light of Imagination: Mavis Gallant's Fiction.* Vancouver: University of British Columbia Press 1988.

Bilan, R.P. "Letters in Canada 1979: Fiction." *University of Toronto Quarterly* 49, no. 4 (Summer 1980): 324–36.

Blodgett, E.D. "Prisms and Arcs: Structures in Hebert and Munro." In *Figures in a Ground: Canadian Essays on Modern Literature*, ed. Diane Bessai and David Jackel. Saskatoon: Western Producer Prairie Books 1978. 99–121.

– *Alice Munro.* Boston: Twayne Publishers 1988.

– "Heresy and Other Arts: A Measure of Mavis Gallant's Fiction." *Essays on Canadian Writing* 42 (Winter 1990): 1–8.

– "The Letter and Its Gloss: A Reading of Mavis Gallant's *A Fairly Good Time.*" *Essays on Canadian Writing* 42 (Winter 1990): 173–90.

Bloomfield, Morton W. "The Elegy and the Elegiac Mode: Praise and Alienation." In *Renaissance Genres: Essays on Theory, History and Interpretation*, ed. Barbara Kiefer Lewalski. Cambridge: Harvard University Press 1986. 147–57.

Bonheim, Helmut. "The Aporias of Lily Littel: Mavis Gallant's 'Acceptance of Their Ways.' " *Ariel* 18, no. 4 (Oct. 1987): 69–78.

Bouson, J. Brooks. *The Empathetic Reader: A Study of the Narcissistic Character and the Drama of the Self.* Amherst: University of Massachusetts Press 1989.

Bowen, Deborah. "In Camera: The Developed Photographs of Margaret Laurence and Alice Munro." *Studies in Canadian Literature* 13, no. 1 (1988): 20–33.

Boyce, Pleuke. "Interview [with Mavis Gallant]: Image and Memory." *Books in Canada* 19, no. 1 (Jan.–Feb. 1990): 29–31.

Brooks, Peter. *Reading for the Plot: Design and Intention in Narrative.* New York: Alfred A. Knopf 1984.

– "Psychoanalytic Constructions and Narrative Meanings." *Paragraph: The Journal of the Modern Critical Theory Group* 7 (1986): 53–76.

- "The Idea of a Psychoanalytic Literary Criticism." In *Discourse in Psychoanalysis and Literature*, ed. Shlomith Rimmon-Kenan. London: Methuen 1987. 1–18.

Bruffee, Kenneth A. "Elegiac Romance." *College English* 32, no. 4 (Jan. 1971): 465–76.

- *Elegiac Romance: Cultural Change and the Loss of the Hero in Modern Fiction*. Ithaca: Cornell University Press 1983.

Bruner, Jerome. "The Narrative Construction of Reality." *Critical Inquiry* 18, no. 1 (Autumn 1991): 1–21.

Buck-Morss, Susan. *A Dialectics of Seeing: Walter Benjamin and the Arcades Project*. Cambridge: MIT Press 1991.

Buitenhuis, Peter. "The Wilds of the Past." *Books in Canada* (May 1990): 19–22.

Cairns, Francis. *Generic Composition in Greek and Roman Poetry*. Edinburgh: Edinburgh University Press 1972.

Caramagno, Thomas C. "Manic-Depressive Psychosis and Critical Approaches to Virginia Woolf's Life and Work." PMLA 103, no. 1 (Jan. 1988): 10–23.

Carriker, Kitti. "Edna O'Brien's 'The Doll': A Narrative of Abjection." *Notes on Modern Irish Literature* 1 (1989): 6–13.

Carrington, Ildikó de Papp. *Controlling the Uncontrollable: The Fiction of Alice Munro*. De Kalb: Northern Illinois University Press 1989.

Carscallen, James. "Alice Munro." In *Profiles in Canadian Literature*, ed. Jeffrey M. Heath. 4 vols. Toronto: Dundurn, 1980. 2:73–80.

Chase, Cynthia. " 'Transference' as Trope and Persuasion." In *Discourse in Psychoanalysis and Literature*, ed. Shlomith Rimmon-Kenan. London: Methuen 1987. 211–32.

Cohn, Dorrit. *Transparent Minds: Narrative Modes for Presenting Consciousness in Fiction*. Princeton: Princeton University Press 1978.

Corsa, Helen. "*To the Lighthouse*: Death, Mourning and Transfiguration." *Literature and Psychology* 21, no. 3 (1971): 115–31.

Culler, Jonathan. "On Apostrophe." *Diacritics* 7, no. 4 (Dec. 1977): 59–69.

Davies, Robertson. "The Novels of Mavis Gallant." *Canadian Fiction Magazine* 28 (1978): 69–73.

de Man, Paul. *Allegories of Reading: Figural Language in Rousseau, Nietzsche, Rilke and Proust*. New Haven: Yale University Press 1979.

- "Autobiography as De-facement." *Modern Language Notes* 94 (Dec. 1979): 919–30.

- "Pascal's Allegory of Persuasion." In *Allegory and Representation*, ed. Stephen J. Greenblatt. Baltimore: Johns Hopkins University Press 1981. 1–25.

- "Sign and Symbol in Hegel's *Aesthetics*." *Critical Inquiry* 8, no. 4 (Summer 1982): 761–75.

– "Anthropomorphism and Trope in the Lyric." In *The Rhetoric of Romanticism*. New York: Columbia University Press 1984. 239–62.

Derrida, Jacques. "*Fors*: The Anglish Words of Nocolas Abraham and Maria Torok." *Georgia Review* 31, no. 1 (1977): 64–116.

– "Freud and the Scene of Writing." *Writing and Difference*. Trans. Alan Bass. Chicago: University of Chicago Press 1978. 196–231.

– *Dissemination*. Trans. Barbara Johnson. Chicago: University of Chicago Press 1981.

– *Memoires for Paul de Man*. Trans. Cecile Lindsay, Jonathan Culler, Eduardo Cadava. New York: Columbia University Press 1986.

– *The Post Card: From Socrates to Freud and Beyond*. Trans. Alan Bass. Chicago: University of Chicago Press 1987.

– *The Truth in Painting*. Trans. Geoff Bennington and Ian McLeod. Chicago: University of Chicago Press 1987.

Deutsch, Helen. "Absence of Grief." *Psychoanalytic Quarterly* 6 (1937): 12–22.

Dictionary of Philosophy. Ed. Dagobert D. Runes. Totowa: Littlefield, Adams and Co. 1968.

Dix, Dom Gregory. *The Shape of Liturgy*. London: Adam and Charles Blac 1945.

Dombrowski, Eileen. " 'Down to Death': Munro and Transcience." *University of Windsor Review* 14, no. 1 (1978): 21–9.

Duras, Marguerite. *Hiroshima Mon Amour*. Trans. Richard Seaver. New York: Grove 1960.

– *The Lover*. Trans. Barbara Bray. New York: Harper and Row 1985.

– *The Ravishing of Lol V. Stein*. Trans. Richard Seaver. New York: Pantheon Books 1986.

– *The War: A Memoir*. Trans. Barbara Bray. New York: Pantheon Books 1986.

– *Practicalities*. Trans. Barbara Bray. New York: Grove Weidenfeld 1990.

Empson, William. *Some Versions of Pastoral*. Harmondsworth: Penguin 1966.

Engelberg, Edward. *Elegiac Fictions: The Motif of the Unlived Life*. University Park: Pennsylvania State University Press 1989.

Fitzpatrick, Margaret Anne. " 'Projection' in Alice Munro's *Something I've Been Meaning to Tell You*." In *The Art of Alice Munro: Saying the Unsayable*, ed. Judith Miller. Waterloo: University of Waterloo Press 1984. 15–20.

Flieger, Jerry Aline. "Proust, Freud, and the Art of Forgetting." *SubStance* 29 (1981): 66–82.

Foster, Dennis A. *Confession and Complicity in Narrative*. Cambridge: Cambridge University Press 1987.

Fowler, Alastair. *Kinds of Literature: An Introduction to the Theory of Genres and Modes*. Cambridge: Harvard University Press 1982.

Frank, Joseph. *The Widening Gyre: Crisis and Mastery in Modern Literature*. New Brunswick: Rutgers University Press 1963.

Freud, Sigmund. *The Complete Psychological Works of Sigmund Freud*. Ed. James Strachey. 24 vols. London: Hogarth Press 1953. Vol. 6, *The Psychopathology of Everyday Life* (1901). Vol. 8, *Jokes and Their Relation to the Unconscious* (1905). Vol. 9, "Creative Writers and Daydreaming" (1908), 141–54. Vol. 12, "The Dynamics of Transference" (1912), 97–108; and "Remembering, Repeating and Working-Through" (1914), 145–56. Vol. 17, "The Uncanny," 217–56.

Friedman, Alan. "Narrative Is to Death as Death Is to Dying: Funerals and Stories." *Mosaic* 15, no. 1 (Winter 1982): 65–76.

Frye, Northrop. *Anatomy of Criticism*. Princeton: Princeton University Press 1957.

Gabriel, Barbara. "Fairly Good Times: An Interview with Mavis Gallant." *Canadian Forum* 66 (Feb. 1987): 23–7.

Gadpaille, Michelle. *The Canadian Short Story*. Toronto: Oxford University Press 1989.

Gallant, Mavis. *The Other Paris*. Boston: Houghton Mifflin 1956.

– *Green Water, Green Sky*. Boston: Houghton Mifflin 1959.

– *My Heart Is Broken*. New York: Random House 1964.

– *A Fairly Good Time*. New York: Random House 1970.

– "Things Overlooked Before." *The Affair of Gabrielle Russier*. Toronto: Popular Library 1971. 9–85.

– *The Pegnitz Junction*. New York: Random House 1973.

– *The End of the World and Other Stories*. Toronto: McClelland and Stewart 1974.

– *From the Fifteenth District*. Toronto: Macmillan of Canada 1979.

– *Home Truths: Selected Canadian Stories*. Toronto: Macmillan of Canada 1981.

– *Overhead in a Balloon*. Toronto: Macmillan of Canada 1985.

– "What Is Style?" *Paris Notebooks: Essays and Reviews*. Toronto: Macmillan of Canada 1986. 176–79.

– *In Transit*. New York: Viking 1988.

Gibson, Graeme. "Alice Munro." *Eleven Canadian Novelists*. Toronto: Anansi 1973. 237–64.

Godard, Barbara. " 'Heirs of the Living Body': Alice Munro and the Question of a Female Aesthetic." In *The Art of Alice Munro: Saying the Unsayable*, ed. Judith Miller. Waterloo: University of Waterloo Press 1984. 43–71.

– "Stretching the Story: The Canadian Story Cycle." *Open Letter* 7, no. 6 (Fall 1989): 27–71.

Gold, Joseph. "Our Feeling Exactly: The Writing of Alice Munro." In *The Art of Alice Munro: Saying the Unsayable*, ed. Judith Miller. Waterloo: University of Waterloo Press 1984. 1–13.

Guillèn, Claudio. *Literature as System*. Princeton: Princeton University Press 1971.

Hancock, Geoff. "An Interview with Mavis Gallant." Canadian Fiction Magazine 28 (1978): 19–67.

− "An Interview with Alice Munro." *Canadian Fiction Magazine* 43 (1982): 75–114.

Hanford, James. "Pastoral Elegy and 'Lycidas.' " PMLA 25 (1910): 403–47.

Harding, D.W. "Psychological Processes in the Reading of Fiction." In *Aesthetics in the Modern World*, ed. Harold Osborne. New York: Weybright and Talley 1968. 300–17.

Harrison, T.P., and H.J. Leon, eds. Introduction to *The Pastoral Elegy: An Anthology*. New York: Octagon Books 1968. 1–24.

Hartman, Geoffrey H. *Saving the Text: Literature, Derrida, Philosophy*. Baltimore: Johns Hopkins University Press 1981.

Hatch, Ronald B. "The Three Stages of Mavis Gallant's Short Fiction." *Canadian Fiction Magazine* 28 (1978): 92–114.

− "Mavis Gallant and the Creation of Consciousness." In *The Present Tense. The Canadian Novel*, ed. John Moss. 4 vols. Toronto: NC Press 1985. 4:45–72.

− "Mavis Gallant and the Fascism of Everyday Life." *Essays on Canadian Writing* 42 (Winter 1990): 9–40.

Hernadi, Paul. *Beyond Genre*. Ithaca: Cornell University Press 1972.

− "Doing, Making, Meaning: Toward a Theory of Verbal Practice." PMLA 103, no. 5 (Oct. 1988): 749–58.

Hoffman, Frederick. *The Mortal No: Death and the Modern Imagination*. Princeton: Princeton University Press 1964.

Holman, C. Hugh, and William Harmon. *A Handbook to Literature*. 5th ed. New York: Macmillan 1986.

Honig, Edward. *Dark Conceit: The Making of Allegory*. London: Faber and Faber 1966.

Hoy, Helen. " 'Rose and Janet': Alice Munro's Metafiction." *Canadian Literature* 121 (Summer 1989): 59–83.

− "Alice Munro: 'Unforgettable, Indigestible Messages.' " *Journal of Canadian Studies* 26, no. 1 (Spring 1991): 5–21.

Hutcheon, Linda. " 'The Pastime of Past Time': Fiction, History, Historiographic Metafiction." *Genre* 20 (Fall–Winter 1987): 285–305.

− *A Poetics of Postmodernism*. London: Routledge 1988.

Irvine, Lorna. "Changing Is the Word I Want." In *Probable Fictions: Alice Munro's Narrative Acts*, ed. Louis K. MacKendrick. Toronto: ECW Press 1983. 99–111.

− "Starting from the Beginning Every Time." In *A Mazing Space: Writing Canadian Women Writing*, ed. Shirley Neuman and Smaro Kamboureli. Edmonton: Longspoon/NeWest Press 1986. 246–55.

Iser, Wolfgang. "The Reality of Fiction: A Functionalist Approach to Literature." *New Literary History* 7, no. 1 (Autumn 1975): 7–38.

– "The Play of the Text." In *Languages of the Unsayable: The Play of Negativity in Literature and Literary Theory*, eds. Sanford Budick and Wolfgang Iser. New York: Columbia University Press 1989. 325–39.

– *Prospecting: From Reader Response to Literary Anthropology*. Baltimore: Johns Hopkins University Press 1989.

Jaeck, Lois Marie. *Marcel Proust and the Text as Macrometaphor*. Toronto: University of Toronto Press 1990.

Jauss, Hans Robert. "Genres and Medieval Literature." *Toward an Aesthetic of Reception*. Trans. Timothy Bahti. Minneapolis: University of Minnesota Press 1982. 76–109.

Jewison, Donald B. "Speaking of Mirrors: Imagery and Narration in Two Novellas by Mavis Gallant." *Studies in Canadian Literature* 10, no. 1–2 (1985): 94–109.

Joyce, James. *Dubliners* (1914). New York: Viking Press 1961.

– *Portrait of the Artist as a Young Man* (1914–15). New York: Viking Press 1964.

– *Ulysses* (1922). New York: Random House 1961.

Joyce, Stanislaus. *My Brother's Keeper: James Joyce's Early Years*. Ed. Richard Ellman. New York: Viking 1958.

Kauffman, Linda S. *Discourses of Desire: Gender, Genre and Epistolary Fictions*. Ithaca: Cornell University Press 1986.

Keefer, Janice Kulyk. "Strange Fashions of Forsaking: Criticism and the Fiction of Mavis Gallant." *Dalhousie Review* 64, no. 4 (Winter 1984–85): 721–35.

– "Mavis Gallant: A Profile." In *The Macmillan Anthology* I, ed. John Metcalf and Leon Rooke. Toronto: Macmillan of Canada 1988. 193–215.

– *Reading Mavis Gallant*. Toronto: Oxford University Press 1989.

Keith, W.J. *Canadian Literature in English*. London: Longman 1985.

– *A Sense of Style: Studies in the Art of Fiction in English-Speaking Canada*. Toronto: ECW Press 1989.

– "The Ethics of Fiction." *Books in Canada* (Aug./Sept. 1990): 15–17.

Kermode, Frank. "Secrets and Narrative Sequence." In *On Narrative*, ed. W.J.T. Mitchell. Chicago: University of Chicago Press 1980. 79–98.

Klibansky, Raymond, Erwin Panofsky, and Fritz Saxl. *Saturn and Melancholy: Studies in the History of Natural Philosophy, Religion and Art*. London: Thomas Nelson and Sons 1964.

Kristeva, Julia. *Desire in Language: A Semiotic Approach to Literature and Art*. Ed. Leon S. Roudiez. Trans. Thomas Gora, Alice Jardine, Leon S. Roudiez. New York: Columbia University Press 1980.

– *Powers of Horror: An Essay on Abjection*. Trans. Leon S. Roudiez. New York: Columbia University Press 1982.

– "On the Melancholic Imaginary." Trans. Louise Burchill. In *Discourse in*

Psychoanalysis and Literature, ed. Shlomith Rimmon-Kenan. New York: Methuen 1987. 104–23.

- "The Pain of Sorrow in the Modern World: The Works of Marguerite Duras." Trans. Katharine A. Jensen. PMLA 102, no. 2 (Mar. 1987): 138–51.

- *Black Sun: Depression and Melancholia*. Trans. Leon S. Roudiez. New York: Columbia University Press 1989.

Lacan, Jacques. "The Mirror Stage." *Ecrits: A Selection*. Trans. A. Sheridan. New York: Norton 1977. 1–7.

- "Homage to Marguerite Duras, on *Le Ravissement de Lol V. Stein*." In *Marguerite Duras by Marguerite Duras*. San Francisco: City Lights Books 1987. 122–9.

Lamont-Stewart, Linda. "Order from Chaos: Writing as Self-Defense in the Fiction of Alice Munro and Clark Blaise." In *The Art of Alice Munro: Saying the Unsayable*, ed. Judith Miller. Waterloo: University of Waterloo Press 1984. 113–21.

Langbaum, Robert. *The Mysteries of Identity: A Theme in Modern Literature*. Chicago: University of Chicago Press 1977.

Leith, Linda. "The Scream: Mavis Gallant's *A Fairly Good Time*." *American Review of Canadian Studies* 18, no. 2 (1988): 213–22.

Macdonald, Rae McCarthy. "A Madman Loose in the World: The Vision of Alice Munro." *Modern Fiction Studies* 22, no. 3 (Autumn 1976): 365–74.

McHale, Brian. *Postmodernist Fiction*. New York: Methuen 1987.

Martens, Debra. "Ghosts and Saints: Notes on Mavis Gallant's *From the Fifteenth District*." *Essays on Canadian Writing* 42 (Winter 1990): 154–72.

- "The Past Projected: Mavis Gallant and Joseph Roth." *Essays on Canadian Writing* 42 (Winter 1990): 41–56.

Martin, W.R. "Alice Munro and James Joyce." *Journal of Canadian Fiction* 24 (1978–79): 120–6.

- "The Strange and the Familiar in Alice Munro." *Studies in Canadian Literature* 7, no. 2 (1982): 214–26.

- *Alice Munro: Paradox and Parallel*. Edmonton: University of Alberta Press 1987.

Mathews, Lawrence. "*Who Do You Think You Are?* Alice Munro's Art of Disarrangement." In *Probable Fictions: Alice Munro's Narrative Acts*, ed. Louis K. MacKendrick. Downsview: ECW Press, 1983. 181–93.

Mepham, John. "Mourning and Modernism." In *Virginia Woolf: New Critical Essays*, ed. Patricia Clements and Isobel Grundy. London: Vision Press 1983. 137–56.

Merivale, Patricia. *Pan the Goat-God: His Myth in Modern Times*. Cambridge: Harvard University Press 1969.

- "The Biographical Compulsion: Elegiac Romances in Canadian Fiction." *Journal of Modern Literature* 8, no. 1 (1980): 139–52.

- "Framed Voices: The Polyphonic Elegies of Hebert and Kogawa." *Canadian Literature* 116 (Spring 1988): 68–82.

Merler, Grazia. *Mavis Gallant: Narrative Patterns and Techniques*. Ottawa: Techumseh Press 1978.

Metcalf, John. "A Conversation with Alice Munro." *Journal of Canadian Fiction* 1, no. 4 (Fall 1972): 54–62.

Miller, J. Hillis. *The Ethics of Reading*. Baltimore: Johns Hopkins University Press 1986.

- *Versions of Pygmalion*. Cambridge: Harvard University Press 1990.

Mills-Courts, Karen. *Poetry as Epitaph: Representation and Poetic Language*. Baton Rouge: Louisiana State University Press 1990.

Moss, John. *A Reader's Guide to the Canadian Novel*. Toronto: McClelland and Stewart 1981.

Müller, Günther. "Bemerkungen zur Gattungspoetik." *Philosophischer Anzeiger* 3 (1928): 129–47.

Munich, Adrienne Auslander. " 'Dear Dead Women,' or Why Gabriel Conroy Reviews Robert Browning." In *New Alliances in Joyce Studies*, ed. Bonnie Kime Scott. Newark: University of Delaware Press 1988. 126–34.

Munro, Alice. *Dance of the Happy Shades*. Toronto: McGraw-Hill Ryerson 1968.

- "Author's Commentary." In *Sixteen by Twelve: Short Stories by Canadian Writers*, ed. John Metcalf. Toronto: Ryerson 1970. 125–6.

- *Lives of Girls and Women*. Toronto: McGraw-Hill Ryerson Ltd 1971.

- "Home." In *74: New Canadian Stories*, ed. David Helwig and Joan Harcourt. Winnipeg: Oberon Press 1974. 133-53.

- *Something I've Been Meaning to Tell You*. Toronto: McGraw-Hill Ryerson 1974.

- *Who Do You Think You Are?* Toronto: McGraw-Hill Ryerson 1978.

- *The Moons of Jupiter*. Toronto: Macmillan of Canada 1982.

- "What is Real?" In *Making It New*, ed. John Metcalf. Toronto: Methuen 1982. 223–6.

- *The Progress of Love*. Toronto: McClelland and Stewart 1986.

- *Friend of My Youth*. Toronto: McClelland and Stewart 1990.

Murray, Heather. " 'Its Image on the Mirror': Canada, Canonicity, The Uncanny." *Essays on Canadian Writing* 42 (Winter 1990): 102–30.

Nietzsche, Friedrich. "The Use and Abuse of History." *The Complete Works of Friedrich Nietzsche*. Ed. Oscar Levy. Trans. Adrian Collins. 18 vols. London: George Allen and Unwin 1910. Vol. 5, 2: 1–100.

O'Brien, Edna. *A Fanatic Heart: Selected Stories of Edna O'Brien*. New York: Farrar Straus Giroux 1984.

- "Long Distance." *Harper's* (June 1990): 43–6.

- *Lantern Slides*. New York: Plume (Penguin Books) 1991.

O'Brien, Peggy. "The Silly and the Serious: An Assessment of Edna O'Brien." *Massachusetts Review* 28, no. 3 (Autumn 1987): 474–88.

Orange, John. "Alice Munro and A Maze of Time." In *Probable Fictions: Alice Munro's Narrative Acts*, ed. Louis K. MacKendrick. Downsview: ECW Press 1983. 83–98.

O'Rourke, David. "Exiles in Time: Gallant's *My Heart is Broken*." *Canadian Literature* 93 (1982): 98–107.

Osachoff, Margaret Gail. " 'Treacheries of the Heart': Memoir, Confession, and Meditation in the Stories of Alice Munro." In *Probable Fictions: Alice Munro's Narrative Acts*, ed. Louis K. MacKendrick. Downsview: ECW Press 1983. 61–82.

The Oxford English Dictionary. 2nd ed. Oxford: Clarendon Press 1989.

Pimentel, Luz Aurora. *Metaphoric Narration: Paranarrative Dimensions in* A la recherche du temps perdu. Toronto: University of Toronto Press 1990.

Poggioli, Renato. "The Oaten Flute." *Harvard Library Bulletin* 11 (1957): 147–84.

– *The Oaten Flute*. Cambridge: Harvard University Press 1975.

Potts, Abbie Findlay. *The Elegiac Mode: Poetic Form in Wordsworth and Other Elegists*. Ithaca: Cornell University Press 1967.

Pound, Ezra. "A Retrospect." *Literary Essays of Ezra Pound*. Ed. T.S. Eliot. Norfolk: New Directions 1954. 3–15.

Reinhard, Kenneth, and Julia Lupton. "Shapes of Grief: Freud, *Hamlet* and Mourning." *Genders* 4 (Spring 1989): 50–67.

Rella, Franco. "Melancholy and the Labyrinthine World of Things." *Sub-Stance* 53 (1987): 29–36.

Ricoeur, Paul. "The Metaphorical Process as Cognition, Imagination, and Feeling." *On Metaphor*. Ed. Sheldon Sacks. Chicago: University of Chicago Press 1979. 141–57.

– "Narrative Time." *On Narrative*. Ed. W.J.T. Mitchell. Chicago: University of Chicago Press 1980. 165–86.

Riffaterre, Michael. *Fictional Truth*. Baltimore: Johns Hopkins University Press 1990.

Robinson, John A., and Linda Hawpe. "Narrative Thinking as a Heuristic Process." In *Narrative Psychology: The Storied Nature of Human Conduct*, ed. Theodore R. Sarbin. New York: Praeger 1986. 111–25.

Rooke, Constance. "Fear of the Open Heart." In *A Mazing Space*, ed. Smaro Kamboureli and Shirley Neuman. Edmonton: Longspoon/NeWest Press 1986. 256–69.

Rosenmeyer, Thomas G. *The Green Cabinet: Theocritus and the European Pastoral Lyric*. Berkeley: University of California Press 1969.

Ross, Malcolm. "Mavis Gallant and Thea Astley on Home Truths, Home Folk." *Ariel* 19, no. 1 (Jan. 1988): 83–9.

Roth, Philip. Foreword to *A Fanatic Heart: Selected Stories of Edna O'Brien*. New York: Farrar Straus Giroux 1984. vii–viii.

Roudiez, Leon S. Introduction to *Desire in Language* by Julia Kristeva. Trans. Leon S. Roudiez. New York: Columbia University Press 1980. 1–22.

Sacks, Peter. *The English Elegy: Studies in the Genre from Spenser to Yeats*. Baltimore: Johns Hopkins University Press 1985.

Schenck, Celeste M. "Feminism and Deconstruction: Re-Constructing the Elegy." *Tulsa Studies in Women's Literature* 5, no. 1 (Spring 1986): 13–27.

– "When the Moderns Write Elegy: Crane, Kinsella, Nemerov." *Classical and Modern Literature* 6, no. 2 (Winter 1986): 97–108.

– *Mourning and Panegyric: The Poetics of Pastoral Ceremony*. University Park: Pennsylvania State University Press 1988.

Schleifer, Ronald. *Rhetoric and Death: The Language of Modernism and Postmodernist Discourse Theory*. Urbana: University of Illinois Press 1990.

Schrank, Bernice. "Popular Culture and Political Consciousness in Mavis Gallant's *My Heart Is Broken*." *Essays on Canadian Writing* 42 (Winter 1990): 57–71.

Scott, D.C. *The Poems of D.C. Scott*. Toronto: McClelland and Stewart 1926.

Siemerling, Winfried. "Perception, Memory, Irony: Mavis Gallant Greets Proust and Flaubert." *Essays on Canadian Writing* 42 (Winter 1990): 131–53.

Slopen, Beverley. "PW Interviews Alice Munro." *Publisher's Weekly* 22 (Aug. 1986): 76–7.

Smith, Barbara Herrnstein. "Narrative Versions, Narrative Theories." In *On Narrative*, ed. W.J.T. Mitchell. Chicago: University of Chicago Press 1980. 209–32.

Smith, Eric. *By Mourning Tongues: Studies in the English Elegy*. Ipswich: Boydell Press 1977.

Smith, Paul. "The Will to Allegory in Postmodernism." *Dalhousie Review* 62, no. 1 (Spring 1982): 105–22.

Smythe, Karen. "*Green Water, Green Sky*: Gallant's Discourse of Dislocation." *Studies in Canadian Literature* 14, no. 1 (1989): 74–84.

– "The Scene of Seeing: Perception and Perversion in *The Ravishing of Lol V. Stein*." *Genders* 6 (Fall 1989): 49–59.

Sontag, Susan. *On Photography*. New York: Farrar, Straus and Giroux 1973.

Spacks, Patricia Meyer. "The Novel as Ethical Paradigm." *Novel* 21, no. 2–3 (Spring/Winter 1988): 181–8.

Spilka, Mark. *Virginia Woolf's Quarrel with Grieving*. Lincoln: University of Nebraska Press 1980.

Squires, Michael. *The Pastoral Novel: Studies in George Eliot, Thomas Hardy, and D.H. Lawrence*. Charlottesville: Virginia University Press 1974.

Stainsby, Mari. "Alice Munro Talks with Mari Stainsby." *British Columbia Library Quarterly* (July 1971): 27–30.

Stevens, Peter. "Perils of Compassion." *Canadian Literature* 56 (1973): 61–70.

Stewart, Garrett. *Death Sentences: Styles of Dying in British Fiction*. Cambridge: Harvard University Press 1984.

Stich, Klaus P. "The Cather Connection in Alice Munro's 'Dulse.' " *Modern Language Studies* 20, no. 4 (Fall 1989): 102–11.

Struthers, J.R. "Reality and Ordering: The Growth of a Young Artist in *Lives of Girls and Women*." *Essays on Canadian Writing* 3 (Fall 1975): 32–46.

– "The Real Material: An Interview with Alice Munro." In *Probable Fictions: Alice Munro's Narrative Acts*, ed. Louis K. MacKendrick. Downsview: ECW Press 1983. 5–36.

– "Alice Munro's Fictive Imagination." In *The Art of Alice Munro: Saying the Unsayable*, ed. Judith Miller. Waterloo: University of Waterloo Press 1984. 103–12.

Todorov, Tzvetan. "The Origin of Genres." *New Literary History* 8, no. 1 (1976): 159–70.

Tolchin, Neal. *Mourning, Gender and Creativity in the Art of Herman Melville*. New Haven: Yale University Press 1988.

Toliver, Harold. *Pastoral Forms and Attitudes*. Berkeley: University of California Press 1971.

Turner, Mark. *Death Is the Mother of Beauty: Mind, Metaphor, Criticism*. Chicago: University of Chicago Press 1987.

Twigg, Alan. "Alice Munro: What Is." *For Openers: Conversations with 24 Canadian Writers*. Madiera Park, BC: Harbour Publishing 1981. 13–20.

Wachtel, Eleanor. "An Interview with Alice Munro." *Brick* 40 (Winter 1991): 48–53.

Watt, Ian. *The Rise of the Novel*. London: Hogarth Press 1987.

White, Edmund. *Nocturnes for the King of Naples*. New York: Penguin Books 1980.

White, Hayden. "The Narrativization of Real Events." In *On Narrative*, ed. W.J.T. Mitchell. Chicago: University of Chicago Press 1980. 249–54.

– "The Value of Narrativity in the Representation of Reality." In *On Narrative*, ed. W.J.T. Mitchell. Chicago: University of Chicago Press 1980. 1–24.

Wilde, Alan. *Horizons of Assent: Modernism, Post-Modernism and the Ironic Imagination*. Baltimore: Johns Hopkins University Press 1981.

Williams, Carolyn. "Virginia Woolf's Rhetoric of Enclosure." *Denver Quarterly* 18, no. 4 (Winter 1984): 43–61.

Willis, Sharon. *Marguerite Duras: Writing on the Body*. Urbana and Chicago: University of Illinois Press 1987.

Woodcock, George. "Memory, Imagination, Artifice: The Late Short Fiction of Mavis Gallant." *Canadian Fiction Magazine* 28 (1978): 74–91.

– "The Plots of Life: The Realism of Alice Munro." *Queen's Quarterly* 93, no. 2 (Summer 1986): 235–50.

Woolf, Virginia. *The Voyage Out*. London: Hogarth Press 1915.

– *Jacob's Room* (1922). London: Hogarth Press 1945.

- *Mrs Dalloway*. New York: Harcourt, Brace and Co. 1925.
- Introduction to *Mrs Dalloway*. New York: Random House, Modern Library 1928. v–ix.
- *To the Lighthouse*. London: Harcourt, Brace and World, Inc. 1927.
- *A Room of One's Own* (1929). Harmondsworth: Penguin 1945.
- "The Narrow Bridge of Art." *Collected Essays of Virginia Woolf*. Ed. Leonard Woolf. 4 vols. London: Hogarth Press 1966. 2:218–29.
- "A Sketch of the Past." *Moments of Being: Unpublished Autobiographical Writings*. Ed. Jeanne Schulkind. London: Chatto and Windus for Sussex University Press, 1976. 71–159.
- *The Diary of Virginia Woolf*. Ed. Anne Oliver Bell. 5 vols. London: Hogarth Press 1977–84.

York, Lorraine M. " 'The Other Side of Dailiness': The Paradox of Photography in Alice Munro's Fiction." *Studies in Canadian Literature* 8, no. 1 (1983): 49–60.

Zeiger, Melissa Fran. *'Lilacs Out of the Dead Land': Changes in the Modern Elegy*. PhD, Cornell University 1986. Ann Arbor: UMI 1989. 8628477.

Index

allegory and mourning, 6, 14, 61–2, 68, 70, 71, 76, 90, 91, 104, 182 n 4, 182 n 5; in Gallant, 26, 35, 42, 55, 61–2, 68, 72, 76, 91, 93, 94, 105, 180 n 5, 183 n 27; and historiography, 91, 98, 104; and irony, 93; in Munro, 123, 126, 141
anagnorisis, 11, 17, 90
analepsis, 17, 18, 136, 139
anamnesis, 18, 82, 164
Aristotle: on catharsis, 3; on praise, 7
Austin, J.L.: on perlocutionary acts, 18; on misfires, 19
autobiography: and elegy, 5, 7, 8, 67, 174 n 21; in Gallant, 31, 62–3, 67, 96, 97, 99, 100, 102; in Munro, 130; in Duras, 157; in White, 163, 164, 165

Barthes, Roland: on photographs, 108, 109, 133; on grief, 111; on death, 128; on bright shadow, 144
Benjamin, Walter: on allegory, 62, 68, 91, 181 n 4; on angels, 80; on ghosts, 80; on thought patterns, 96; on history, 97; on photography, 109; on stories, 135, 136, 143; on melancholy, 142; on memory, 143
Bion, "Lament for Adonis," 6
Brooks, Peter: on analysis, 28; on plotting, 29; on mortality, 31

catharsis, 3, 21, 165, 180 n 108; in Gallant, 29, 36, 45; in Munro, 130, 140; in Duras, 157; in O'Brien, 166; in Joyce, 192 n 3
closure, 8, 10; and modernism/late modernism, 5, 14; in Woolf, 15; in Joyce, 18; and consolation, 66; in Gallant, 66, 87, 89, 96–7; and sequence, 66; and historiography, 66–7; and autobiography, 67; Munro, 135, 137; in O'Brien, 168
confession, 44; in Gallant, 44, 74
consolation, 3, 7, 8–10 passim, 12; in Gallant, 10, 29, 32, 36, 38, 58, 66; in Munro, 10, 107, 109, 113, 117, 123, 126, 133, 135, 137, 138, 140, 141, 142, 144, 146, 148, 150, 152; and metaphor, 13, 29; in Woolf, 16; and closure, 17, 66; and epiphany, 18; and the think-act, 18; and temporality, 20; and the image, 21; and the symbol, 32, 33, 58; and memory, 41, 42, 72, 73; and allegory, 62; and sequence, 65; and consolation/closure, 66;